Innovations and Institutions

This book is the meeting point of two seemingly incongruous schools of theoretical thought: that of institutional theory and the literature of innovation. Whereas the former struggles with explaining the mere existence of innovation, the latter has not been able to fully explain the inherent problems of the innovative efforts of established firms. As the authors argue however, opposites attract.

Taking an institutional perspective, Vermeulen and Raab illustrate how institutional forces come to shape the interest, priorities and behaviour of organizational members in the development and implementation process of incremental product innovation, investigate the failed innovative attempts of established organizations and demonstrate the importance of organizational and intraorganizational forces for innovative success.

The conceptual models developed by the authors in this book will be of considerable interest to managers and consultants in the financial sector, whilst the utilization of institutional theory to explain innovation will be extremely useful for students taking courses in innovation management.

Patrick Vermeulen is Associate Professor of Organization Studies at Tilburg University in the Netherlands.

Jörg Raab is Assistant Professor of Policy and Organization Studies at Tilburg University in the Netherlands.

RIOT!

Routledge Studies in Innovation, Organization and Technology

1. **Innovation in the U.S. Service Sector**
   Michael P. Gallaher, Albert N. Link and Jeffrey E. Petrusa

2. **Information and Communications Technologies in Society**
   E-living in a digital Europe
   Edited by Ben Anderson, Malcolm Brynin and Yoel Raban

3. **The Innovative Bureaucracy**
   Bureaucracy in an age of fluidity
   Alexander Styhre

4. **Innovations and Institutions**
   An institutional perspective on the innovative efforts of banks and insurance companies
   Patrick Vermeulen and Jörg Raab

Innovations and Institutions

An institutional perspective on the innovative efforts of banks and insurance companies

Patrick Vermeulen and Jörg Raab

Routledge
Taylor & Francis Group
LONDON AND NEW YORK

First published 2007
by Routledge
2 Park Square, Milton Park, Abingdon, OX14 4RN

Simultaneously published in the USA and Canada
by Routledge
270 Madison Avenue, New York, NY 10016

Routledge is an imprint of the Taylor & Francis Group, an informa business

Typeset in Sabon by
Bookcraft Ltd, Stroud, Gloucestershire

Printed and bound in Great Britain by
TJI Digital, Padstow, Cornwall

British Library Cataloguing in Publication Data
A catalogue record for this book is available from the British Library

Library of Congress Cataloging in Publication Data
Vermeulen, Patrick Alexander Maria, 1970–
Innovations and institutions: an institutional perspective on the innovation efforts of banks and insurance companies/Patrick Vermeulen and Jörg Raab
p. cm – (Routledge studies in innovation, organization and technology)
Includes bibliographical references and index
1. Financial services industry–Technological innovations.
2. Insurance companies–Technological innovations. 3. Institutional economics. I. Raab, Jörg. II. Title.
HG173.V45 2007
332.1–dc22 2006029370

ISBN10: 0–415–39073–7 (hbk)
ISBN10: 0–203–96405–5 (ebk)

ISBN13: 978–0–415–39073–6 (hbk)
ISBN13: 978–0–203–96405–7 (ebk)

Contents

Illustrations

Figures

Tables

Preface

This book is about a new combination of existing theories. In our definition this means that this book is an innovation. Writing an innovative book is, as we argue in our book, inherently difficult and requires careful framing of the arguments used in order to not be too innovative and unwittingly break down our own institutionalized realities. Every innovative attempt is about trying to steer a middle ground between Charybdis, who would swallow the innovator and then spit him up again, and Scylla, who would devour any attempt to approach her rugged cliffs. Hence, we have been cautious not to drift too far into unknown territory.

We have been fascinated by the idea of combining the literature on innovation and institutional theory, which at first sight might be typified as colliding scientific paradigms. One thrives upon inventions, newness and change, whereas the other merely arouses passion for inertia, stability and sameness. However, opposites attract, and this is exactly what triggered us to write this book, which is the result of an enduring unsatisfactory feeling with both literatures. Whereas one has not been able to fully explain the inherent problems of new things, the other struggles with explaining the emergence of new things. We are, however, modest in our goals. A wealth of scholars has been active in both fields and their contributions may far exceed ours. We merely try to bring together two strangers that could actually become a happy couple. This first conversation is intended to open up the debate and look for mutual interests and starting-points.

Tilburg, July 2006
Patrick Vermeulen
Jörg Raab

Acknowledgements

The authors and publishers would like to thank the following for granting permission to reproduce material in this work: Sage Publications for permission to use material from the forthcoming essay 'Complex Incremental Product Innovation in Established Service Firms: a micro institutional perspective?' by P. A. M. Vermeulen, F. A. J, van den Bosch and H. W. Volberda, to be published in *Organization Studies* (2007). Taylor & Francis for permission to use material from 'The Organization of Product Innovation in the Financial Sector: an exploration in The Netherlands' by P. A. M. Vermeulen and B. Dankbaar, originally published in *The Service Industries Journal*, 22(3): 77–98 (2002) www.tandf.co.uk/journals

We would like to express our appreciation to the members of the organizations studied who gave generously of their time and patience. The ideas presented in this book also benefited from discussions with, and feedback from, many colleagues. We wish to mention a few in particular: Shazad Ansari, Jos Benders, Frans van den Bosch, Ben Dankbaar, Deborah Dougherty, Royston Greenwood, Jac Geurts, Jeroen de Jong, Patrick Kenis, Anoop Madhok, K. C. O'Shaughnessy, Henk Volberda, David Wicks and Charlene Zietsma. We also would like to thank Alice de Kok and Rogier Havelaar for their support in the tiresome but necessary editing and referencing work.

Patrick would like to thank Afke and Hugo for their patience during the last weeks of finishing this book. It's done! Jörg would like to thank Rachel, who has spent many evenings alone while her husband worked on the computer.

1 Introduction

Developing new products and services on a regular basis is one of the key activities for many organizations. New products are a means to gain market share and ensure the viability of companies. They have been referred to as the crucial sources for competitive advantage (Tushman and O'Reilly 1997; Dougherty 1999). This is also the case for incremental product innovations. Incremental product innovations are not radically different from the current product portfolio, but are often refinements and extensions of existing products of a company and seem to involve primarily exploitation-oriented activities (cf. March 1991). Incremental product innovation is, therefore, a critically important competitive factor in established industries and focuses on leveraging a firm's existing resources and capabilities and, as such, requires primarily routine procedures and capabilities (Nelson and Winter 1982; Leonard 1998). Although the relation between incremental product innovation and competitiveness has largely been reported in studies on the manufacturing industry (e.g. Clark and Fujimoto 1991; Wheelright and Clark 1992; Banbury and Mitchell 1995; Pisano 1997), we will demonstrate in this book that it is also the case for companies in the service sector such as banks, insurance companies, airlines or travel companies.

Undoubtedly, during the last three decades services have moved to the center of economic activities in modern societies. Both the commercial services and the non-profit/government sector have grown to the point that they employed well over 70 percent of the working population in most advanced countries by the mid 1990s (Quinn *et al.* 1997). In the course of this growth process, many of these industries have changed beyond recognition. In the financial services sector, the rapid development of information technology (IT) has not only enabled an enormous increase in transactions per employee, but also created numerous opportunities for the development and marketization of new processes and products. As a consequence, banks and insurance companies have been confronted with new standards for the organization, speed and flexibility of their operations, but also with new distribution channels, new forms of competition and different types of products. Next to these technological changes, in the European context, there are the powerful forces of economic and monetary integration as well as the liberalization and deregulation of markets within the European Union. In the financial sector, these developments have caused an ongoing process of mergers and acquisitions (De Leeuw 1996). Although most mergers and acquisitions have taken place within national boundaries, cross-border activities are increasing and the financial institutions of smaller countries such as the Netherlands are moving to the forefront, because they can no longer survive, let alone expand, in their home markets alone (Sijbrands and Eppink 1994; De Leeuw 1996).

Apart from being affected by technological and general economic trends (globalization), the Dutch financial sector has been influenced by changing national government policies in at least two fields (Den Hertog 1995). The first concerns the deregulation of the sector, which contributed to the fading of the boundaries between banks and insurance companies. Historically, the financial sector was known for its tight institutional control and high entry barriers (Scott 1998). The collaboration between banks and insurance companies had always been strictly regulated by the Structure Policy[1] of the national government, and although it was legally possible for banks and insurance companies to cooperate (to some extent), they were not interested in each other (De Leeuw 1996). Although the Central Bank (*De Nederlandsche Bank* or *DNB*) objected to the collaboration between banks and insurance companies in the early 1970s, in 1981 a discussion round the Structure Policy led to an adjustment of this policy (De Leeuw 1996). Today, this situation has changed dramatically and we can observe a whole new spectrum of cooperative forms and integrated products. This change is still ongoing as the search for a profitable interpretation of 'bancassurance' is still in progress. Second, there have been some changes in social security legislation, which implies a movement away from a collective welfare state towards a more individualized 'insurance state' (Den Hertog 1995). This development creates numerous opportunities for new product development by banks and insurance companies.

As a result of all these changes, the Dutch financial services sector has changed radically in a relatively short period of time. As in many other countries, it has changed from a fairly closed sector, with conservative and slowly operating companies, to an extremely dynamic one with several Dutch banks and insurance companies becoming leading actors in the global financial market. ABN-AMRO, for instance, took over Banco Real in Brazil and ING bailed out Barings Bank after its Singapore disaster.

Inside these dynamically growing companies, product development is gradually acquiring a status as a separate, identifiable activity. Due to the rapidly increasing level of (international) competition there is a growing need for product innovation. New products are a means to keep the customers loyal to the organization and to increase the visability in the market. As will be shown in this book, most product innovation in the financial services sector takes place in the form of incremental product innovation, because such a strategy minimizes the risk if compared to the introduction of radically new products. Since established insurance companies and banks have traditionally been characterized as rather risk averse (Vermeulen 2005), this kind of strategy does not come as a surprise.

Incremental product innovation leverages existing resources and capabilities, which should make it a relatively easy task for established firms (McDermott and O'Connor 2002). It is typically carried out within the organization using the existing organizational arrangements. None the less, empirical evidence suggests that many firms seem to struggle with this type of innovation, which often results in diminished company performance, lengthened development times or even complete failure of the new product (Banbury and Mitchell 1995; Song and Montoya-Weiss 1998). Despite the numerous studies suggesting how incremental product innovation should be successfully undertaken, firms still seem to struggle with this type of innovation (e.g. Griffin and Hauser 1996; Adams et al. 1998; Tidd and Bodley 2002). Cooper (1999: 115) even claims that 'project teams and leaders seem to fall into the same traps that their predecessors did back in the 1970s'.

Past research on product innovation in both manufacturing and service industries has taken a predominantly rational perspective and focused on key determinants that lead to successful product innovation.[2] This large body of literature has examined what the development process looks like, what steps firms must carry out and what models could support the development process (Cooper and Kleinschmidt 1987, Cooper 1999; Cooper *et al.* 2002). Furthermore, product factors that separate winners from losers have been identified, such as a clear product definition (Cooper 1984, 1999; Cooper and De Brentani 1991), a differentiated product with unique customer benefits (De Brentani 1989, 1991; Cooper *et al.* 1994; Cooper 1999), and sufficient market knowledge (Thwaites 1992; Cooper 1999; De Brentani 2001). Additionally, important organizational issues such as working with and listening to lead users (Von Hippel 1988; Leonard 1998); the involvement and cooperation of multiple functions during the development process (De Brentani 1989; Moenaert and Souder 1990; Griffin and Hauser 1996; Avlonitis et al. 2001); the use of flexible organizational structures and cross-functional teams (Souder 1987; Thwaites 1992; Griffin and Hauser 1996); communication processes (Allen 1977; Lievens and Moenaert 2000); the overall execution of the project (Song and Montoya-Weiss 1998; Tidd and Bodley 2002); and a close fit between the firms' strategy and resources (Crawford 1994; Lievens and Moenaert 2000; De Brentani 2001) have all been cited as contributing to the success of incremental product innovation.

However, as was mentioned previously, these determinants have not been able to fully explain the persistence of problematic innovation efforts. We aim to contribute to the literature on incremental product innovation by adding a complementary perspective. In this book we take an institutional perspective and will illustrate how *institutional forces* come to shape the interests, priorities and behavior of organizational members (cf. Selznick

1957; Meyer and Rowan 1977; Zucker 1983, 1987; Scott 2001) in the development and implementation process of incremental product innovation.

We focus our study on those institutional forces that affect incremental product innovation efforts in the financial services sector in the Netherlands. We are not only interested in how incumbent firms shape the rules and legitimize the behavior of managers and employees (cf. Vermeulen *et al.* 2007), but we also try to understand how the external or macro institutional environment legitimizes incumbent behavior regarding incremental product innovation. We assume legitimacy to be a complementary factor that determines the ability or willingness to innovate, but we believe (cf. Aldrich and Fiol 1994) its importance has not been fully recognized in the innovation literature [see Dougherty and Heller (1994) for a valuable exception]. By simultaneously analysing multiple institutional forces (regulative, normative and cultural-cognitive) at both organizational and intraorganizational levels, we investigate how these forces influence the development and implementation of incremental product innovation in established financial services firms. Moreover, few empirical studies have addressed the simultaneous impact of these institutional forces on organizational members (Wicks 2001), which leads us to the following research question: How do organizational and intraorganizational institutional forces affect the development and implementation of incremental product innovations in financial services firms in the Netherlands?

Managing innovation

During the last decades, innovation has received a lot of attention in many scientific disciplines and is generally considered as the major engine for economic growth in the OECD countries (Geroski 1995). However, what innovation actually means is not always clear. In the beginning of the twentieth century, Schumpeter was one of the first to elaborate on the importance of innovation for economic development. An innovation was defined as a new combination and one of its features was that innovations do not appear gradually over time but are clustered in periods of time (Schumpeter 1939). The reason for this clustering, Schumpeter argued, is that if company A introduces a new type of product, company B can not wait long to introduce the same (or a similar but improved) product.

After Schumpeter's groundbreaking work, numerous definitions have been proposed in order to capture the essence of innovation. Researchers and practitioners are far from consensus regarding a formal definition of innovation [see Chapter 2 for an overview of definitions and Garcia and Calantone (2002)]. However, there is some agreement that an innovation usually involves something new. Various types of innovation are distinguished in the innovation literature, e.g. product versus process innovations and administrative (new procedures, policies and organizational forms) versus technological (new technologies, products and services) innovations (Ettlie *et al.*

1984; Utterback 1994, Garcia and Calantone 2002). One of the key distinctions is that between incremental and radical innovations (Ettlie *et al.* 1984; Dewar and Dutton 1986). Incremental innovations are relatively minor changes to existing products or processes that reinforce current capabilities of firms, whereas radical innovations deviate from existing products, open up new possibilities and require a new set of capabilities (Henderson and Clark 1990).

Implicit in almost all definitions of innovation is the emphasis on processes of development and implementation. Innovation is a process of interrelated activities. This makes it often highly complex, no matter what the nature of the innovation. The process of developing new ideas into actual products usually demands an enormous amount of time, energy and financial investments. When it comes to innovation, to a considerable extent, it does not matter whether organizations are concerned with banking, transporting people, manufacturing chairs or automobiles; the underlying processes are similar in all firms. Organizations constantly seek for optimal ways of organizing their innovation processes. Most researchers also seem to agree that the innovation process does not 'unfold in a simple linear sequence of stages and substages. Instead, it proliferates into complex bundles of innovation ideas and divergent paths of activities by different organizational units' (van de Ven 1995: 275).

Product innovation processes consist of the range of stages and activities that have to be undertaken in order to bring about a new product as extensively described in the literature on product development. Zaltman *et al.* (1973) distinguished two subprocesses in the innovation process: initiation and implementation. Both these subprocesses consist of several sequential stages: agenda setting and matching (initiation) and redefining/restructuring, clarifying and routinizing (implementation). Soon after, several other notions on the essence of innovation processes appeared. Daft (1978) claims that there are four essential steps that bring about a new product: conception of idea, proposal of idea, decision to adopt, and implementation of the innovation. Booz, Allen and Hamilton (1982) developed one of the most cited product development models, which consisted of seven stages: new product development strategy, idea generation, screening and evaluation, business analysis, development, testing and commercialization. Extensions based on these early ideas eventually led to lengthy descriptions of all the activities needed to develop a new product (Cooper 1983). Underlying most of these models is a highly generic process of signal processing, strategic concepts, product and market development and launch (Tidd *et al.* 1997). Most researchers seem to agree that the innovation process does not 'unfold in a simple linear sequence of stages and substages. Instead, it proliferates into complex bundles of innovation ideas and divergent paths of activities by different organizational units' (van de Ven 1995: 275). The underlying process is suitable for both product and service development. Financial service companies will also follow a process of signal processing, strategic concepts, product and market development and launch (Tidd *et al.* 1997).

Organizations constantly seek for optimal ways of organizing their innovation processes. In order to streamline innovation processes and effectively manage processes of innovation, specific organizational structures have been designed. Organizational structure can be a leverage or a constraint for managing product innovation processes. In their classic study of the Scottish electronics industry, Burns and Stalker (1961) emphasize that an innovative organization is characterized by an organic structure, with open communication lines, few sharply defined tasks and little emphasis on hierarchy. An organic structure is the necessary capability for an organization to be able to respond to a dynamic and changing environment. Burns and Stalker place the organic structure on one side of a continuum. On the other side is the mechanistic structure. Specialization, hierarchy and the strict following of rules and procedures characterize the mechanistic structure. A mechanistic structure is mainly directed towards control and flourishes in static environments. Although the work of Burns and Stalker has been cited many times in the innovation literature, there are several scholars who abandoned the idea of innovation being tightly coupled with organic structures. Tidd et al. claim that 'not all innovation works in organic, loose, informal environments or "skunk works"' (1997: 305). Schoonhoven and Jelinek (1997) pointed out that they did not even find organic structures in the innovative organizations they investigated. Instead, they found organizational structures with clear job descriptions and lines of authority. They also noted a frequent use of project teams and product committees in the innovation process, which they call 'quasi-formal' structures, reserving the word 'formal' for the structure of the more routinized primary processes. They further argue that innovation management should focus on managing these quasi-formal structures.

Despite these claims that innovation can also take place in more stable and routinized organizational structures, a large part of the innovation literature argues that firms have to embrace radical change in order to be innovative (Souder 1987; Davenport 1993; Tidd *et al.* 1997; Afuah 2003). This also includes reconsidering the organizational structure and culture. Achieving sustained product innovation (a continuous stream of innovations) requires alterations at the deepest levels of the organization (cf. Dougherty 1990; Dougherty and Heller 1994). It is further argued that it is not enough that project organizations are clear, that top management supports the innovative enterprise during the whole development process, and that product champions run the projects. These means are generally regarded to improve the chance for successful innovation and they are probably appropriate in many instances. However, being continuously innovative requires an atmosphere and vision directed towards exploring new things. The organization should breath innovation if it wants to be successful at multiple innovative efforts. For many organizations it is not possible to create this kind of atmosphere and culture. Most organizations will not be able to continuously rejuvenate and fundamentally alter the course of their strategic directions. Partly this may be caused by a lack of resources and capabilities. Another explanation we want to develop in this book is derived from institutional theory, which is introduced in the next section.

An institutional perspective

In the context of this study, we apply institutional theory as an overarching perspective to explain innovation and its related problems in financial services, because it represents one of the more robust sociological perspectives within organizational theory (Perrow 1979). Institutions and institutionalization are considered the core concepts of general sociology (Jepperson 1991: 143). Institutional theory provides a rich, complex view of organizations. It is claimed that organizations are influenced by regulative, normative and cognitive pressures arising from external sources or from within the organization itself (Zucker 1987; Scott 1995). These pressures lead towards conformity to institutional norms among organizations. In the last decades, institutional theory has developed prominently in the field of organizational analysis, starting with the work of Selznick (1949, 1957). In contrast to other organizational theories that emphasize the behavior of rational actors, this theory does not see an organization as a mechanical instrument of rational actors, designed to achieve specified goals. Instead, organizations are viewed as adaptive, organic systems, affected by the social characteristics of their participants as well as by the varied pressures imposed by their environment. Because organizations are seen as social systems, goals or procedures tend to achieve an established, value-impregnated status, leading towards the institutionalization of those organizations (DiMaggio and Powell 1991). Early institutionalism focused mainly on the intraorganizational level, analysing group conflict, influence patterns, competing values, coalitions and political trade-offs, highlighting informal interaction (Selznick 1949, 1957). Organizations were embedded in local communities through organizational ties with other organizations and their preferences were shaped by social institutions.

Starting with the seminal works of Meyer and Rowan (1977) and Zucker (1977) a new approach towards the institutionalization of organizations was formed, called 'new institutionalism' (DiMaggio and Powell 1991). The main difference from the 'old institutionalism' is that within new institutional theory the emphasis is 'on legitimacy, the embeddedness of organizational fields, and the centrality of classification, routines, scripts and schema' (Greenwood and Hinings 1996: 1023). The concept of legitimacy has been a focal point of study in new institutional theory. Legitimacy has been defined as a generalized perception or even assumption that certain actions are desirable, proper or appropriate within a certain organization (Suchman 1995) and refers to the degree of cultural support for that organization (Meyer and Scott 1983). Organizations incorporating legitimated elements maximize social acceptance and increase their capabilities for survival (Meyer and Rowan 1977). These rules and practices that prevail within an organizational field create powerful pressures for organizations to seek legitimacy and strive for social conformity (Orrù *et al.* 1991). In other words, for something to be considered legitimate it has to be in accordance with accepted rules and procedures. As such, organizations that innovate and refrain from accepted rules and procedures might suffer in terms of legitimacy (Deephouse 1999) and, especially in established organizational fields, might run the risk of failing. Most often this concept is studied in terms of the relationship between organizations and their institutional environment (Ashforth and Gibbs 1990; Suchman 1995; Ruef and Scott 1998), but it has been suggested that legitimacy is also concerned with intraorganizational processes (Elsbach 2002). When key players within a specific organization become dissatisfied with the activities of the organization, they may reduce the quality of their input needed for executing the activities.

Institutional theory is often viewed as a break from rational-actor models (see, for instance, Zucker 1983, 1991; Scott 1987). Conforming to institutional rules may even conflict with organizational efficiency criteria (Meyer and Rowan 1977). Institutionalized organizational behavior is seen as being based on ideas, values, norms and beliefs embedded in the institutional environment. Oliver (1992) speaks of a 'force of habit' that, alongside an organization's history and tradition, creates a certain degree of value congruence among its members. Institutions have a high 'taken-for-granted' degree of current practices that are re-enacted, which means that they 'acquire a rule-like status' (Oliver 1992: 563). They are treated as 'relative fixtures' in a certain environment and are hardly ever the subject of scrutiny (Jepperson 1991). Institutions guide individual actions in a specific direction due to the predefined patterns of which the institution is constructed and therefore constrain and enable individual behavior.

Although institutional theorists have, in the past, struggled with explaining change (Leblebici *et al.* 1991), institutional theory neither denies nor conflicts with the notion of change (Greenwood *et al.* 2002). However, institutions have, for a long time, been viewed as sources of stability and order. Institutionalized practices were seen to have a natural tendency to perpetuate themselves through either deliberate or unintentional processes. This emphasis on persistence and homogeneity resulted in institutional theorists being heavily criticized by other academics within and outside the scholarly domain of institutional theory (see Scott 2001). Early institutional studies that did refrain from the notion of stability mostly emphasized the creation or construction of institutions and convergent change processes (Oliver 1992; Greenwood and Hinings 1996; D'Aunno *et al.* 2000; Dacin *et al.* 2002). The prevailing nature of this type of change is one of constant reproduction and reinforcement of existing modes of thought and organization (Greenwood and Hinings 1996). Organizations must be responsive to external demands and expectations in order to survive, and therefore they constantly adapt to their environment and go through change processes in order to obtain stability and legitimacy.

Relevance of the study

The study contributes to the following four discussion topics in the area of innovation and institutions. First, the financial services sector is one of the industries driving economic growth in most developed countries (Quinn *et al.* 1997; Alic 2001). Yet, the innovation literature is still dominated by examples from manufacturing (e.g. Clark and Fujimoto 1991; Wheelwright and Clark 1992; Dougherty 1992; Christensen 1997; Meeus and Oerlemans 2000).[3] There is some logic in this fixation on industrial innovation because service sectors have been lagging for years concerning innovation, but recent technological and institutional changes in various industries such as transportation, travel or financial services deem it interesting to have a fresh look. Especially the financial services sector has undergone a major transformation driven by the forces of globalization, European integration and the revolutionary developments in information and communication technology, which in our view more than justifies a shift towards service-based research. As stated previously, the rapid developments in information technology not only enabled an enormous increase in transactions per employee, but also created opportunities for combining existing products and subsequently improving these so-called combi-products. It has been argued in the innovation literature that innovation differs across industries and countries. The financial services industry is highly regulated, which makes it extremely interesting to transfer the results of this study to other highly regulated industries such as utilities, public school systems, childcare and airlines. In some countries, innovation may in itself prove to be more legitimate as the national government provides an environment that is conducive to innovation (Afuah 1998). Thus, the results of this study provide the opportunity to increase understanding of innovative processes within the service as well as across different sectors.

Second, the regulatory changes the financial sector has undergone in the last two decades had a major impact on the innovative context of the companies involved. In the late 1980s and early 1990s, restrictions on domestic competition were eliminated, the scale and scope of financial activities changed, and the external competitive position of financial firms improved. These changes challenged the leadership of the firms to invest in new products (cf. Volberda *et al.* 2001) and revise their structures and processes. The study analyses these developments and gives an insight into specific features of innovation processes in the financial services sector. Moreover, the study sheds light on the roles of various actors (departments) during the innovation process and enhances our understanding of how financial firms handle their innovation processes. It further looks at the influence of contingent factors on the development of new products that may enhance the opportunities to profit from the potential of new products in the market. This knowledge will increase the possibility for banks and insurance companies to restructure their processes in the future.

Third, a large part of the innovation literature is based on describing innovation processes in view of formal steps or procedures (e.g. Booz, Allen and Hamilton 1982; Cooper 1983). This type of literature has a predominantly prescriptive nature and is oriented on how these steps should be taken. It pays less attention to what actually happens in innovation processes and who is involved in the process. The present study tries to enhance our understanding of the underlying mechanisms that inhibit the innovative performance of incumbent firms and adds a distinctively analytical perspective to the literature on innovation.

Fourth, the present study further integrates the literature of two fields of research, which have previously rarely talked to each other: namely innovation and neo-institutional theory. Innovations, especially competence-destroying innovations, cause major problems for established firms in mature populations and thus lack initial legitimacy (Tushman and Anderson 1986; Christensen 1997; Aldrich 1999; Tripsas and Gavetti 2000; Hill and Rothaermel 2003). Innovations can be distinguished between competence-enhancing and competence-destroying innovations. While competence-enhancing innovations tend to reinforce competitive positions, competence-destroying innovations go beyond current organizational competencies and create new opportunities (Tushman and Anderson 1986; Henderson and Clark 1990). The financial innovations in our study are not competence-destroying innovations: they mainly combine existing components in line with existing activities (see Chapter 2). However, when innovations meet institutions two social forces collide – one that stimulates stability and the other that stimulates change (Hargadon and Douglas 2001: 476). Our study points out that the acceptance of incremental or competence-*enhancing* innovations is problematic, because, although incremental innovations can be labeled 'familiar' (to all parties in an organization) and have therefore stayed on well-traveled paths, actors that try to champion these products do not always succeed in acquiring the necessary legitimacy for their product.

Outline of the book

In Chapter 2 we give an overview of the most relevant literature regarding institutional theory on the one hand and innovation on the other. Since extended literature reviews already exist in both fields, we concentrate on the most relevant contributions and direct the reader to the relevant overview articles. We then try to merge the two streams of literature and develop an analytical framework for the institutional analysis of innovation mainly based on the work by Scott (2001). Chapter 3 describes the specific features of services and the new service development process. In Chapter 4 we lay out the research design and the methodological framework of the study. In this chapter, the reader will also find a short description of the financial services companies that served as comparative cases. Chapter 5 is devoted first to three basic organizational notions that are widely expected to influence the success of product innovation: (1) project organization; (2) development approach and (3) teamwork. Second, based on this analysis the results of an exploratory study, which looked at innovation efforts of 39 financial services companies in the Netherlands at the end of the 1990s, are presented. We conclude this chapter by identifying the barriers for incremental product innovation these firms encountered. Chapter 6 contains an in-depth comparative description of incremental innovation processes in three large Dutch financial services companies. These empirical findings, and the results from case studies in nine more firms, are subsequently analysed in Chapter 7 on the basis of the neo-institutional approach. In Chapter 8, we present a theoretical framework for the analysis of innovation processes based on institutional theory and suggest that it could, in the future, serve as a complementary approach in the field of innovation. Chapter 9 concludes the book by listing the major findings and contributions to the innovation and institutional literature. We close with a discussion of the limitations and suggestions for future research.

2 Innovations and institutions

Introduction

The main purpose of this chapter is to develop a framework for understanding innovation from a neo-institutional perspective. In order to set the stage, we provide a brief overview of the literature on innovation and contemporary institutional theory. As most of the relevant literature regarding institutional theory has already been covered in review papers, we do not think it necessary to review the existing literature [see, for example, Scott (1995, 2001), who presented an excellent overview of research on institutions and organizations, and Lawrence and Suddaby (2006), who have carefully constructed an overview of the role of actors in creating, maintaining and disrupting institutions]. Our contribution lies in presenting a broad overview of the objects and subjects of innovation studies and exploring the possible contribution of institutional theory in explaining innovation. For the literature on innovation, we provide an overview of review articles covering a broad range of innovation topics.

Innovation[4]

Innovation is considered crucial for firm survival. Firms need to invest in new products and services before their competitors do. It is argued in much of the innovation literature that those firms that refrain from taking innovative actions will not remain viable in the long term (e.g. Soni *et al.* 1993; Banbury and Mitchell 1995). Innovation has been a consistent buzzword in the academic literature and has been receiving attention for over 70 years starting with the groundbreaking work of Schumpeter (1939, 1942). Thus, labeling innovation as just another fad or fashion does little justice to the body of literature that developed after Schumpeter's initial work. Yet, the perceived importance of innovation, especially in economics, management and organization studies, seems to have increased given the expanded attention in the academic literature over the last decades. Numerous publications have appeared in the academic journals covering a broad range of topics including technology development, product innovation, new product/service development, R&D, innovation diffusion, organizational innovation and innovation indicators.

Despite all the valuable contributions in the innovation literature, a clear overview of what innovation actually is and what innovation researchers are studying is lacking. The variety in the innovation literature is enormous, making it difficult and sometimes confusing for those new to the field to figure out what the important or interesting topics are and what innovation is all about. In this chapter we try to eliminate some of this confusion by presenting the reader with an overview of review articles that are categorized into two distinct approaches to innovation: an object and a subject approach (cf. Archibugi and Sirilli 2001). The key distinction between the two approaches is the unit of analysis. Whereas object-based studies focus on the innovation itself, subject-based studies focus on specific levels on which innovation is studied. Examples of innovation as objects are new products, services or processes, radical or incremental innovations, the transfer of technologies, patterns of diffusion, and measurement systems. Studies following the object approach mainly collect information about a certain category of innovation. These studies do not, for instance, measure or compare the innovativeness of actors. They are grouped under the same heading because of the lack of an actor perspective. Subject-based studies include research conducted on the national and international level, industry or sector studies, organizational-level, team-based and individual innovation studies. These studies often focus on the role of actors (nations, industries, organizations, teams and individuals) and try to derive best practice scenarios for these actors in order for them to become more innovative. The distinction between object- and subject-based studies is clearly analytical, meaning that there is considerable overlap between some of the categories identified in the two approaches.

Object-based approaches

The first group of studies focuses on *types of innovation*. There are many different types of innovation studied in the literature. For instance, new technologies, product lines, product features, processes, services, skills and uses are identified [see Garcia and Calantone (2002) for a complete overview]. In these studies it is described what exactly is new (often combined with to whom it is new). Furthermore, scholars in the marketing-oriented tradition concentrate on new product or service development, process development, product augmentation development, market development and offer development (Johne and Storey 1998). Each of these types is described in terms of its key features. For instance, product augmentation development deals with repositioning existing products, whereas process development comes in the form of cost reductions due to re-engineering efforts.

The second group of object-based studies is concerned with the degree of innovativeness. Perhaps even more than identifying different types of innovations, innovation researchers have elaborated on the degree of newness of innovations. Innovations can be new to the world, industry, scientific community, market, firm or customer (Garcia and Calantone 2002). The relevant unit of adoption is central in these studies. The majority of research takes a firm perspective as the relevant unit of adoption. Yet, others focus on markets or industries as the unit of adoption. Other studies look at the level of risk associated with innovations and distinguish between cost reductions, product repositioning, improvements, line extensions, new to the company products and new to the world products (Johne and Storey 1998). Other well-known distinctions have been made in the literature as well: radical versus incremental, evolutionary versus revolutionary, competence-enhancing versus competence-destroying, and discontinuous versus continuous innovation.

A third field of literature relates to measures of innovation. Several indicators for innovative activity are distinguished: R&D expenditures, patents, product announcements, number of R&D employees, expert judgments, and actual versus predicted market value (Clark and Guy 1998). These indicators are often used in national studies of innovation (see p. 15) to determine the competitive position of industries and countries. Data for these studies are collected on the basis of questionnaires (Community Innovation Surveys) that ask firms about the sources and objectives of innovation, costs and sales percentage of innovation, factors obstructing innovation, R&D activities, the impact of innovation, and technology transfer. Over time, the strengths and weaknesses of these indicators have been reported in the literature.

The fourth group of object-based studies is concerned with the adoption, implementation and diffusion of innovations. The development of innovations can be a daunting task. However, once the innovation is fully developed it needs to be implemented. Given the high failure rate of implementation, this is again a difficult task (Linton 2002). Implementation is one of the last steps in the innovation process. It involves the decision to adopt, and the use of, an innovation. Studies focusing on implementation describe the various steps in this part of the innovation process and focus on key success factors that lead to successful implementation (Linton 2002). After innovations are adopted and implemented by single firms, widespread diffusion takes place. The diffusion pattern refers to the spread of an innovation through a population of potential adopters (Wolfe 1994). The main objective of this type of research is to explain or predict adoption patterns over time. There are several key factors that affect diffusion patterns: characteristics of the adopter, the social network of the adopter, innovation attributes, environmental characteristics, communication process, characteristics of those promoting the innovation (Wolfe 1994).

The last group of object-based approaches deals with technology transfer. The literature on technology transfer deals with 'the movement of know-how, technical knowledge, or technology from one organizational setting to another' (Bozeman 2000: 629). Research in this field mainly covers technology policy paradigms and determinants of effectiveness of technology transfer. Three competing paradigms are identified in the literature: market failure, mission and cooperative technology. The market failure paradigm is based on the free market as the most efficient allocator of goods and services. There is, however, a role for the government in science and technology policy in order to remove barriers to the free market (Bozeman 2000). The mission technology paradigm argues that the government should perform R&D, whereas in the cooperative technology paradigm different actors should cooperate in technology development and transfer. Literature dealing with the effectiveness of technology transfer can be described in terms of dimensions and criteria (Bozeman 2000). The dimensions include characteristics of transfer agents, media, objects, demand environment and the transfer recipient. Criteria for effectiveness include 'out-the-door' (was technology transferred?), market impact (did transfer affect sales?), economic development (did transfer lead to economic development?), political (has the agent benefited politically?), opportunity cost (what was the impact of transfer on alternative use of resources?), and human capital (did transfer lead to increased capacity to perform?).

Subject-based approaches

The first subject approach can be found in international/national innovation studies. Research on this level is mainly focused on measuring inputs and outputs of innovation and 'traces the development of ... indicators derived by academics and researchers, through to the collection of more comprehensive and standardized national and international statistics' (Clark and Guy 1998: 368). Measures such as R&D expenditures, patent counts, new product announcements and other indicators of R&D activity are used to describe the innovative ability of industries and nations. The Community Innovation Survey (CIS) is an often-used data source for these studies. Notable is the shift of the traditional input-output models towards more holistic approaches to study innovation. Other studies on this level include explorations of the relationship between innovation and economic performance (these can also be related to the other levels described below). Most studies on the national level include policy implications to stimulate innovation. There are three broad areas for which innovation policies are developed: the supply of technologies, stimulating demand for technologies, and improving information flows through networks (Clark and Guy, 1998). Clark and Guy (1998) not only reviewed the literature, they also circulated a survey to researchers in the field of innovation. From the results of this study it appeared that the national level of analysis was most comprehensively covered in the field of innovation. Studies that include international issues are focused on comparisons of historical, economic and socio-cultural differences between countries and their respective effect on innovation (West and Altink 1996).

The second group of subject-based studies can be found on the level of industries and sectors. Sector studies are still relatively scarce. There are studies that consider differences between different industries or sectors (De Jong and Vermeulen 2006), but most researchers include services or manufacturing activities in their sample (Hoffman *et al.* 1998). Most research in this area is aimed at uncovering factors that lead to innovation success in specific industries. Also, a specific sample of firms has been considered, for instance small and medium-sized enterprises (Hoffman *et al.* 1998). Again a broad range of innovative activities is studied in relation to this specific sample of firms. These studies often include items derived from both national- and organizational-level studies, meaning that input and output factors are measured, as well as organizational factors that contribute to increase innovative performance. A second category of industry studies focuses on innovation diffusion (Da Silveira 2001). In these studies the mechanisms that determine the speed (how long it takes for the innovation to be adopted by a certain number of innovations) and pattern (changes in the number of adopters over time) of adoption of innovations are examined across industries (Da Silveira 2001).

The third group of studies is concerned with organizational innovations. Literature on innovation in single firms deals with attributes or factors that determine the innovativeness of organizations and products, and innovation processes (Wolfe 1994; Cumming 1998). The research on success factors deals with identifying key attributes that determine an organization's ability to innovate (Wolfe 1994). The organizational structure is an important variable that is studied since it is expected to be of major importance, but there is no agreement on what set of factors truly affect the innovative performance of individual firms (West and Altink 1996). Studies that focus on the process of innovation (Wolfe 1994) examine how and why innovations develop. The key activities and steps to be undertaken to successfully develop an innovation are closely examined. At first the focus was on stage-gate models that described a set of linear activities, whereas later the messiness of the development process was more accurately described.

The literature on new product and service development (which we include in this third group of organization-related literature) focuses on similar issues, yet the unit of analysis differs. Individual projects or products/services are studied rather than the organization as a whole. Brown and Eisenhardt (1995) presented an overview of the new product development (NPD) literature in three streams: success factors, development process, and communication web. Although their distinction has been a valuable contribution it does not clearly distinguish between different levels of analysis. The first stream deals with factors that contribute to the success of new products or projects. Factors such as product advantages, market attractiveness, product-market fit, internal organization, top management support, supplier and customer involvement, a creative climate, a well-designed process and sufficient resources have been identified as key issues that increase the success of NPD/and new service development (NSD) attempts (Brown and Eisenhardt 1995; Griffin 1997; Johne and Storey 1998; De Jong and Vermeulen 2003). A second stream of research deals with the development process itself. The development process consists of several distinct activities. How these can be organized and what should happen during these activities is central to this stream of research (Brown and Eisenhardt 1995; Griffin 1997; Johne and Storey 1998). Besides describing the development process, there is also attention for broader issues are considered such as the organizational conditions in which the development process is embedded (De Jong and Vermeulen 2003).

The fourth group of subject-based approaches deals with innovation at the team level. Brown and Eisenhardt's (1995) third area of research, communication web, deals with communication issues that are mainly related to team-based work in NPD projects. It highlights boundary-spanning activities of individuals in order to link various development activities, problems of communication between people with different functional backgrounds and the degree of communication between team members. Communication problems between people with different functional backgrounds have also been the focus of Griffin and Hauser's (1996) study. These authors review the literature that focused on the R&D and marketing interface. This interface has been identified as one of the most crucial interfaces in the development process. It is believed that people from these departments have different 'thought-worlds' and personalities, and speak different languages, which leads to problematic communication. Also, cooperation patterns are strongly hindered due to these problems (Griffin and Hauser 1996; McDonough 2000). This is partly related to different task priorities and responsibilities. These organizational barriers are often increased by lack of top management support in team efforts and perceived illegitimacy of product development. Furthermore, it appears that functional departments involved in NPD/NSD projects are often physically separated, which further increases cooperation and communication problems.

Other team-related innovation studies focus on antecedent variables that play an important role in the NPD/NSD process, such as empowerment of team members, setting project goals, establishing a project climate, and available resources of the team (West and Altink 1996; McDonough 2000). Another set of studies has focused on enablers of team success. These studies often focus on certain individuals that play an important role in the NPD/NSD process. Support from top management, team leadership, the presence of product champions, commitment from team members and ownership are important issues studied in this type of research (West and Altink 1996; McDonough 2000). A final group of studies is related to creativity in teams or groups (West and Altink 1996; McAdam and McClelland 2002). These studies focus on the effects of leadership style and cohesiveness between team members and how these eventually affect creativity in teams. Furthermore, as is the case in many innovation studies, key determinants for facilitating group innovation are studied, including vision, participative safety, a climate for excellence, and practical support (McAdam and McClelland 2002). Another stream of creativity literature focuses more on the idea generation techniques firms use to increase teams' innovative potential. Providing adequate structures for individual members to freely discuss their ideas is important in improving an overall climate of innovation (McAdam and McClelland 2002).

The final group of subject-based approaches studies individuals in relation to innovation and creativity. Researchers focusing on creativity regard individuals as the foundation of the organization (Mumford 2000; McAdam and McClelland 2002). This body of research has been split into several distinct areas. McAdam and McClelland (2002) focus on three areas: characteristics of creative people, preferred cognitive style for problem solving, and stimuli for individual creativity. The traits of creative individuals are often discussed in early research on creativity. Researchers tried to isolate the characteristics of creative people in order to understand why they were creative. These traits include a desire for autonomy and social independence, tolerance for ambiguity, and a propensity for risk taking. Preferred cognitive styles of individuals are analysed with Kirton's adaption-innovation theory (McAdam and McClelland 2002), which consists of an inventory list of statements against which individuals are scored. Enablers of individual creativity include expertise, creative-thinking skills and task motivation. Mumford (2000) argues that research on creativity stresses three key considerations: knowledge, process and work styles. He argues that creativity involves the creation of knowledge, which is achieved through a process of acquiring and manipulating information. Combining and reorganizing information is a complex process that is closely related to specific work styles of creative individuals. Hence, Mumford also pays attention to the traits of creative people.

We began this chapter by noting that a clear overview of what innovation researchers are studying is lacking. The large variety of studies in the innovation literature makes it difficult for those new to the field to figure out what the important or interesting topics are and what innovation is all about. We presented an overview of review articles that are categorized into two approaches to innovation: an object and a subject approach. Although we presented these approaches as clearly distinct, there is considerable overlap. Many studies include issues covering both approaches. Our study can best be described as following a subject-based approach on the organizational level. Before we continue with a description of how innovation can be organized, we first provide a working definition of what we mean by incremental product innovation in this book.

Defining incremental product innovation

The following overview represents a short summary of definitions concerning innovation that serve as a point of departure for the present study. According to Rogers (1962: 13) 'an innovation is an idea that is perceived as new by an individual'. Later, Rogers extended this early definition into 'an idea, practice, or object that is perceived as new by an individual or another unit of adoption' (1995: 11). Zaltman *et al.* define an innovation as 'any idea, practice, or material artifact perceived new by the relevant unit of adoption' (1973: 10). This means that an innovation does not necessarily have to be a novelty to the world, a country or an industrial sector but solely to a company, a business unit or even an individual. The rationale for defining innovation in this way is explained by Rogers (1995). He claims that it is the perception of the individual of the 'new' idea that will influence his or her behavior when he states that 'It matters little, so far as human behavior is concerned, whether or not an idea is objectively new as measured by the lapse of time since its first use or discovery. The perceived newness of the idea for the individual determines his or her reaction to it. If the idea seems new to the individual, it is an innovation' (1995: 11).

Barnett defines innovation as the invention of something new, and according to Mansfield an 'innovation represents an organization's "first use ever" of a new product, service, process, or idea' (in Pierce and Delbecq 1977: 28). Rickards (1991: 105) defines innovation as 'a social problem-solving process of a non-routine kind', while van de Ven (1986: 591) simply says that 'an innovation is a new idea'. Following the definition of Zaltman *et al.* mentioned above, West and Farr (1990: 9) elaborate on an innovation as 'the intentional introduction and application within a role, group or organization of ideas, processes, products or procedures, new to the relevant unit of adoption, designed to significantly benefit the individual, the group, organization or wider society'. West and Altink (1996) note that innovation is intentional and the success of the innovation is not only measured by its economic benefits (other benefits could be personal growth, increased satisfaction and improved cohesiveness). Besides this, innovation is not restricted to technological change and can also be found in procedures or processes and 'requires an application component' (1996: 5). The final aspect is about the novelty of the innovation, where the main focus is on the idea being new to the relevant unit of adoption. Although these definitions differ to some extent, they share at least one similar feature: an innovation always implies something new or perceived new, non-routine or a discovery and in most cases the newness relates to the unit of adoption.

However, these definitions do not give any information on what kind of innovations are involved. In Chapter 1 we mentioned various types of innovation that are distinguished in the literature. In this study, innovations are product innovations that are new combinations of (existing) products. The basic assumption in developing a new product is that several (meaning more than one) organizational functions are involved. This leads to the following definition of product innovation:

> A new combination of (existing) products that is perceived new by the relevant unit of adoption and of which the development involves multiple organizational functions.

Product innovation does not happen overnight. It involves many people from different departments who collaborate for a long time and a large amount of money and energy is spent on these efforts. For this study, we also narrow the type of product innovation to incremental product innovation. Most new products in financial service firms are modifications of existing products that build on current competencies (Avlonitis *et al.* 2001). This type of innovation mainly is concerned with improvements in existing 'combi-products'. Combi-products resemble architectural innovations (Henderson and Clark 1990). The separate component parts of these products already exist, yet either the combination is new or one of the components is changed, which creates new linkages with the other components. As such, they also resemble Garud and Nayyar's (1994) notion of transformative capacity in which firms combine resources spread over the organization. In our case, we are interested in improved versions of these products. This means that the linkages between the components remain unchanged and the core concepts are reinforced. Therefore, these improved combi-products are labeled incremental innovations. Although we are dealing with incremental innovations, there is complexity involved in these processes. The complexity of these innovations is concerned with the reorganization of interdependent administrative procedures and the co-ordination of the multiple departments involved (MacMillan *et al.* 1985).

Organizing for sustained innovation

It has often been said that large, mature organizations lack sufficient innovative capabilities and that there is a love-hate relationship between the two (Burgelman and Sayles 1986). However, large US companies such as 3M, General Electric, Johnson and Johnson and Wal-Mart have shown that 'large size need not be antithetical' to innovation (Block and MacMillan 1993: 2). Yet, large firms often do have more difficulties with the development of new products than smaller firms do. The most important changes that are needed for these organizations to become more innovative concern the organizational structure and the underlying values and beliefs. One of the key issues in becoming more innovative in the financial services sector is to explicitly designate a 'place' for product development. Different types of innovation-enabling structures have been designed over the last decades. The venture organization, for instance, has a dual structure. Besides the structure of the (functional) parent organization, a second structure, a new product division, can be identified. This division is a place that provides a 'safe haven' for product development projects and consists of a pool of employees that originate from the functional departments in the parent organization (Block and MacMillan 1993). These employees have volunteered for the new product division and can be considered the entrepreneurs of the organization. The venture organization combines a relatively organic culture that coexists under the same corporate skin with traditional, proceduralized business (see Burgelman and Sayles 1986; Block and MacMillan 1993). It is characterized by the structural separation of product development from the parent organization. The hypertext organization (as described by Nonaka and Takeuchi 1995) consists of three organizational layers: a business-system layer, a project-team layer and a knowledge-base layer. The business-system layer is the central layer in the hypertext organization in which the routine activities are carried out. These routine activities can be conducted in a bureaucratic structure. Therefore, the business system is shaped like a traditional hierarchical pyramid. The project-team layer hosts all the project teams that work on innovative or non-routine activities. The team members are drawn from the business system and work on the project on a full-time basis until the project is finished. The knowledge layer is a virtual aspect of the hypertext organization. It does not exist as a separate unit, but is embedded in the organizational strategy and vision of top management. It is a virtual place where knowledge from the other two layers is stored and shared.

For many large firms the solution to becoming innovative was found in behaving like small entrepreneurial ventures (Quinn 1985). These firms tried to keep their organizations flat and worked in project teams with members from different departments who complemented each other's skills. Under the labels of skunkworks, corporate venturing teams, product development teams and new business development teams many new products have been developed. These approaches are believed to have reduced bureaucracy, allowed fast communication, reduced throughput times and lowered costs (Clark and Fujimoto 1991). However, besides creating structures that facilitate the development of new products, these firms also had to invest heavily in altering the basic assumptions and underlying values by using vision and leadership and an active external orientation. Changing current assumptions and values will probably be the most difficult task for organizations that want to achieve sustained product innovation, since these are taken for granted and implicitly guide individual behavior. These kind of changes require the articulation of a new vision (Tidd *et al.* 1997).

Whether the basic assumptions and values will be changed depends, to a large extent, on the behavior of top management. A clear vision that underlines the importance of innovation is needed and innovative behavior should be rewarded accordingly (Schein 1997; Tushman and O'Reilly 1997). By sending out clear signals to the organization it should be stressed that the traditional norms and values are no longer sufficient to survive. Management could even consider creating dissatisfaction with the status quo (Tushman and O'Reilly 1997) as long as employees realize that innovation is a necessity for their organization and needs to be incorporated in the organizational value system. At all levels of the organization continuous attention must be placed on these new values. The change efforts are still rather gradual and incremental, but nevertheless they eventually reshape the organization's culture. Organizational leaders are often initiators of change. They feel that the prevailing ideologies need to be adjusted with the belief that innovation is (sometimes) necessary and as such should receive specific attention at certain times. Besides the use of reinforcement mechanisms (Schein 1997) such as the organization structure, supporting systems and procedures, rites and rituals, and formal statements, organizational leaders can also use other mechanisms for communicating what they believe in. Employees will notice what leaders pay attention to, what criteria they use to allocate resources (i.e. what is important), what kind of behavior is stimulated and rewarded, and what kind of new members are recruited. Consistent behavior is a very powerful tool for communicating new values and assumptions. When managerial behavior is experienced as consistent, employees might copy this behavior.

Organizing for innovation also means a more active external orientation. Markets are scanned more actively and additional methods are used to collect customer information. A clear focus on customer needs is crucial for success or failure of new products (Rothwell 1992). Although customers might find it difficult to express their needs, which is certainly the case in financial services, close attention should be paid to what the customer desires. A widespread awareness of customers has to be developed in the organization in order to improve the quality (and the match with customer demands) of new products (Nijssen *et al.* 2006).

There are many examples of mature firms that have been able to develop new products successfully. Similarly, there are many examples of firms who have not been successful at delivering new products. This is especially the case when firms try to engage in sustained innovation, i.e. the development of a continuous stream of new products (cf. Dougherty and Hardy 1996). The key challenge is to connect these consecutive innovation attempts with routine practices. Developing the capacity for sustained innovation requires resources, collaborative structures and processes (such as described previously) and new innovation-related values and beliefs that are considered meaningful (Dougerhty and Hardy 1996). However, being capable of sustained innovation is not simply a matter of assigning resources to projects, changing structures, processes and values. Van de Ven (1986) has lamented on the strategic problem of creating an infrastructure that would be conducive to innovation. We draw on the notion of organizational practice (cf. Kostova and Roth 2002) to explain this. Underlying the activities of organizations is a routine use of knowledge for conducting the essential functions of the organization that has evolved over time under the influence of the organization's history, people, interests and actions (Kostova and Roth 2002: 216). Organizational practices in mature, established firms have become taken-for-granted and are increasingly difficult to change because they are accepted by organizational members and are highly legitimate. Sustained innovation requires a new way of working and hence a new set of organizational practices. We argue that organizational practices are institutionalized and have required a rule-like status, which constrains the ability to deviate from these practices. When innovations meet institutions two social forces collide; one that stimulates stability and the other that stimulates change (Hargadon and Douglas 2001: 476). Our study points out that the acceptance of incremental or competence-enhancing innovations can be problematic, because, although incremental innovations can be labeled 'familiar' (to all parties in an organization) and have therefore stayed on well-traveled paths, actors that try to champion these products do not always succeed in acquiring the necessary legitimacy for their product.

In many established financial services firms, organizational practices seem heavily institutionalized and new innovative products that generate changes in these practices are considered illegitimate (Vermeulen 2005). The unique features of services (see Chapter 3) lead to the unavoidable adaptation of organizational procedures, even in the case of incremental innovations. Hence, the introduction of new products leads to adjustments and alterations in organizational practices. The adaptation of these organizational practices is an example of how organizations that are heavily institutionalized may change. Incremental product innovations are building on existing practices and, as such, resemble convergent change. Convergent change, however, which is similar to improving existing practices, is not sufficient to break down institutionalized practices and achieve sustained product innovation. The shift towards a more innovative company is not an easy one. Many organizational members find it difficult to change. The resistance to change will be higher when drastic changes are needed. However, firms that want to fundamentally change their current practices and implement and internalize new innovative practices to achieve a level of sustained product innovation need alterations at the deepest institutionalized levels of the organization. Radical change or 'frame bending' (Greenwood and Hinings 1996: 1024) is needed to transform the organization and overcome the constraints that the organizational trajectory imposes on organizations. When confronted with pressures from within or outside the organization the adoption of new practices will be influenced by perceptions and interpretations shaped by intra- and organizational institutions (Kostova and Roth 2002). In the next section we elaborate on the institutional perspective underlying our study.

Institutional theory

Some 15–20 years ago it was noted that institutional theory had reached adolescence (Scott 1987) and experienced a renaissance in the social sciences (DiMaggio and Powell 1991). Today, a steady stream of institutional research is still published in a large variety of academic journals, such as Administrative Science Quarterly, Academy of Management Journal, Academy of Management Review, American Journal of Sociology, Organization Science, Organization Studies and many more. It seems that we are far from decline. One reason for this continued interest is the high level of interdisciplinarity that characterizes the underlying assumptions of institutional theory (DiMaggio and Powell 1991). We have seen institutional ideas being used in political science, economics, sociology, psychology, social movement studies, and organization studies. The integration of different scientific disciplines has resulted in a broad and extensive research field that enforced the opportunities within organizational theory to analyse problematic issues from different perspectives. This broad interest has led to a variety of definitions of what institutions are. North (1990: 3) defines institutions as 'the rules of the game in a society, or more formally ... the humanly devised constraints that shape human interaction'. Jepperson (1991: 143) also talks about rules of the game and claims that institutions are organized, established procedures represented as constitutive rules. According to Jepperson an 'institution represents a social order or pattern that has attained a certain state or property; institutionalization denotes the process of such attainment' (1991: 145). A more elaborate description has been provided by Scott (1995: 33) who claims that 'Institutions consist of cognitive, normative, and regulative structures and activities that provide stability and meaning to social behavior. Institutions are transported by various carriers – cultures, structures, and routines – and they operate at multiple levels of jurisdiction'. This 'omnibus' definition immediately demonstrates the complexity of institutional theory in terms of its pervasiveness of institutions at distinct levels of analysis, the distinct features of various carriers and a variety of potential institutional forces. This complexity causes the difficulty in understanding institutions (van de Ven and Hargrave 2004). Scott (2001) explained that important differences exist among institutional scholars, which has resulted in varying emphases on the different institutional elements. These elements could be regulative, normative or cultural-cognitive, and their impact on the innovative activities of banks and insurance companies will be discussed later in this chapter. Hence, in this section, we only address the carriers of institutions and the levels of analysis to further lay the foundation of our theoretical framework.

Institutions are embedded in various types of carriers. Jepperson (1991) distinguished between formal organization, regimes and culture. Formal organization has received much attention as one of the main carriers of institutions (e.g. Meyer and Rowan 1977). Regimes refer to 'institutionalization in some central authority ... without primary embodiment in a formal organizational apparatus' (Jepperson 1991: 150). Regimes are codified rules and sanctions, which can be found in a legal system or a certain profession (e.g. the police or medics). There is often some monitoring and sanctioning involved to make sure that there is no deviation from the regime by any of its members. Culture can also be a carrier of institutions, although it is not formal and monitoring and sanctions are lacking, which produces expectations about the behavior of individuals. Scott (1995) has revised this set suggested by Jepperson and argues that social structures, routines and culture are the carriers of institutions. Cultures, according to Scott (1995:

53), are carriers that primarily rely on interpretive schemes (codified patterns of meaning and rule systems) that inform and constrain ongoing behavior, but at the same time they can be reinforced and changed by this behavior. Different emphasis is given to various aspects of culture depending on the institutional elements stressed. Rules and laws are typical when emphasizing regulatory elements, values and expectation fall under the normative elements, and categories and typifications are mainly found when cognitive elements are stressed. The second carrier distinguished by Scott is social structure, meaning the 'patterned expectations connected to networks of social positions: role systems' (1995: 53). The aspects of social structures that are addressed also depend on the three possible elements. Regulatory elements view structures as governance or power systems in which coercion is dominant. In a normative setting, structures are authority systems or regimes. Cognitive elements stress structural isomorphism and distinct identities (e.g. departments within an organization). Institutions can also be 'carried' by routines (Scott 1995: 54) namely patterned actions that reflect the deeply ingrained habits and procedures based on tacit knowledge. Again, we see distinctions between the emphases of the institutional elements. Regulatory elements look at routines as protocols and standard procedures, normative elements are mainly concerned with conformity and the performance of specific duties, and cognitive elements view routines as consisting of performance programs and scripts.

Levels of analysis

Institutional theory has been applied at various levels of analysis. Scott (2001) has distinguished six levels: world system, societal, organizational field, organizational population, organization, and organizational subsystems. All of these levels have been used in institutional analysis, but the organizational field has been identified as the most significant level of analysis for institutional theory. Organizational fields are communities of organizations that constitute a recognized area of institutional life and whose interactions are regularized and 'fateful' (Scott 1994). Fields thus comprise suppliers, resource and product consumers, regulatory agencies, professional associations as well as organizations that produce similar services or products (DiMaggio and Powell 1983: 148). Regulatory agencies of the state and professional associations have the ability to endorse or reject strategies from members of the field, and in doing so they play an important role in defining organizational fields and their behavior (Scott 2001). Fields are sustained through shared 'institutional logics' (Friedland and Alford 1991) that draw boundaries around field constituents, defining membership, role identities and exchange relationships (Lawrence 1999).

Fields are often conceived as highly stable. Indeed, studies of field evolution emphasize how regularized patterns of exchange (markets) become amplified and reproduce themselves through processes of structuration (e.g.

Leblebici *et al.* 1991). However, over time, fields are subject to considerable discussion and change (Brint and Karabel 1991; White 1992; Hoffman 1999; Scott 1995, 2001; Greenwood *et al.* 2002). Fields contain 'contradictions' that become opportunities for change (Seo and Creed 2002). Furthermore, constituents of a field may be 'armed with opposing perspectives rather than with common rhetorics ' (Hoffman 1999: 352). Organizational fields comprise groups of organizations differentially advantaged by prevailing institutional structures: powerful groups impose their preferred logics (Brint and Karabel 1991: 355) but insurgent logics are contained within less advantaged players who seek a more powerful position. Stability in the market patterns of a field, therefore, may be temporary rather than absolute.

A less fine-grained approach to distinguishing between various levels can be found in Baum (2002); in this edited volume a distinction is made between intraorganizational, organizational and interorganizational institutions. Intraorganizational institutions are taken-for-granted beliefs that arise within organizations and delimit acceptable and normative behavior for its members (Elsbach 2002: 37). Elsbach (2002) distinguished three types of intraorganizational institutions: value, structure and process institutions. Value institutions include norms about core values of organizational units. They can refer to norms about certain organizational practices, such as quality management or responsible use of resources. Much of the work on value institutions has examined group identities and subcultures that aid group members to maintain positive self-images. Through value institutions organizational members seek affirmation of their identity, which, once institutionalized, is strongly adhered to even though this may be irrational or highly inefficient. Weick (1993) eloquently describes the case of a group of firefighters that refuse to drop their heavy tools in a situation that eventually led to the death of 13 men in 'The Mann Gulch Disaster'. Because they did not drop their tools in time, or at all, they were not able to outrun the fire that chased them. Later, Weick claimed that 'the reluctance to drop one's tools when threat intensifies is not just a problem for firefighters' (1996: 301), but a more common problem that relates to all human beings. Dropping one's tools means unlearning, adapting to new situations, being flexible, accepting mutation and modernizing old values. As such, value institutions can be strong inhibitors of change. Process institutions include protocols, standard operating procedures and routines. These may be created intentionally by managers who develop manuals on how to engage in specific activities (such as product development) or they develop informally over time. In the latter case, examples are routines about how people communicate in the organization (phone, email, face-to-face) or how public facilities are used. When taken-for-granted by organizational members, protocols and routines can be seen as a type of intraorganizational institution. Many product development projects are routinely executed through the use of a product development manual. Such manuals not only guide the process, but have become entrenched as routine problem solving (Clark and Fujimoto 1991). Structure institutions involve the norms about roles, composition, power and status of groups. These are particularly strongly developed in professions, such as in a medical or accounting setting. The struggle of midwifes or psychologists to become legitimated in the medical environment serve as illustrative examples of the problems that may rise when powerful groups are reluctant to change their taken-for-granted beliefs. Meyerson (1994) provides an example of the low status of social work departments in hospitals dominated by traditional medical models.

Palmer and Biggart (2002) elaborate on another type of institution: organizational institutions. Research that focuses on these institutions is mainly focused on the institutional environment that affects organizations. Regulative, normative and cognitive institutions shape and guide the behavior of individuals within organizations. Palmer and Biggart (2002: 260) address three questions: Where do institutional constraints on organizations come from? What are the effects of institutional structures on organizations? How does change in institutional environments come about and diffuse? The sources of institutional constraints can be found in supra-organizations such as the state. The states' laws and regulations set boundaries for organizational behavior. Industry associations and professions may also be a source of institutional constraint. Professional and trade associations, for example, promulgate institutional rules (DiMaggio and Powell 1983; Greenwood et al. 2002). These associations try to protect and advance the interests of their members and evaluate and monitor conformity to their rules. Associations can obstruct governmental actions directed at institutional change. Lounsbury (2001) argued that field-level associations are critically important both in legitimating new organizational practices and in evoking resistance to deviating practices. The effects on organizations are varied. Institutions can have an effect on the form of an organization when founded. In the 1990s, new accountancy firms were likely to shape their organization according to the dominant organizational form of multidisciplinary practice that was broadly diffused at the time (Greenwood and Suddaby 2006). Institutions may also affect the birth rate and survival of organizations. Ultimately, they also trigger change in organizations. Below, we further elaborate on the notion of institutional change.

Interorganizational institutions are the third type of institutions. Research on this type of institution focuses on relations between and networks of organizations. It tries to shed more light on the dynamic interplay between institutionalized structures. The role and importance of collective actors is stressed in attempts of institutional resistance or change (Strang and Sine 2002). Collectivities such as communities play a dominant role in the way their members behave and respond to changes in the environment. For institutional challengers to be successful, it is often argued that a collective effort is needed to bring about change (Fligstein and Mara-Drita 1996). The mobilization of groups is considered a necessary condition for successful institutional change efforts.

In short, institutional theory is often viewed as a break from rational-actor models (see, for instance, Zucker 1983, 1991; Scott 1987). Conforming to institutional rules may even conflict with organizational efficiency criteria (Meyer and Rowan 1977); they may appear in different forms and at different levels. In this book we will mainly focus on intraorganizational institutions, but we also devote ample attention to organizational institutions. Before we turn to the influence of institutional forces on innovation we briefly address the notion of institutional change. We think it is necessary to understand that institutions can change, before we continue describing the relation between institutions and innovation.

Do institutions change?

It was mentioned earlier that institutional theory neither denies nor conflicts with the notion of change (Greenwood *et al.* 2002). The heavy criticism by other academics within and outside the scholarly domain of institutional theory (see Scott 2001) has probably had its effect on the inclusion of change and agency in institutional theory. There is a growing number of studies on institutional change (Oliver 1992; Goodstein 1994; Goodrick and Salancik 1996; Dorado 2005) and it has been argued that the topic of institutional change has emerged as a central focus for organization scholars interested in institutional phenomena (Dacin *et al.* 2002: 45). The processes of institutional transformation involve both the decomposition and disappearance of given institutions (Scott 2001: 182) or deinstitutionalization (Oliver 1991, 1992) and the re-composition of a new set of institutional arrangements (Lounsbury 2002; Reay and Hinings 2005).

Although there is still a tension in institutional theory with respect to the issues of agency and change, also termed the 'paradox of embedded agency' (Seo and Creed 2002), the focus of institutional theory has shifted towards understanding the process 'by which the legitimacy of an established or institutionalized organizational practice erodes or discontinues' (Oliver 1992: 564). Oliver (1992) distinguished between political, functional and social pressures that might lead to deinstitutionalization. Political pressure can be increased by performance problems (crisis) that threaten the legitimacy of an organization and its rules and procedures. Because of these problems, internal conflicts may arise. When power is shifted to people with different visions, they might try to use their influence to gain political support from other organizational members to change the course of the organization (i.e. to deinstitutionalize). Other political pressures are 'innovation' pressures that can be enforced by customers or competitors and changes in external dependencies (as in the case of deregulation as is described below).

Functional pressures are more concerned with changes in the 'perceived utility or technical instrumentality' of institutionalized practices (Oliver 1992: 571). This can relate to economic utility (when it is no longer rewarding to perpetuate institutionalized practices) or to increased technical specificity or goal clarity. Institutionalization thrives on ambiguity and uncertainty. The less clear the mission and goals of the organization, the more chances for organizational myths and beliefs concerning the legitimacy of organizational practices to prevail, and thus for institutions to remain intact (Selznick 1957). In other words, 'when means-ends relations in any organization become clearer ... , when methods for evaluating outcomes become more precise ... or when organizational objectives become more technically specific ... , then institutionally prescribed activities and modes of operation will tend to be displaced by more technical criteria of organizational effectiveness' (Oliver 1992: 573). This is in line with the view of institutions not being driven by rational actors. It is not until these functional pressures become visible that people question the validity of institutionalized practices and wonder how efficient these practices are. Increased competition for resources is also considered a functional pressure. If the organizational performance is to be kept at an acceptable level and the organization wants to be competitive, the organization needs to adapt in order to be distinct from competitors and obtain the scarce resources. The last functional pressures that are described by Oliver are unexpected events that 'discredit or challenge the utility of the operating assumptions of organizations' (1992: 574).

Social pressures are of a different nature than the political and functional pressures described above. According to Oliver (1992: 575), political and functional pressures assume that actors 'consciously acknowledge the need' to challenge current institutionalized practices, which means that they are actively involved in the deinstitutionalization process. This is not the case when social pressures affect institutionalized practices. Normative fragmentation, the loss of agreement among organizational actors due to new leadership, and increased turnover or workforce diversity, changes the course of the organization. New employees bring their own set of ideologies into the organization. Some of these new ideologies might get lost due to socialization processes, but some will affect the other organizational members, leading to deinstitutionalization.

Political, functional and social pressures, technological innovations and regulatory changes, presenting themselves as 'environmental jolts' (Meyer *et al.* 1990), are important drivers for disrupting institutionalized practices and provide alternatives on which the foundations for new institutions are created (Oliver 1992; Greenwood *et al.* 2002). This will most likely be a difficult and lengthy undertaking, as established fields may feel threatened and undermine the legitimacy of the new institution through disinformation or the active suppression of alternatives (Aldrich and Fiol 1994). Widespread adoption of new alternatives or innovation is therefore not likely at this stage. For widespread adoption and diffusion of new arrangements to occur, it needs to be justified as a possible solution before actual diffusion may take place (Greenwood *et al.* 2002). This involves the development of consensus among organizational decision makers and the subsequent adoption by other organizations (Tolbert and Zucker 1996). Additionally, institutional entrepreneurs may enhance the diffusion of innovations. Institutional entrepreneurs try to actively establish changes in the existing institutional arrangements (DiMaggio 1988). These change agents are expected to be 'marginalized or less powerful participants within the existing institutional arrangements' (Seo and Creed 2002: 236). In order to be successful, these entrepreneurs require social skills to be able to motivate cooperation from other actors (Fligstein 1997). However, a single individual will often not be capable of disseminating an innovation, but instead an entrepreneurial group is needed (Colomy 1998). By crystallizing broad symbolic orientations in new ways and articulating specific goals, such groups work to persuade other players to adopt the innovation. The change process is 'completed' when cognitive legitimacy sets in and the new arrangements become taken-for-granted (Greenwood *et al.* 2002).

These mutually constitutive and interactive processes of change are widely seen to follow a 'sequential' model. In their study of the Canadian accounting profession, Greenwood *et al.* (2002) document a process model of institutional change that includes the following stages: a precipitating jolt that disturbs existing practices; deinstitutionalization, in which the established consensus is challenged and new actors and practices enter; pre-institutionalization, in which actors innovate; theorization, in which deviations from prevailing conventions are legitimated and made available for wider adoption; diffusion, which follows successful theorization; and re-institutionalization, when new practices become fully institutionalized. The literature has long emphasized institutional change as a 'sequential' process comprising of different 'stages' (Lawrence *et al.* 2001; Greenwood *et al.* 2002). However, such a portrayal masks the dynamism and complexity of the change process, whereby the ideas, values and logics of different 'stages' may vacillate, cross, coexist, fuse, conflict or remain unresolved (Fiss and Zajac 2004). Several scholars have argued that the changes process is represented not by complete, distinct or sweeping shifts, but rather 'sedimentation' – a layering of one logic on another (e.g. Cooper *et al.* 1996; Pinnington and Morris 2003). This makes change an erratic process with many steps, partial steps and missteps. In short, the sequential model does not fully capture the dialectic of continuity and transformation (Pettigrew 1985). The process of institutional transformations is not necessarily 'sequential' and progressive but iterative and recursive, especially in the early stages.

Although we do not explicitly address the notion of institutional change, we have considered our brief outline important for understanding the relation between institutions and innovation and the possibilities for institutionalized organizations to engage in innovation. Next we explain how institutional forces may affect the innovative activities of financial services firms.

Institutional forces affecting incremental innovation

In this book we build on Scott's (2001) framework of regulative, normative and cultural-cognitive institutional pillars. This framework converges around multiple themes combining the 'old' and 'new' institutionalism into 'neo-institutionalism' (Greenwood and Hinings 1996). Research in the regulative school has focused on institutional elements that constrain and standardize behavior through explicit regulative processes. These elements are distinguished by the prominence of rules, systems, laws and sanctions that are developed as a result of conflicting interests of individuals and organizations, eventually leading to the pursuit of self-interest (Scott 2001). The normative school emphasizes aspects that are prescriptive, evaluative and considered obligatory. These normative elements include values and norms that deal with preferences for certain desired behaviors or outcomes and tell us how things should be done, for example which behaviors or outcomes are expected, acceptable and appropriate (March and Olsen 1989). The cultural-cognitive school concentrates on shared conceptions constituting the nature of reality and the frames through which meaning is conveyed (Scott 2001: 57).

The evolution of three separate schools of thought in the institutional literature serves as an example of the fragmentation of the field. Besides the varying emphasis on specific pillars, there is much variety in the levels of analysis on which institutions are studied (Scott 2001). There are, however, few studies that have combined both the three pillars and multiple levels. In this book, we will investigate institutional pressures from a variety of sources (cf. Wicks 2001) and, in developing our conceptual framework, we will make a distinction between intraorganizational (micro) and organizational (macro) institutional forces (cf. Zucker 1991).

Based on a review of the literature, in the remainder of this section regulative, normative and cognitive factors that are assumed to have a strong impact on the innovative activities of financial services companies on both levels will be discussed. We do not intend to provide an exhaustive overview of all the institutional literature available, but want to indicate illustrative references that focus on these issues (see Table 2.1).

Regulative forces

Intraorganizational forces

The organizational structure is probably one of the most frequently studied institutional elements (Scott 1987). Whereas classic organization theory emphasized the problems of coordination and control of work activities (Tolbert 1985), Meyer and Rowan (1977) argued that formal structures reflect myths and ceremonies of their institutionalized environments. Formal structures that adhere to myths are designed to fit with collectively valued

Table 2.1 References for institutional forces

Regulative	*Normative*	*Cultural-cognitive*
Organizational level		
Regulation at the governmental or professional association level (DiMaggio and Powell 1983; North 1990; Dobbin and Dowd 1997; Oliver 1991; Hoffman 1999; Greenwood *et al.* 2002)	Societal pressures that affect the organization, such as customer expectations (Parsons 1951; Selznick 1957; DiMaggio and Powell 1983; Ashforth and Gibbs 1990; Friedland and Alford 1991)	Mimetic behavior (isomorphism) from competitors (DiMaggio and Powell 1983; Galaskiewicz and Wasserman 1989; Fligstein 1991; Haveman 1993; Scott 1995)
Intraorganizational level		
Regulatory processes that establish rules to influence future behavior, such as organizational structures and systems (Meyer and Rowan 1977; Tolbert and Zucker 1983; Tolbert 1985; North 1990; Scott 1987, 1995, 2001; Dijksterhuis *et al.* 1999; March et al. 2000)	Norms, values and roles directed at social obligation (Selznick, 1957; March and Olson, 1989; Dougherty and Heller 1994, Scott 1995, 2001, McDermott and O'Conner 2002)	Shared conceptions and frames of references that construct reality and create social identities (Berger and Luckmann 1967; Zucker 1977, 1983, 1987; Prahalad and Bettis 1986; Dougherty 1992; Trice 1993; Scott, 1995, 2001; Dijksterhuis *et al.* 1999; Wicks, 2001; Seo and Creed 2002)

purposes, thereby increasing their legitimacy in the wider social structure (Tolbert and Zucker 1983; Dijksterhuis *et al.* 1999). Although this conception of structure has a cognitive connotation, we believe that many formal authority structures have clearly defined, specified procedures to follow, as well as associating penalties in the case of failure (March *et al.* 2000). This latter conception clearly emphasizes the regulatory force of organizational structures. Furthermore, many organizational structures are still directed at obtaining compliance with the pursuit of self-interest, which has been ascribed to the regulative pillar. North (1990) stresses the use of formal and informal rules and enforcement mechanisms in order to obtain this compliance. When these rules are violated, punishment is administered (North 1990). Unwritten rules or codes of behavior are, therefore, as important in determining the regulative properties of institutions as formal structures are (North 1990). Formal, quasi-formal (see Schoonhoven and Jelinek 1997) and informal structures prohibit and enable individual behavior. Organizational structures and information systems are examples of regulative forces on the micro level. These systems exert strong controls on innovative activities in financial companies. Information systems were designed in the 1970s (Flier *et al.* 2001) and have been referred to as legacy systems, based on what now is considered old or even obsolete technology. Legacy systems are the core substance of banks and insurance companies. These systems have been developed to support organizational functions and are focused on optimizing local efficiencies, without considering the wider organizational system (Singh 1997). Thus, they contain sedimented regulatory elements that may be as hard to change as the mere technical aspects. We believe that micro regulatory forces exert strong controls on innovative activities in established companies (cf. North 1990). In the case of radical innovation, these structures and their supporting information systems may lead to fierce problems in the development process (e.g. Dougherty and Heller 1994; Christensen 1997; Tushman and O'Reilly 1997). Incremental innovations, however, seem to benefit from more traditional structural arrangements (Ettlie *et al.* 1984; McDermott and O'Connor 2002), which means that intraorganizational regulatory forces are supposed to have a positive impact on the development of incremental product innovation.

Organizational forces

Regulatory agencies, such as the national government and professional associations, have been identified as critically important in the process of institutionalization (North 1990; Hoffman 1999; Greenwood *et al.* 2002). North (1990) describes the role of the state in third-party enforcement. Third-party enforcement involves a 'neutral' party, an enforcer that has to make sure that contracts between parties are not violated. In the case of the Dutch financial services industry, up to the end of the 1980s the national government had imposed strict regulations on the collaboration between banks and insurance companies by means of a so-called 'structure policy', which defined the limits of collaboration between banks and insurance companies (Flier *et al.* 2001). Policy has often shown direct effects on organizations, causing firms to adopt specific practices or encouraging managers to invent new practices (Dobbin and Dowd 1997). In this respect, the state could be seen as a coercive force steering organizations in a certain direction (DiMaggio and Powell 1983). However, most policies do not dictate firm behavior, but create constraints and incentives that managers take into account in formulating strategies (Dobbin and Dowd 1997). Due to the regulatory changes at both the European Union and country level, in the early 1990s banks and insurance companies were allowed to integrate. This regulatory change led to an enormous increase in financial products (Flier *et al.* 2001). Therefore, the national government has had a strong impact on the number and type of new products that were developed in Dutch financial services companies. As a consequence, we expect these organizational institutional forces to have a positive impact on the development of new services in these firms. In countries where the government still imposes restrictions on the collaboration between banks and insurance companies, this force will negatively affect sustained incremental product innovation.

Normative forces

Intraorganizational forces

Normative forces introduce a prescriptive, evaluative and obligatory dimension into social life, reflecting the values (what is preferred) and norms (how things should be done) of the social system (Scott 2001). People in specific organizational roles are expected to fulfil certain social obligations (Selznick 1957; March and Olson 1989). Expected behavior follows the logic of appropriateness. Appropriate behavior reflects the normal, routine way in which people do what they are supposed to do and is based on behavior that is expected by other actors (March and Olson 1989: 21). Specific roles (or positions) held by certain actors in the organization lead to expectations held by other organizational members. These expectations are often perceived as external pressures to which one must conform. The basis for this type of confirmation is described as social obligation, which can be either constraining or enabling to social action. The social context is able to specify certain guidelines for individual conduct, which means that it is not necessarily rational (Scott 2001). In financial services companies we expect that social obligations point in the direction of risk avoidance and uncertainty reduction. Traditionally, managers in these companies are not expected to take risks, which is often needed for innovation. Uncertainty reduction and risk avoidance are examples of normative forces that have been identified as some of the main barriers to innovation (Dougherty and Heller 1994; McDermott and O'Connor 2002). However, since incremental innovation is of an evolutionary nature, few uncertainties are involved. We therefore assume that top managers in established firms that display a high degree of uncertainty reduction and risk avoidance behavior will still engage in incremental innovation.

Organizational forces

Organizations looking for legitimacy need to find congruence between organizational values and wider societal values. It has even been argued that organizational behavior cannot be understood without locating it in a wider societal context (Friedland and Alford 1991). Organizations also fulfil certain roles that lead to associated expected behavior, which among others reflects customer expectations. Understanding customer values and needs is crucial for the success of new products (as has been argued at length in the innovation literature, e.g. Dougherty 1990; Cooper 1999; Ulwick 2002). Adhering to customer values is especially important to organizations whose claims to legitimacy are predicated on high levels of trust, such as financial services companies (Ashforth and Gibbs 1990). Radical innovation is not necessarily an activity these 'high-trust' organizations should conduct since these innovations are extremely difficult to make sense of. However, incremental innovations building on 'well-traveled paths' do lead to customers' understanding and appreciating the new product (Hargadon and Douglas 2001). As such, organizational-level forces, expressed as customer expectations, should provide incentives for incremental product innovation in firms that are supposed to deliver a high level of trust.

Cultural-cognitive forces

Intraorganizational forces

Cultural-cognitive forces include shared systems of meaning that arise in processes of interaction between organizational members (Berger and Luckmann 1967; Scott 2001). Eventually these systems are taken for granted by individual actors because humans tend to habitualize their actions. By repeating actions they become patterns that can be reproduced and transmitted to new entrants (Berger and Luckmann 1967; Zucker 1983, 1987). These taken-for-granted patterns are the core of social action (Zucker 1987) and are maintained for long periods of time without further justification; they are highly resistant to change (Berger and Luckmann 1967; Zucker 1977, 1983, 1987). Constitutive rules, which are rules applied to thought and action that cast subjective roles with accompanying expectations on individuals, serve not only the creation of value through group membership, but also sustain group characteristics (Wicks 2001). Group membership provides the members of the group with a sense of social identity that defines who an individual is and subsequently guides collective action (Dougherty 1992; Trice 1993; Dijksterhuis *et al.* 1999). We expect that groups with distinct identities, based on professional disciplines or functional areas such as accounting and marketing, will respond differently to incremental product innovation [cf. the extensive literature on managing the R&D/marketing interface as described in Souder (1987), Olson *et al.* (1995) and Olson *et al.* (2001)]. The more 'traditional' identities in established financial services firms, such as accounting, will most likely have a negative attitude towards innovation, whereas relatively 'new' identities (such as marketing and product development) will have a more positive stance towards innovation. The most dominant and powerful discipline has the strongest impact on the ability to redefine institutional arrangements. This dominant group deems incremental product innovation either legitimate or illegitimate (cf. Prahalad and Bettis 1986; Seo and Creed 2002).

Organizational forces

Organizations model themselves after similar organizations within their field that are perceived to be more successful or legitimate (DiMaggio and Powell 1983). These organizations seek to behave conventionally, which will cause them not to be noticed as different (Scott 1995), meaning that they try to become isomorphic, as a means of increasing legitimacy, with similar organizations in their environment. Organizations try to imitate companies that are generally considered industry leaders as a way to reduce uncertainty (Galaskiewicz and Wasserman 1989; Fligstein 1991; Haveman 1993). These companies have been successful through time and have acquired legitimacy as industry leaders. Most of the established financial services companies existing today have been able to survive for a long time. We expect that the established banks and insurance companies resemble each other closely. Product portfolios will, therefore, not differ to a large extent and competitors will follow new product introductions by one firm within weeks or months. The legitimacy of new products will, to a large extent, depend on the overall attitude towards innovation. If industry leaders have a very dominant discipline (un)favorable of innovation, competitors will mimic this companies' strategy and (il)legitimate product innovation.

The above discussion of the impact of regulative, normative and cultural-cognitive forces at both organizational and intraorganizational levels on the possibilities for successful incremental product innovation suggests a conceptual framework as depicted in Figure 2.1. In our empirical study we will investigate the impact of each of these forces for incremental innovation in the context of the Dutch financial services sector.

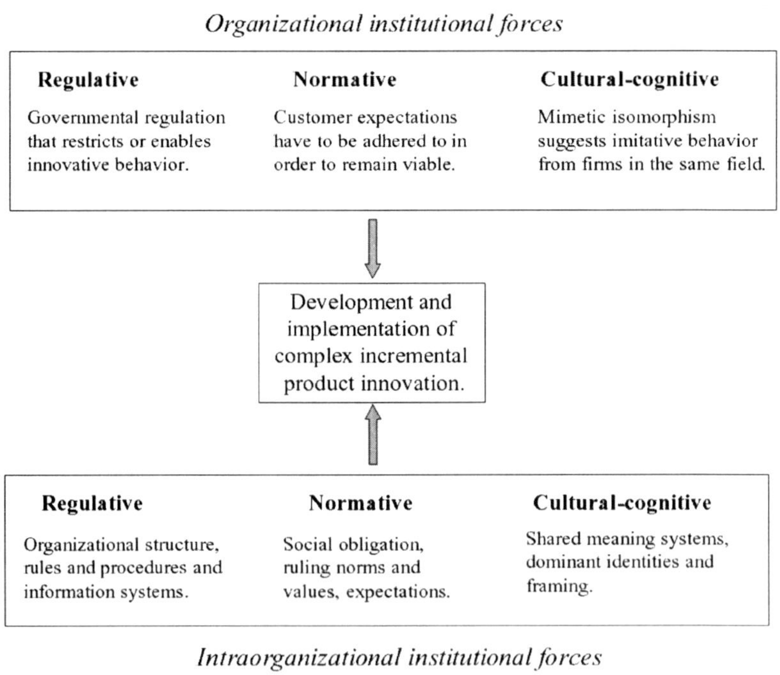

Figure 2.1 The impact of intraorganizational and organizational institutional forces on incremental product innovations

3 Intermezzo

A service environment

Services

Services have been described and classified in several ways (Lovelock 1983). A service can be 'a deed, act or performance' (Berry 1980) or, in more detail, 'any act or performance that one party can offer to another that is essentially intangible and does not result in the ownership of anything' (Kotler 1994: 464). An even more extensive definition is provided by Grönroos (1990: 27):

> A service is an activity or series of activities of a more or less intangible nature that normally, but not necessarily, take place in interactions between the customer and service employees and/or physical resources or goods and/or systems of the service producer, which are provided as solutions to customer problems.

Two specific characteristics can be identified from these definitions: intangibility and simultaneity. With respect to these definitions it is possible to state that a service is only then a service when it is being delivered. Consumers can only evaluate the quality of a service once it is actually delivered and often they have to pay beforehand, meaning that services are, to a large extent, based on trust. For instance, a tourist expects that his ticket, which has already been paid for, will give him access to the plane and if, for any reason, something goes wrong he expects that the insurance company will compensate for the loss since he has already paid the premium. Research on services has often focused on intangibility and on other characteristic features that distinguish them from physical products (e.g. Bateson 1977; Shostack 1977; Lovelock 1983; Zeithaml *et al.* 1985). These differences are displayed in Table 3.1.

Intangibility

Flipo (1987) argues that intangibility is the only feature common to all services and best differentiates services from goods.[5] Because of this intangibility, customers will always have to face some uncertainty concerning the

Table 3.1 Differences between services and goods

Services	*Goods*
A performance or activity	A physical object
Intangible	Tangible
Simultaneous production and consumption	Separation of production and consumption
Heterogeneous	Homogeneous
Services are perishable: a service cannot be kept in stock	Goods can be consumed at a later point in time: they can be kept in stock

purchase; there is no transfer of ownership. Ennew *et al.* (1992) argue that intangibility can be both physical and mental. The first relates to the untouchable aspect of a service, whilst the latter means that people cannot understand the service. This especially seems to be the case with financial services, which are very complex, meaning that they are not easily defined and understood. Services may be seen as performances instead of objects, because they cannot be seen or touched (Zeithaml *et al.* 1985). It is important for companies to emphasize the product's characteristics and what it will do (Meidan 1996). The degree of intangibility will, however, differ between services. The service itself will remain intangible, but tangible products (for instance credit cards) more and more accompany services.

Simultaneity

The second feature of services is the simultaneity of production and consumption (e.g. Zeithaml *et al.* 1985; De Brentani 1991). This simultaneity means that services are produced and consumed in the presence of customers or 'require substantial interaction' (Cooper and De Brentani 1991: 77) in contrast with goods that are first produced, then sold and then consumed. In producing services, the customer takes part in the production process; this is rarely the case in manufacturing. Exceptions to the simultaneousness of production and consumption might be found in financial services (e.g. continuous credit, mortgage loans, life insurance). These services are produced in interaction with the customer, but once a (mortgage or life insurance) contract is signed, the actual consumption lacks substantial interaction. The degree of overlap between production and consumption varies from service to service. Many financial services show only a small degree of overlap in production and consumption.

Heterogeneity

Heterogeneity is concerned with the variability of services. According to several researchers (e.g. De Brentani 1991; Kotler 1994), services appear to differ substantially because of personal perceptions. Individuals might have different expectations of the service. Three reasons for these differences can be pointed out. First, the impact of the service provider. De Brentani argues that 'the degree of heterogeneity depends on whether the service is people- or equipment-based' (1989: 243). The role of company personnel is often crucial, as they 'deliver' the service to the customer in people-based services. People often are unable to standardize the output (the actual service). However, an ATM, as an equipment-based service, is able to provide the same services over and over again. Second, the interpretation of the customer. People differ in their expectations and perceptions. What might be perceived as 'good service' by person A on day X might be perceived as 'mediocre service' by person B on day X. Or to make it even more complicated, person A might have different perceptions on days X and Z. This often has to do with the third reason, which is that external factors can influence the perception of the customer. If you go to a bank and have to wait a long time before getting served, this will increase your level of irritation. Minor problems might evolve into serious conflicts between the customer and the service provider.

Perishability

Services that are available but are not being consumed can not be stored and therefore are perishable (Zeithaml *et al.* 1985; De Brentani 1989). Because services cannot be stored, it can be difficult to synchronize supply and demand. Some service sectors are highly dependent on seasonal fluctuations (e.g. tourism), meaning that periods of high and low demand will alternate. The available seats in a plane might not all be filled, which means that all the empty seats are 'lost'; they cannot be used as a buffer for a period of high demand.

Although the 'specific' service characteristics seem obvious they should not be over-emphasized. Easingwood (1986) argues that 'not all services are intangible, produced simultaneously, heterogeneous, and perishable and some manufactured goods may possess one or more of these characteristics' (1986: 265). Travel documents, (insurance) policy conditions and investment contracts can be thought of as the physical parts of the service. For several of the characteristics there is a 'degree' to which the features are related to the service concerned. This means that services differ from each other and are not all alike. In the empirical part of this study it was noticed that people who work in the financial services sector often talk about their 'products' and the 'factory' in which they work.

Developing New Services: an overview of the literature

Research on NSD has only started to grow in the last fifteen years. Before the second half of the 1980s, publications on developing new services only appeared occasionally (Berry and Hensal 1973; Shostack 1981, 1984; Haaroff 1983; Lovelock 1984; Johne and Harborne, 1985; MacMillan *et al.* 1985). However, the number of publications grew rapidly in the 1990s. The greatest bulk of these publications concerns the development of new financial services. The existing body of literature on new service development can be divided into three areas of inquiry (based on Lievens 1996; Johne and Storey 1998):

1 different types of new service developments;
2 the new service development process;
3 factors for success or failure.

Different types of new service development

The first area of inquiry is concerned with the different types of service development. Lovelock (1984) distinguishes six types of new services (major innovations, start-up business, new products for the currently served market, product line extensions, product improvements and style changes), which are similar to the classification of new products by Booz *et al.* (1982).

Johne and Storey (1998) provide an alternative classification that stretches earlier attempts to categorize new services. Product development is used as an 'umbrella term embracing improvements and also radical alterations' (1998: 189). The repositioning of products is a separate category of development, named product augmentation development. According to Johne and Storey, 'repositioning involves making changes to the way core product features are promoted and made available to customers' (1998: 190). Augmentation, which among other things involves changes in the delivery system and supplier support to the customer, is a key factor that contributes to the success of new services (Easingwood and Storey 1993; Johne and Pavlidis 1996). Together with product development augmentation development is labeled 'offer development'. There are several types of offer development that can be compared to the types of new services distinguished by Lovelock (1984). When redesigning business processes leads to a reduction in costs, this is named process development. As indicated by Utterback (1994), companies first develop new products and subsequently try to produce these products as efficiently as possible. If business processes can be optimized, product development can benefit by offering better prices to the customer, which may lead to an increase in customer demand, lower costs and higher profits. Although Utterback conducted his research in manufacturing, the line of reasoning can be extended to the financial services sector. The discovery of new markets is labeled as market development. Market development is mainly concerned with 'improving the mix of target markets into which newly developed offers can be sold, thus enhancing the mix of customers served by the organization' (Johne and Storey 1998: 192). The role of market development is crucial, since new products have to be offered to the right market segment. Market opportunities should be closely examined by the company to avoid launching products in the wrong market.

Product and product augmentation development, process and market development are the input for business development. These four types of development have to be combined in order to maximize business opportunities. The emphasis on a certain type of development depends on the type of organization. Direct writers, for instance, may focus on market development. They are in direct contact with the customer and do not use intermediaries to offer products to the various market segments. All marketing efforts have to be oriented directly towards the final consumer. The more traditional companies working with intermediaries have to focus on product augmentation. The better the organization is capable of supporting intermediaries, the more likely it is that the intermediary will sell the companies' products. Therefore, the distribution channel available is a main driver for emphasizing a certain type of development.

The new service development process

The second area of literature is based on the NSD process and is split into six themes: corporate environment, the process itself, the people involved, analysis of opportunities, development, and implementation (Johne and Storey 1998). Literature on corporate environment mainly deals with the lack of corporate vision and strategy on NSD in many service organizations. The corporate environment is responsible for possible barriers to innovation (Reidenbach and Moak 1986; Drew 1995). It seems that the services sector is lacking an appropriate organizational structure for NSD. Empirical data, however, suggest that so-called 'top performers' have more formalized and better structured approaches to NSD than the 'low performers' (Reidenbach and Moak 1986; Johne and Pavlidis 1996). Some other 'corporate' problems involved project ownership, leading to departmental conflicts and coordination problems (Edvardsson *et al.* 1995). An important aspect of corporate environment is organizational culture. It is argued that the organization has to support innovation and, for instance, link its reward systems to NSD.

Process literature is concerned with the activities that lead to a new service, resulting in normative models of NSD (Scheuing and Johnson 1989) or complex descriptions of the development process (Shostack 1984). Process literature is mainly interested in how the different activities, or stages, in the NSD process are carried out. In the light of this study, where literature on New Product Development (NPD) serves as an important reference, it is interesting to note that NSD 'has to follow the same generic process as NPD' (Johne and Storey 1998: 201). However, how each activity is carried out depends on the characteristic features of services, meaning that the development processes of goods and services appear similar but differ when it comes to the performance of certain development activities or stages.

Johne and Storey (1998) also stress the crucial role of people in NSD. Different groups of people are involved in a development process and they have to be managed in an effective way in order to be successful. Cross-functional teams have been implemented, but they are run on a committee basis or dominated by single functions, which often leads to conflicts between functional departments (Johne and Storey 1998). The integration of departments is a key problem in many service organizations. Individuals from different functional departments do not speak the same language nor do they share a common understanding of the organization. The so-called 'human factor' still seems to be problematic in managing NSD (Scheuing and Johnson 1989; Edvardsson and Olsson 1996). Besides the functional departments, front-office personnel contributes, or should contribute, to NSD. Front-office involvement helps to identify customer requirements, increases the likelihood of positive implementation, stops process efficiency considerations overwhelming the needs of customers and leads to better customer treatment (Schneider and Bowen 1984 in Johne and Storey 1998). Front-office personnel is, however, only a minor player in NSD. Customers are the last, but certainly not the least, group of people that should be involved in NSD. On the whole, customer involvement has been low in NSD (Martin and Horne 1995; Vermeulen and Dankbaar 2002). One reason for low customer involvement is that many banks and insurance companies consider their branch network or insurance agents (intermediaries) as the main customer. These customers are being involved in NSD, at least to some extent. However, the final consumer has little or no involvement in developing new products. 'The final consumer does not know what he wants' is an often heard excuse for not asking him what his financial needs are.

A thorough analysis of opportunities (through market research and test marketing) is needed to develop new services that the market requires. Although it seems easy for many service companies to generate new ideas (Easingwood 1986), the main sources for ideas for new services are competitors. This is probably one of the reasons for the high number of 'me-too' products. Another source is governmental regulation, which has created a lot of new opportunities for banks and insurance companies. Idea generation is, to a large degree, reactive and rarely based on market research (Edgett 1993).

As was shown previously, developing a new service not only consists of the service itself but also includes an augmented service. It is important to understand that the two parts of development are strongly connected and they cannot be separated.

One of the main problems in service development is how to balance new business operations with the existing line of business (Langeard *et al.* 1986). Coordination of activities is necessary, all the more because several functions are involved in developing the new service. In many financial services organizations, the product departments (not marketing) have overall responsibility for NSD, but the product departments are not responsible for all activities (for instance IT-related tasks). Close coordination between functions is needed in NSD.

Implementation is the last theme in the second research area. It is considered one of the most crucial phases in NSD and consists of implementing an operations plan and a communication strategy and market introduction (Shostack 1984). Employees need to be trained in order to understand the new service. When this is properly done customer expectations can be controlled (Edvardsson and Olson 1996). Extensive testing (of both product and market) is required before introduction, but service companies seem to fall short on this part of NSD, especially test marketing (Edgett 1996). Several reasons appear in the literature: financial loss is low compared to the costs of testing; ease of copying; lack of time; little difference between cost of testing and going 'live'; many new services are introduced to complete the existing product line (Johne and Storey 1998).

Factors for success or failure

It has been argued that a large number of new services fail (e.g. Storey and Easingwood 1993). The third area is therefore concerned with key success factors that distinguish top performers from low performers (De Brentani 1989; Cooper and De Brentani 1991; Cooper *et al.* 1994). A perfect execution of one or two single activities, however, will not be enough for products to be successful; several supporting activities are needed that can be classified into opportunity analysis, project development and offer formulation (Johne and Storey 1998).

Opportunity analysis mainly concerns the importance of synergy. Synergy is needed between the new product and the company strategy, the new product and the available resources/expertise, the new product and the market. Conducting market research and understanding customer needs is also part of opportunity analysis. Many service companies, however, still lack a thorough market orientation (Cooper *et al.* 1994; Edgett 1994, 1996). In project development, a formalized process is advocated. Several studies indicate that service organizations rarely use a formally structured approach for their new development projects (e.g. Easingwood 1986; De Brentani 1991; Johne 1993; Edgett 1996). Project development also concerns functional coordination between the disciplines involved in the development, the use of customer contact personnel in the development process, top management support, speed of the development, testing, and a well-prepared formal launch. Offer formulation is concerned with the features of the service product and augmented service product (Johne and Storey 1998). Not only is the uniqueness of the product important, but it also has to be understandable for the customer. In order to achieve the latter, delivery is considered crucial.

Front-line personnel need the expertise to explain the benefits of the more complex products and must deliver high service quality in an enthusiastic way (Cooper *et al.* 1994; Edgett 1994). In obtaining the 'best' offer formulation, customer participation is necessary. In offer formulation it becomes clear that not only the 'what' is important but also the 'how'. Since (financial) services are low-interest and complex products, the role of the 'how' can be crucial. One more key factor that leads to new service failure is the lack of customer attention. Regard for the customer therefore needs to be a central element in the development process (Edvardsson 1997).

Until now, little has been said about the actual organization of the NSD process. A large body of literature on NSD dealt with various types of new services, success factors, and aspects of the NSD process. Research in this third area is already more concerned with the organization of NSD, but generally does not pay much attention to issues such as organizational structures, integration and coordination. Organizational factors have been studied in relation to their impact on new financial services success. Variables such as formalization and (de)centralization have been researched for their impact on the performance of new financial services (Lievens 1996). Studies by De Brentani (1991) and Edgett and Parkinson (1994) point to organizational factors as the second most important success factors. Edgett and Parkinson (1994) claim that successful services 'exhibited strong interfunctional cooperation and coordination', implying that organizational factors were found to be a major leverage for success. Compared to research in manufacturing, research on the organization of innovation in financial services has remained limited (some valuable exceptions are Thwaites 1992; Drew 1995; Lievens 1996; Sundbo 1997; Lievens *et al.* 1999; Lievens and Moenaert 2000). It may be that there are very few differences between developing new goods and new services, but it should be considered if and how the specific features of services affect the development process.

Consequences of service features for developing new services

In Section 3.1 the various characteristics of services have been described. Several authors (Shostack 1984; Easingwood 1986; De Brentani 1991; Thwaites 1992; Terill and Middlebrooks 1996) have argued that these specific features affect the new service development process. In this section we take a closer look at whether this is also the case for the organization of the NSD process.

Although the specific service characteristics seem obvious, the influence on the organization of new service development processes should not be overemphasized (Easingwood 1986). As indicated before, Easingwood argued that 'not all services are intangible, produced simultaneously, heterogeneous, and perishable and some manufactured goods may possess one or more of these characteristics' (1986: 265). The intangibility of services is considered a key factor for distinguishing services from products. Some scholars argue that developing new services is easier than developing industrial products because of their intangibility (De Brentani 1991). But from an organizational perspective, similar issues arise. As in manufacturing, several people are needed to develop the new service. These individuals are representatives from functional departments and have to work together for some time in a project team. It may be more difficult to perceive that different understandings of the same product are used in the group, because there is no physical object on which all can direct their thoughts. On the other hand, the extent to which a new product idea differs from existing products will probably be the main determinant of the level of communication problems. In the financial services sector, very few projects are concerned with radically new offerings. If we concentrated on the more radical product innovations, however, we would expect similar problems of communication between the various functional specialists in, for example, manufacturing.

Furthermore, services are fairly easy to imitate. According to Easingwood (1986), this results in a too casual approach for developing new services, although they are often highly complex (the latter is especially true for financial services). However, copying services that are developed by another competitor does not mean that the organization is capable of organizing a development process. Most organizations will try to adjust the competitor's product. Thus, De Brentani (1991) and Shostack (1984) are right if they refer to the ease of imitating new financial services. However, they overlooked the effects of intangibility for the internal organization of the development process, which will be more difficult because the people involved cannot see, feel or touch the product being developed. Therefore, it will be difficult, even for employees, to understand the new service (Ennew *et al.* 1992).

Easingwood (1986) argues that the simultaneity of production and consumption has an important impact on the organization of new service development activities. He refers to the need for the front office to be involved in the decision-making process due to the relative proximity to the customer. Front-office personnel produce the service in more or less close interaction with the customer. The development of the production process (e.g. supportive software in the financial sector) is therefore just as important as the elaboration of the product concept. Close involvement and integration of front- (but also back-) office personnel in new service development is therefore considered highly desirable (Edgett and Parkinson 1994).

The heterogeneity and perishability of services do not appear to give rise to important differences between physical products in the realm of product development. The fact that quite different perceptions may come to exist of the same service will obviously make it more difficult to develop, but to some extent this also holds for the development of new physical products and is, in fact, one of the core issues in any marketing exercise. Another aspect of this heterogeneity is the delivery of the product by the front-office personnel. Because many services are people-based, the service will be different each time it is delivered. The fact that services cannot be stored (referred to as the perishability of services) obviously does not mean that they cannot be developed in advance at the conceptual level.

The literature on new service development also shows that many factors for the successful development of new services and products are similar. Successful service companies show a commitment to service development and generally have aligned their culture and systems to support innovation efforts. NSD programs in these organizations are more formalized, proactive and the whole process is better structured than that of their less successful counterparts. Moreover, they have high-quality development staff and a clear strategy for new services as well as an aim beyond short-term financial objectives (Johne 1993; Edgett 1994; Drew 1995; Johne and Storey 1998).

However, because 'NSD [requires] integrating the needs of new service operations and processes with those of existing business activities' (Johne and Storey 1998: 207) there are also important differences between NPD and NSD. Fit between the new service and existing systems, internal co-ordination, internal marketing and staff involvement are some of the factors that appear to be more important for creating new services than products. Moreover, research findings suggest that, particularly for radically new services, internal organizational factors are of prime importance (De Brentani 2001). Thus, more than NPD, NSD involves managing organizational change processes. For instance, Thwaites (1992) shows that successful service organizations are particularly good in mastering organizational structures and are able to create organizational climates to support innovation. The importance of the internal organizational factors is also reflected in the emphasis in the service literature on the service delivery system, indicating that NSD, is for a large part, developing an organization to deliver the service (cf. Edvardsson and Olsson 1996). Finally, Johne and Storey (1998: 223) note that less successful service organizations face 'multiple organizational hindrances, mainly because the predominant focus in them is running yesterday's business'.

This leads to the conclusion that the specific features of services may have implications for the organization of new service development. However, there is no reason to assume that all insights developed by research in a manufacturing environment will be inapplicable in a services context. On the contrary, it is likely that many similar issues will arise and that many manufacturing concepts will also be useful in services. The Product Management Association's best practices research states that 'many of the key factors for service NPD are identical to those identified for manufacturing firms' and 'there are almost no organizational NPD practice differences between service and product producing firms' (Griffin 1997: 434, 446). Sundbo (1997) also argues that innovation theories developed in manufacturing are applicable to services. Therefore, we use both the NPD and NSD literature to guide our first exploration in the field of new service development (see Chapter 5).

4 Methodological considerations

Qualitative research

Qualitative research has been present in the scientific community for a long time and is widely acknowledged as a field of inquiry that crosses disciplines. In organizational science there are several examples of qualitative research that have been published in the 'top-ranked management journals'[6] (Larsson and Lowendahl 1996 in Lee 1999: 15). Due to its nature, a clearly accepted definition of qualitative research is not at hand.[7] Several authors explain what they mean by qualitative research, but the definitions are not unequivocal. However, they exhibit several shared characteristics:

> Research that produces findings not arrived at by means of statistical procedures
>
> (Strauss and Corbin 1990: 17)

> Qualitative research is multimethod in focus, involving an interpretive, naturalistic approach to its subject matter
>
> (Denzin and Lincoln 1998: 3)

> Qualitative research is many things at the same time. Its practitioners are sensitive to the value of the multimethod approach. They are committed to the naturalistic perspective, and to the interpretive understanding of human experience
>
> (Nelson *et al.* 1992: 4)

These definitions contain three key characteristics. First, qualitative research is considered interpretive. This means that the studied artifacts are not statistically countable and that they can not be objectively determined. Instead, multiple subjective perceptions are possible. Second, multiple methods are used. Most qualitative researchers use several methods in the same study, for instance interviews, observations and document analysis. Third, it is naturalistic (*in sito*). 'Things' are studied in their natural environment. The researcher often visits the object of study (e.g. an organization) to gather data, taking the setting of the studied object into account in the data analysis.

Some further explanations of what qualitative research is are provided by Maso and Smaling (1990) and Wester (1995). There are three central issues in qualitative research that distinguish it from quantitative research. First, the collected empirical materials[8] are unstructured and contain the personal perspectives ('inner world') of the people involved in the research. One of the goals of qualitative research is to describe the way people make sense of their environment. The empirical materials need to reproduce this sensemaking aspect of the people that are studied, meaning that the actor's point of view must be made explicit as well. Second, there is an open relation between empirical materials and concepts. The relation between empirical materials and concepts is open because it is this relation that has to be proven in the research. Qualitative in this sense means that the researcher looks at the world with an open mind and tentatively tries to connect the findings to the theory to be developed (Wester 1995). Third, the research design is cyclical or interactive, which means that the collection of empirical materials, the analysis and reflection continuously interchange.

Qualitative research strategies

A research strategy can be defined as the complete range of interrelating decisions about how the research is conducted. There is no such thing as *the* qualitative research strategy. Several qualitative strategies can be identified in the literature. An ethnographic study, for instance, is mainly focused on the construction of a specific culture and is often descriptive in nature. Ethnographers participate for some period of time (which can be several years) in the studied culture. Ethnographic studies are the heart of anthropology, where researchers could be 'members' of some tribe and study the members of the tribe. Participant observation is one of the main data sources in ethnographic studies (Atkinson and Hammersley 1998). A more philosophical approach would lead to a phenomenological strategy. This approach focuses on descriptions of 'the reality, which seems self-evident to men remaining within the natural attitude' (Schutz and Luckmann 1974: 3). The main goal of this type of research strategy was to 'explicate how objects and experience are meaningfully constituted and communicated in the world of everyday life' (Holstein and Gubrium 1998: 140). In this section two research strategies, case study and grounded theory, will be elaborated because this study focuses on case study research with grounded theory principles for the analysis of the data.

Case study research

Conducting a case study means intensively studying a phenomenon in its natural environment, which means that the dynamics present within the setting are also studied (Eisenhardt 1989). The main distinction between the case study and ethnographic studies can be found in the nature of the research question; research questions in a case study focus on a specific problem. In a case study, observations are conducted with various elements of the object of study (e.g. departments or team members) and these observations (opinions, statements etc.) are compared with each other (Wester 1995). Case study research is mostly used when the researcher tries to answer the 'how' and 'why' questions. Usually these questions resemble complex processes in which case study research can offer in-depth understanding of the formal and informal processes, interactions and behaviors (Yin 1994). A case study is therefore a 'holistic' approach; it tries to uncover a broad range of issues. Because of the labor-intensiveness of a case study it is not possible to select a large number of cases. The selection of cases therefore is very important. A pilot study is suggested by several researchers to explore the not yet visible problem. There is, however, a disadvantage in using a single pilot study as a foundation for research propositions. The pilot case can differ to a large extent from the 'average' case and therefore is not an exact representation of 'reality'. To avoid the risk of selecting future cases on the wrong propositions this research started with a qualitative survey to explore innovation processes in the financial services sector in a broad range of companies.

Several variants of case study research are distinguished in the literature (see Yin 1994). A sequential comparative study is closest to this study. In a comparative case study, several cases are studied and compared. In the sequential model, a first case is studied, and based on the results of this study a second case is selected. The results of these two cases are subsequently compared and a third case is selected. This method resembles the grounded theory approach. We also have applied the principles of grounded theory research to the analysis of the empirical materials (see below).

Grounded theory research[9]

Researchers might also be interested in adjusting, building, or discovering theories, which they try to derive inductively from the studied object. A grounded theory study is based on some initial idea that is studied in the field. The process of discovering theory from data has been developed by Glaser and Strauss in *The Discovery of Grounded Theory: Strategies for Qualitative Research* (1967). One of the main characteristics of grounded theory is the researcher's inquisitive attitude. The researcher embarks on a journey, without a detailed description of the course he is traveling. He tries to keep an open mind at all times. This 'theoretical sensitivity' 'indicates an awareness of the subtleties of meaning of data' and 'refers to the attribute of having insight, the ability to give meaning to data, the capacity to understand, and capability to separate the pertinent from that which isn't' (Strauss and Corbin 1990: 41–2).

A second characteristic of grounded theory research is the process of continuous comparison. As was explained previously, a comparative case study is closely related to grounded theory research. However, in a comparative case study the results of two individual cases are compared after the data for both cases have been collected. In a process of continuous comparison, the researcher does not wait until all the data is gathered before comparing the cases. In this study we tried to combine these two methods for comparison. Continuous comparison was not considered an option because the people that were interviewed worked in a large number of different departments and on various hierarchical levels. Directly comparing the remarks of someone from marketing with those of an actuary would lead to a very distorted comparison. It was expected that such a comparison would not contribute to theory building. Rather, the remarks from all people representing marketing in different companies were compared with those of all the actuaries interviewed in the various companies. Besides these empirical comparisons, the collected data were also compared with existing theories: first, with the literature that was used as a starting point for this study (the NPD literature), and, second, with additional literature that was studied in order to explain some of the problems that the banks and insurance companies in this study experienced.

The data that are used for theory building have to be systematically obtained via a set of coding procedures. The grounded theory method is applied in this study, which makes it necessary to elaborate on the research process as described by Glaser and Strauss, and later by Strauss and Corbin (1990). This study does not attempt to develop a 'new' theory, but it uses the grounded theory procedures as a means to collect and analyse qualitative empirical materials by using 'a systematic set of procedures' (Strauss and Corbin 1990: 24). According to Strauss and Corbin, a grounded theory is 'inductively derived from the study of the phenomenon it represents (…) it is discovered, developed, and provisionally verified through systematic data collection and analysis of data pertaining to that phenomenon' (1990: 23). Collecting and analysing data is therefore directly linked to theory building.

The use of literature

As was argued by Eisenhardt (1989), it is probably impossible for a researcher to have no theoretical knowledge on the object of study. Moreover, the use of literature is very important in Strauss and Corbin's (1990) conception of grounded theory. Literature can either be technical or nontechnical (Strauss and Corbin 1990). Technical literature, theoretical papers or reports of research studies are often used as background material against which the collected empirical materials are compared. Nontechnical literature can be used as primary data, but is often used to complement interviews or observations. Studying an organization's documents might increase a researcher's understanding of certain phenomena. Although they can be used as primary data, nontechnical literature should be cross-checked with other data because sources can be hard to track down.

Technical literature serves a different purpose than is common in other qualitative (and quantitative) studies. Since the main goal of grounded theory research is discovering categories and relationships between categories, an existing list of identified categories is likely to get in the way of this discovery (Strauss and Corbin 1990). A grounded theory researcher should not be constrained by a previously developed theory. However, he or she must be aware of its existence in order to adjust or extend it, if necessary. This implies that a researcher will not enter the research scene without any theoretical background. Since most researchers have some kind of educational background in which exams had to be passed, entering the research scene as a blank screen is unlikely to happen. The theoretical assumptions guide the researcher in the observation of the studied organizations. The same holds for a researcher's ontological and epistemological 'Weltanschauung' (world-view).

Keeping an open mind in data collection is key to a grounded theory study. Knowledge of all categories is not required and therefore should not be looked for in existing theories. After the emergence of a category, however, the researcher might want to revisit the technical literature in order to determine what has been written about it. Strauss and Corbin argue that full knowledge of the relevant literature is detrimental in grounded theory because the researcher is likely to be 'constrained and even stifled in terms of creative efforts' by knowing 'everything' (1990: 50).

There are various uses of technical literature in grounded theory research (Strauss and Corbin 1990). First, literature can be used to enhance theoretical sensitivity. Some knowledge on recurring variables, which appear to be significant, might be useful and can be compared with the data from the research object. One might be interested in a theory that has been applied to certain situations and attempt to find out if it also applies to the new situation. For instance, sociotechnical systems design originally focused on redesigning primary processes in manufacturing organizations. Later, the main principles were applied in banks and insurance companies. More recently, there has been an extension of the theory towards new product development. Second, literature can be used as a secondary source of data. Research that has already been published may include quoted material from interviews, which can be used as a secondary source of data. Third, literature can stimulate questions. Reading an article or book often leaves the researcher with several questions, which can be asked in an interview. It is also possible that there are discrepancies between the data and the existing literature, which in turn might lead to the question of why there are discrepancies. Fourth, literature can direct theoretical sampling by giving the researcher ideas he/she normally would not have thought of. Fifth, existing literature can be a source of validation. After gathering and analysing the empirical materials, literature can be an additional validation to the accuracy of the findings. This does not mean that everything has to be validated by published literature.

A sensitizing concept serves the double purpose of keeping an open mind *and* focusing attention while empirical materials are collected (Glaser and Strauss 1967). Blumer claims that sensitizing concepts provide a 'general sense of reference and guidance in approaching empirical instances' and 'merely suggest directions along which to look' (1969: 148). A sensitizing concept 'offers a way of seeing' (Charmaz 2000).

After every case, the sensitizing concepts, also referred to as 'rough ideas', can be adjusted and refined. A sensitizing concept can be very useful in keeping an open view, which is possible when analysis of data is conducted after collecting all the data. In this study the grounded theory approach will not be conducted in the purest way. The qualitative survey is based on the three sensitizing concepts (see Chapter 5). The analysis of, and reflection on, the gathered data will be performed after the data from all thirty-nine companies in the first phase was collected. The reason for this adjustment is twofold. First, there is probably no 'one best way' to organize the process of innovation and multiple solutions exist in practice. Because of these variations it is not possible to describe *the* innovation process. Several processes seem viable. These can only be visible after completing the survey. Second, a distinction has been made in company size (large, medium, small) and type of company (bank or insurance). In order to discover possible differences between the companies involved, the analysis was postponed until the survey was completed. The qualitative survey eventually helped to identify several barriers for innovation. These barriers, which partly were refinements of the sensitizing concepts, served as new sensitizing concepts for the case studies. In the second phase, the analysis of the collected empirical materials was conducted after data collection for each case was complete.

Data collection

To gain more insight into the impact of the micro institutional forces on incremental product innovation, we conducted an inductive study using multiple qualitative data collection methods (cf. Eisenhardt 1989). In five phases, exploratory research activities were conducted in the period 1997–2004: panel group sessions, exploratory interviews, interviews with IT experts, and case studies. In total, over 175 people were interviewed. All the people interviewed, except one, agreed on the use of a tape recorder that was used in the writing of transcripts. These transcripts were sent back to the respondents in order to give them the opportunity for factual corrections. The final version of all transcripts and the documents based on meetings with the twelve case organizations covered more than 1400 pages of empirical material. The panel group sessions served as input for the exploratory interviews and the interviews with IT managers, which in turn served as input for the case studies. Table 4.1 provides an overview of the five research

Table 4.1 An overview of the empirical research activities (1997–2004)

Research phase	*Research activity*	*Companies involved*	*Goals*	*Research instruments*
Phase 1	Panel sessions	10	To get acquainted with the sector and financial services	4 Panel sessions with 6–10 people
Phase 2	Exploratory interviews	39	To obtain preliminary insights in product innovation process and forces affecting the process	39 interviews (tape recorder used for transcripts)
Phase 3	Interviews with IT experts	10	To explore IT-related forces	10 interviews (tape recorder used for transcripts)
Phase 4	Panel sessions	10	To discuss results of stages 2 and 3 and select cases	2 Panel sessions with 6–10 people
Phase 5	Case studies	12	To obtain in-depth insight of institutional forces affecting product innovation processes	125 interviews (5 CEOs, 12 business-unit managers, 5 IT managers, 12 product managers, 24 project leaders, 24 IT project members, 45 team members), observations, internal documents (tape recorder used for transcripts)

phases, the conducted research activities, and displays the number of companies involved, the main goals, and the research instruments for the various activities. Direct quotes from the interviews are given to illustrate important aspects. Since the interviews were conducted in Dutch, the respected passages were translated into English by the authors.

Panel group sessions

In the first phase of the empirical research in 1997, a panel of company experts was formed. Representatives from ten of the largest Dutch financial services companies, i.e. firms with more than 2500 employees such as ING, ABN-AMRO, Rabobank and AEGON, participated in this group. Members of the group were actively involved in product innovation processes in their organization, as business-unit managers, product managers or new product development managers. In the first year the group met three times and discussed several aspects of new service development and the characteristic features of services. Later the frequency of the meetings was reduced. In each meeting, a short presentation with some questions was followed by a lively discussion between the participants. Together with the members of the panel it was decided to study the development of the latest generation of combi-products. The panel considered these products as the most appropriate examples of incremental innovations, because they build on the first generations of combi-products. The panel group also assisted in the design of the questionnaire that was used for the qualitative survey (see below). A first draft was discussed in a meeting with the group. The members of the group made various suggestions concerning the answer categories for the closed questions.

The panel group was again consulted in the fourth phase. We wanted the opinion of the experts in the field as to whether our projects were examples of complex incremental innovations. This would strengthen our argument that were really looking at complex incremental projects.

Qualitative survey

In the second phase an exploratory round of interviews was conducted in 39 incumbent and non-incumbent companies. The number and size of the participating banks and insurance companies (the latter were life insurance companies or the life insurance departments of larger insurance companies) are shown in Table 4.2.[10] All companies were located in the Netherlands. For the purposes of the study, this geographical limitation does not appear to be problematic, especially since several Dutch companies have proved to be competitive on the world market. These companies were selected using criterion sampling (Miles and Huberman 1994). The sampling criterion used was to focus on companies that had recently introduced an *improved combi-product*, which was reported in the media and professional journals. It is therefore possible that innovative companies were over-represented in this study, but in the light of the research aims this was not problematic. Forty-two companies were contacted by phone, of which thirty-nine agreed to cooperate. The initial contact focused on finding the persons responsible for the development of the new product. Referring to reports on new products in the media turned out to be a most useful method of gaining access to these organizations. The initial contact focused on finding the persons responsible for the development of the improved combi-products. Once these people were identified, interview appointments were made. The interviews focused on the respondents' understanding of product innovation processes and the surrounding forces affecting the development of new products. All the interviews followed a common protocol: people were first asked to tell the story of product development processes and subsequently generic questions were asked to find out more about the stages in the NSD process, who was involved, and potential problems in these processes. The questions that were

Table 4.2 Size of the companies involved in the exploratory study

	No. of employees			
Companies	*< 100*	*100–500*	*> 500*	*Total*
Banks	4	6	4	14
Insurance companies	6	14	5	25
Total	10	20	9	39

asked in this round were based on the existing NPD literature. This was, however, not the core of our study. At this stage, we were only interested in obtaining a general overview of product innovation processes in financial firms. Hence, we only used this information as a first exploration. The results from the exploratory interviews in phase two did show that incumbent firms (the larger and older firms in the industry) especially, experienced problems in complex incremental product innovation projects. Therefore, in the final stage of data collection (see p. 58), we focused on the incumbents.

Interviews with IT experts

In phase three and in addition to these exploratory interviews in thirty-nine companies, ten interviews were conducted with IT experts in the ten companies from the panel group. This type of convenience sampling (Miles and Huberman 1994) saved time and effort in gaining access to firms. The reason for conducting these interviews was twofold. First, the data from the exploratory interviews was rather one-sided, because only people from marketing or product developers were interviewed. Second, the results from the exploratory interviews indicated that information systems had a strong impact on the possibility of developing new products. This was verified in the panel. Before starting the in-depth case studies, some additional insight was needed. The IT interviews were thus used as an additional starting point for the in-depth studies. As a matter of convenience, we then asked these companies to participate in a short round of interviews with IT representatives to find out more about this specific role before the case study stage started. These interviews followed a similar protocol to that mentioned above. Furthermore, the IT experts were asked to provide a detailed description of the companies' information systems. The interviews with the ten IT persons were taped; the authorized transcripts amounted to approximately seventy-five pages of empirical materials. Authorizations involved only factual corrections, but respondents were not allowed to change the texts, as they were literal transcripts of what had actually been said.

Case studies

We make a distinction between two groups of cases. The first three case organizations were used for an in-depth understanding of how product development projects are actually conducted (as described in Chapter 6). The exploratory survey indicated that the large mature organizations, especially, suffered from problems with organizing product development. Two large (BanCo and FinCo) and one medium-sized (SureCo) organization that had recently introduced new products were studied. Special attention was paid to the problem areas in these organizations. Several research instruments were used: interviews, observations and internal documents. In the interviews, recently finished projects were taken as example cases. Most respondents spoke about the organization and tried to explain their thoughts with examples from the selected projects. During the interviews the respondents were asked to 'tell the story of the project'. Table 4.3 presents an overview of the number and the level of people interviewed in the three in-depth cases.

All participants, except one, agreed on the use of a tape recorder, which was used in producing the transcripts. These transcripts were sent back to the respondents in order to give them the opportunity to make factual corrections, but respondents were not allowed to change the texts, as they were literal transcripts of what had actually been said. Three respondents had some remarks, which led to a few minor adjustments in the transcripts. The final version of all transcripts and the documents of meetings from the three organizations covered more than 600 pages of empirical material.

In addition to the interviews, additional empirical material was gathered from all these companies through the attendance of meetings, evaluation sessions and by studying documents. For each case the use of additional empirical materials will be indicated.

Table 4.3 An overview of the number of people interviewed

Case	*Project team level*	*Project manager level*	*Managerial level*	*Total number of people interviewed*
BanCo	14	3	4	21
FinCo	17	3	4	24
SureCo	8	1	4	13
Total				58

BanCo

At BanCo the development process of two products was more closely examined. Product MGH, the unsuccessful project, and product SWK, the successful project, had both been introduced to the market in 1998. Seventeen interviews were conducted at BanCo at the project team and project leader level. The fourteen interviews at the project team level were divided between four SWK respondents (since there was no project team, these four respondents covered the majority of the work that was done in the SWK project) and ten MGH team members. Three project leaders (one from SWK, an external consultant who was the 'informal' project leader in the beginning of the MGH process, and an official project leader) were also interviewed. The project leaders also provided the project documents, such as minutes of meetings, planning schedules etc. Four additional interviews with managers were carried out after the data from the project teams was collected. These interviews focused on the innovative potential of the organization and were more reflective than descriptive.

FinCo

The FinCo case also focused on two products. The first development project, product ABC, was known as a success in the organization, whilst the second project, product XYZ, was considered a 'problem child'. Product ABC had been successfully introduced to the market almost two years prior to the interviews. Product XYZ had not yet been introduced. Several attempts had been made, but all failed in the early stages of development. Twenty open-ended interviews were held with project team members and project leaders. In addition to the interviews and the documents of the two projects, several other documents were studied, including an in-company handbook on project management. Four additional interviews were held with general managers, focusing on the innovative potential of FinCo. Since the two projects had started two years prior, these interviews were retrospective in nature. For product ABC this was no problem. All team members were still in the organization and because of the unusual project approach, the team members were able to describe the development process very accurately. The project leader documented all the activities in the minutes of team meetings. These documents were used as a check to confirm the descriptions of the respondents. In the case of product XYZ this was more complicated because few documents or minutes of meetings and little written material existed. However, the latest attempt to introduce XYZ was less than a year before the interviews, so most team members could remember the development process. The fourth attempt to develop XYZ was closely observed. All project team meetings were attended and the new team members were interviewed. After a few months, the development process was evaluated with the team members and the project leader. The evaluation session led to some valuable insights into why certain problems arose during the process.

SureCo

At SureCo, thirteen interviews were conducted at various levels of the organization. The project team members had been involved in a development process that was about to be evaluated. The team developed a new product, CLR (new for SureCo), and it had just been introduced to the market. The development process of CLR was very troublesome. SureCo management claimed that the problems in CLR were similar to many of the problems that occurred in product development projects. The project leader and the members of the management team were also interviewed. All the interviews focused on product innovation at the company level. CLR only served as an example. The evaluation of the development process was observed and taped. The main problems that were identified during the interviews were also raised in the evaluation. During the evaluation session it became clear that there was some confusion about the contents of the product specifications (the descriptions of the product that are transformed into business specifications for the IT department). According to some of the team members a certain aspect of the product was missing in the business specifications, which led to delays in the development process. In order to find out what went wrong, a small survey was conducted (in cooperation with a SureCo employee who was not involved in the CLR project). Following up on the survey, an additional session to evaluate this specific problem was organized.

In the final phase of data collection, selected business units from nine more incumbent companies were studied (see table 4.4). We selected respondents from two different business units in each of these firms. Because the 12 companies had already participated earlier (in the exploratory survey) and expressed their interest in the research project, we felt that it would be relatively easy to get access for the case studies as well. Since we tried to study organizational and intraorganizational institutional forces, we needed data on both the firm level and the project level. We were interested in discovering how and why *incumbents* experienced problems; we used theory-based sampling (Miles and Huberman 1994) for this final phase. These companies (see Table 4.4) were all founded more than seventy-five years ago; however, they differed in size (number of employees) and focus (global versus national). Our sample is equally divided into banks and insurance companies.

This round of data collection represents a multiple-case design (cf. Yin 1994) and consisted of studying business units in twelve companies in which exemplary product development projects were studied (see Table 4.5). Two product development projects in separate business units were selected in each of the firms in close consultation with a business-unit manager. Three selection criteria were used. The first criterion for the choice of a project was the

Table 4.4 Demographic profile of case study organizations in 2001–2004

*Company**	*Company age (years)*	*Company focus*	*Company size*	
			No. of employees	*Net Profit (in million euros)*
BanCo	> 100	Global	> 10,000	> 500
FinCo	> 100	National	5,000 ≤ 10,000	250 ≤ 500
SureCo	> 100	National	1,000 ≤ 5,000	100 ≤ 250
RealCo	> 100	National	1,000 ≤ 5,000	100 ≤ 250
PayCo	> 100	National	1,000 ≤ 5,000	100 ≤ 250
RiskCo	75 ≤ 100	National	1,000 ≤ 5,000	100 ≤ 250
CashCo	> 100	National	750 ≤ 1,000	75 ≤ 100
LifeCo	> 100	National	750 ≤ 1,000	75 ≤ 100
HypCo	> 100	National	500 ≤ 1,000	50 ≤ 100
CreditCo	75 ≤ 100	National	500 ≤ 1,000	50 ≤ 100
AssurCo	> 100	National	250 ≥ 500	< 50
ChipCo	75 ≤ 100	National	250 ≥ 500	< 50

* Due to confidentiality issues company names have been changed.

nature of the product. The products had to be so-called improved combi-products, which means that besides functional departments (such as actuaries, marketing, IT and legal affairs) more than one product department was involved in the development process due to the multiple aspects of the product.

The second criterion was whether the project was perceived as a troublesome or smooth development process; meaning that one of the projects was developed quite easily and the other project faced serious problems during development. The main idea in selecting a successful and a less successful project was to find out if there were fundamental differences in the development of incremental product innovations within a single firm. Internal documents were used, when available, to verify the data if serious doubts arose during the interviews. The business-unit managers were asked to provide an exemplary project that best illustrated the way innovation projects were carried out in their business unit. The third criterion was the development stage of the project. The development process had to be either finished within the last year or had to be in progress in order for the respondents to be able to recall the details about the development process. Three companies were not able to present two product development projects in distinct business units. In these firms we chose the two most recent incremental development efforts

Table 4.5 Extended profile of projects

Project	*Features of product innovation**	*Development time months*	*Number of departments involved*
Unsuccessful projects			
BanCo 1	Improved combi-product; new version of an existing mortgage product with existing linkages.	>24	8
FinCo 1	Improved combi-product; investment annuity of which several existed in the company. This product had several new investment features.	>24	7
SureCo 1	Improved combi-product; single-premium policy with investment opportunities. Similar products already present in the company.	$12 \leq 24$	6
RealCo 1	Improved combi-product; investment annuity of which several existed in the company. This product had several new investment features related to pensions.	$12 \leq 24$	7
PayCo 1	Improved combi-product; extension of already existing flexible life insurance product.	$6 \leq 12$	6
RiskCo 1	Improved combi-product; mortgage product with extra features. Consumers can choose between saving and investing. Similar linkages between products already exist.	$6 \leq 12$	5
CashCo 1	Improved combi-product; mortgage product with extra features. Consumers can choose between saving and investing. Similar linkages between products already exist.	$12 \leq 24$	7
LifeCo 1	Improved combi-product; extension of already existing flexible life insurance product.	$6 \leq 12$	6
HypCo 1	Improved combi-product; mortgage product for capital accumulation. New version of existing product with several adjustments.	$6 \leq 12$	6
CreditCo 1	Product improvement; minor extension of original mortgage product.	$1 \leq 6$	3
AssurCo 1	Improved combi-product; mortgage product with extra features. Consumers can choose between saving and investing. Similar linkages between products already exist.	$6 \leq 12$	6

Table 4.5 Extended profile of projects

Project	*Features of product innovation**	*Development time months*	*Number of departments involved*
ChipCo 1	Improved combi-product; investment annuity of which several existed in the company. This product had several new investment features.	6 ≤ 12	4
Successful projects			
BanCo 2	Improved combi-product; extension of original investment product with savings account.	1 ≤ 6	4
FinCo 2	Product improvement; minor extension of original mortgage product.	6 ≤ 12	7
SureCo 2	Improved combi-product; mortgage product with extra features. Consumers can choose between saving and investing. Similar linkages between products already exist.	6 ≤ 12	7
RealCo 2	Improved combi-product; new version of investment and savings product. Product is revised every two years.	6 ≤ 12	6
PayCo 2	Improved combi-product; extension of original savings product combined with pension product.	1 ≤ 6	4
RiskCo 2	Product improvement; minor extension of original investment product.	1 ≤ 6	4
CashCo 2	Improved combi-product; mortgage product for capital accumulation. New version of existing product with several adjustments.	6 ≤ 12	6
LifeCo 2	Product improvement; minor extension of original life insurance product.	1 ≤ 6	3
HypCo 2	Improved combi-product; flexible mortgage product with many options for consumers to choose from. Improved and extended version of an already existing flexible mortgage product.	6 ≤ 12	6
CreditCo 2	Improved combi-product; new version of investment and savings product.	1 ≤ 6	5
AssurCo 2	Product improvement; minor extension of original pension product.	1 ≤ 6	4
ChipCo 2	Improved combi-product; life insurance product with additional features, closely linked with investment product.	1 ≤ 6	4

* Combi-products are improved combinations of already existing products. Product improvements are minor adjustments to an existing combi-product.

in one business unit and added these to our sample. The 125 interviews (see Table 4.1 on p. 53) were conducted with people in different departments and at various hierarchical levels in the organization from 1998 to 2003. The same protocol as mentioned above was again used. During the interviews, people were first asked to tell the story of the project on which they had been working. Subsequently more detailed questions were asked about the specific problems and where these originated from according to the respondent.

Data analysis procedures

The transcripts describe the experiences and opinions of the respondents regarding complex incremental product innovation projects. As such, they reflect specific characterizations of the respondents' version of reality. These characterizations referred to the respondents' opinion on why certain events and activities occurred. Several steps were taken in the analysis of the transcripts. Coding is synonymous with analysis in many qualitative studies. It 'represents the operations by which data are broken down, conceptualized, and put back together in new ways'. Coding plays a crucial role for 'it is the central process by which theories are built from data' (Strauss and Corbin 1990: 57). The coding procedures can be seen as a set of tools or techniques to assist the researcher in making use of his creative capacities and to develop theoretical sensitivity. There are three types of coding: open, axial and selective. The 'usual' coding cycle starts with open coding and is followed by axial coding and finally selective coding. However, it is also possible that open or axial coding might be conducted at the end of the research process when the researcher discovers, in selective coding, that some concepts are poorly developed.

Open coding

The first part of analysis, open coding, is mainly concerned with the naming and categorizing of phenomena through close examination of data (Strauss and Corbin 1990: 62). A piece of data, for example a transcript of an interview, is broken down and conceptualized by assigning labels to sentences, paragraphs or entire documents. The label should represent the content of the piece of data under review. These labels can be 'counted' more easily than raw data, and it is easier to talk about a label or a concept. The next step is to group the concepts, like with like. Although it is possible to identify hundreds of labels in the raw data, several of these can be grouped together since they are more or less similar. They will be grouped around an identified phenomenon. The process of grouping is called 'categorizing' (Strauss and Corbin 1990). Categories are classifications of concepts that are discovered in the comparison of concepts that relate to the same phenomenon. A category is a conceptual, high order, element of a theory (Glaser and Strauss

1967). One remark has to be made about the name of the category. The researcher has two options when naming a category: choose a name that he finds most logically related to the data it represents or use an existing concept. The latter, 'borrowed' concepts are often loaded with meaning and association, which can be either an advantage (it requires less explanation) or disadvantage (because these names are familiar to a lot of other researchers, they will attach the standard meaning and are not able to see the actual meaning of the category).

It is possible to reduce the disadvantage of borrowed concepts. Categories are developed in terms of properties and dimensions. A property is an element or a characteristic of a category (Glaser and Strauss 1967). Dimensions represent the location of a property on a continuum. By assigning properties and dimensions to a category, it will be much clearer what the essence of a category is. Open coding is therefore not only concerned with discovering categories, but also with their properties and dimensions (Strauss and Corbin, 1990).

Thus, we engaged in an open coding procedure in which labels were assigned to text units (sentences or paragraphs). These labels represented the key issues mentioned by the respondents. During this initial stage we mainly used descriptive codes to get a broad overview of key issues in the innovative efforts of banks and insurance companies. These codes entail little interpretation since they closely resemble the text of the transcripts; in our case descriptive codes such as cooperation (COP), division of labor (DOL), sanctions (SAN), informal meetings (IME), formal meetings (FME), and coordination (COR) are examples of descriptive codes that were attributed to 'organizational structure'; codes that were used to describe 'expectations' included novelty as burden (NAB), need for innovation (NEI), employee perspective (EPE), managerial perspective (MPE), lack of incentives (LOI) and core activities (COA). We used the abbreviations to aid in grouping data from the interviews in order to be able to compare the contents of our codes.

Axial coding

Whereas open coding was mainly concerned with dividing data, axial coding 'puts those data back together in new ways by *making connections between a category and its subcategories*' (Strauss and Corbin 1990: 97; italics in original). Axial coding is a very different kind of coding when compared with open coding. The main idea is to focus on a category (phenomenon) and describe it until it has 'sufficiently materialised into satisfactory, clear concepts that cover important aspects of the field of study that is to be analysed' (Verschuren and Doorewaard 1999: 175). Categories and subcategories are correlated in cause-and-effect diagrams. The phenomenon is the central idea that needs to be managed or, since it often reflects a problem, solved. Causal conditions are events that lead to the occurrence of the phenomenon. Single causal conditions rarely lead to the occurrence of a phenomenon; instead the combination of causal conditions and the characteristics of these conditions produce phenomena (Strauss and Corbin 1990). The phenomenon causes all kinds of effects. Strategies of action or interaction are directed to managing the phenomenon (solving the problem). Once the context, meaning a particular set of conditions, of the phenomenon has been clarified, strategies can be thought of to solve the problem. However, there are always intervening conditions that either constrain or facilitate the strategies taken within a certain context (Strauss and Corbin 1990: 103).

We identified underlying patterns by grouping the initial codes into a smaller number of themes, which is often referred to as axial coding. These patterns were first compared across interviews. An example of a pattern that appeared from our data is the so-called expectancy gap. While examining our data we discovered that the unsuccessful projects suffered from major differences between the managerial and employee level. CEOs and senior managers thought innovation was crucial for the viability of their companies, whereas the employees considered developing new products as a burden. There were no incentives for working on these projects, which led to the belief that these were not core activities that were highly valued. Passages from the transcripts related to each of the patterns were highlighted. Next, we grouped passages relating to the same patterns. We were eventually able to identify several patterns that appeared to be dominant (we counted the appearance of all the patterns in the interviews) in either the regulatory, normative or cultural-cognitive perspective.

Selective coding

The last step in the coding procedure is called selective coding. Selective coding is 'the process of selecting the core category' (Strauss and Corbin 1990: 116) and relating it to other categories. All the categories, phenomena and concepts that were described in the open and axial coding stages are to be reduced to a core category. The core category is the central phenomenon of the study. The first step in the selective coding process is to identify the story by presenting a general descriptive overview of the core category in a few sentences. From this descriptive overview of the core category we have to move to conceptualization. This conceptualization of the story is called the story line (Strauss and Corbin 1990).

5 Exploring new service development

This chapter explores both the literature on product innovation and the practices of new service development (NSD). Sensitizing concepts (described on p. 52) were derived from the innovation management literature. As was explained in Chapter 4, an exploratory study was conducted at thirty-nine companies in the financial services sector. The results of this study are described in this chapter. This chapter ends with a discussion of the main barriers to innovation that were discovered in the exploratory study.

Organizing new service development: some basic notions

Much of the innovation literature has a long tradition of being 'manufacturing-based'. Industrial product development received widespread attention in academia, which was to a large extent caused by the available empirical evidence. Many lessons have been learnt about how to organize new product development (NPD) processes. Many of these lessons have been incorporated in the growing amount of research regarding the NSD processes. The explicit focus on the organization of such processes has received less attention in the NSD literature. Hence, the concepts and issues originally raised in manufacturing-based innovation literature were chosen as a starting point for this study, if only to guide the search. Three (broad) organizational notions that are widely expected to influence the success of product innovation are described below: (1) project organization; (2) development approach and (3) teamwork.

Project organization

Product development is often conducted in projects. People from different functional departments are brought together in a project organization that tries to integrate these departments. These project organizations are an important determinant to the success of product development projects (Larson and Gobeli 1988; Clark and Fujimoto 1991; Wheelwright and Clark 1992; Tidd *et al.* 1997). Four modes of organizing product development have received widespread attention in the product development literature (Wheelwright and Clark 1992): functional structure, lightweight team structure, heavyweight team structure and autonomous team structure [these four modes are similar to Clark and Fujimoto's (1991) classification of functional structure, lightweight product manager structure, heavyweight product manager structure and project execution team]. The following descriptions of these structures are to a large extent based on Wheelwright and Clark (1992).

The product development function in a *functional structure* is divided into functional areas and is often found in large, mature firms. Previous research has indicated that functional structures were predominant in the financial sector (Johne 1993). These structures group people together by discipline. These disciplines all agree on an idea that will be developed through a set of product specifications. The functional managers coordinate the activities in the development process. The specifications pass every discipline in order for a representative from the discipline to contribute to the specifications. Sometimes meetings are held to talk about issues that are related to multiple disciplines (Wheelwright and Clark 1992). The responsibility during the development process passes, with the product that is being developed, from function to function. There are several advantages of these functional product development structures (Wheelwright and Clark 1992). First, the functional manager controls the resources and the performance of the tasks that occur in his functional area. Second, career paths follow functional lines, therefore, people participate in this kind of project under supervision of the functional manager, which ensures that the same manager that makes decisions concerning the future career path also evaluates the work done in a project. Thirdly, the functional structure ensures that specialized knowledge is present at key tasks.

In the *lightweight team structure* the team members conduct project activities, as in the functional structure, in their own department. However, the various functional managers appoint liaison persons to represent the department in a special new product committee (Wheelwright and Clark 1992). The lightweight project manager is sometimes a member of the product committee and works closely with the liaison persons. A lightweight project leader is usually someone from middle or junior level who has enough experience to lead a project, but lacks status or influence in the organization. Although the project leader is formally in control of the project, the functional managers have to allocate the resources for the project. As a consequence, the lightweight project leader has little power. This type of structure is similar to the functional structure described above. Wheelwright and Clark argue that this structure 'usually occurs as an add-on to a traditional functional organization' (1992: 193). However, the main difference is the project leader who tries to coordinate the project across the functional disciplines. This is the main strength, in addition to the strengths of the regular functional structure and the lightweight team structure. There is at least one person who has an overview of the entire process and is, to some extent, able to look across functions. This project leader has to make sure that people are not working in isolation without paying attention to the contributions of the other disciplines. Communication and coordination are important. The project leader has little influence or power. Resource allocation, thus power, still resides with the functional managers.

A response to this problem was the *heavyweight team structure*, in which a heavyweight project leader is assigned to coordinate the project. This project leader does have the necessary formal status and power and has direct access to all the resources needed to finish the project. The project leader is also responsible for finishing the project in time without exceeding financial means. The main difference between lightweight and heavyweight project leaders is that the latter are senior managers who have earned their credits in the organization. They have the same, or sometimes an even higher, rank than the functional managers and have a lot of expertise and experience (Clark and Fujimoto 1991). These heavyweight project leaders have also been referred to as product champions (Chakrabarti 1974; Maidique 1980) and are an important determinant for success. Product champions are often senior managers, for example heads of functional departments with formal status (Clark and Fujimoto 1991; Wheelwright and Clark 1992). They need to be able to inspire the team members and commit them to the task. The project team is under the direct supervision of the heavyweight leader; team members have to report to the heavyweight leader. The functional manager's influence over team members is strongly reduced in this structure. This is due to the managerial position of the project leader and to the physical location. The team members no longer conduct project activities in their department, but are co-located with the other team members and the project leader instead. Often a few core team members are assigned to the project full-time. As the development process proceeds, additional team members are added to the team when needed.

The heavyweight team structure also operates in a functional organization and, as such, team members are still appraised and rewarded by the functional members. Working in project teams is still on a temporary, not permanent, basis. Despite the fact that the functional structure is not changed, a heavyweight team structure requires behavioral changes of functional managers and their employees. The position of the heavyweight project leader has to be formalized and the core team members have to accept responsibility for the overall team results (Wheelwright and Clark 1992).

The last structure, *autonomous team structure*, is also referred to as the 'tiger team' (Wheelwright and Clark 1992: 196). In a tiger team, representatives from various functional departments are assigned to the project on a full-time basis and they share the same location. A heavyweight project leader has full control over all the resources and the team members (who will be evaluated by the project leader). Tiger teams are often not allowed to use the current organizational procedures and practices. They are considered 'green fields' and are started without constraints imposed by the existing organization. According to Wheelwright and Clark (1992), there is a potential risk in starting these 'green fields'; because team members can develop the new product without restrictions it will be difficult to integrate the new product in the existing organization. One solution to this potential risk is to start a new business unit or even a new organization based on the new product. The main advantage of the autonomous team structure is focus. Both team members and the team leader are fully concentrated on the project because they have no other responsibilities besides the project. The speed of development will rapidly increase in the autonomous team structure due to increased efficiency and cross-functional integration, and full-time availability.

In these four types of project organization, product development is carried out in project teams. Other scholars have also argued that additional integration mechanisms might be needed to increase the amount and intensity of coordination in interfunctional interaction. Several of these integration mechanisms, or boundary-spanning solutions, have been suggested. They mostly provide the opportunity to overcome 'barriers between departments' (Daft 1995: 195). Direct contact, liaison roles, task forces, full-time integrator, matrix structures, design teams and design centers are alternatives that can improve horizontal communication (Lawrence and Lorsch 1967; Galbraith 1973; Tushman 1977; Mintzberg 1979, 1983; Olson *et al.* 1995; Ancona and Caldwell 1997). The first option is direct contact between managers or workers who perceive a problem. A liaison person is located in a department, but has the responsibility to communicate with, mostly, interdependent departments. A task force links more than two departments, in contrast with the two prior options, and consists of representatives from each department involved in a problem situation. Task forces are, however, temporary. A more structural solution is the full-time integrator position. This integrator, a product or project manager, is located outside the departments and is responsible for coordinating activities concerning several departments (Daft 1995). In a matrix organization, activities are structured by product or market and by function (Mintzberg 1979, 1983). A dual authority structure is the main feature of the matrix, which means that people who work on new product development report to both a project manager and a functional manager. Design teams bring together a group of specialists from various departments that work together on a development project. They have some degree of autonomy, which means that they, for instance, can establish their own operation procedures (Olson *et al.* 1995). Design centers are added to the functional structure as an additional structure in which employees engage in different product development projects (Olson *et al.* 1995).

These integration mechanisms are in some way embedded in the project organizations that were described earlier (except for the design center).

Because it was expected that, in practice, the project organization terminology was more common, the empirical part of this chapter will concentrate on the types of project organization in use by banks and insurance companies.

The development approach

Researchers have focused frequently on the description (or prescription) of the various steps that have to be taken in the development of a new product. Many formal procedures or processes which have been described at length in the NPD literature, seemingly contribute to the success of a new product (Cooper and Kleinschmidt 1987, 1990). Cooper (1983) provides an overview of several models ranging from four to over twenty steps in developing a new product. Although there is no consensus, most of these models consist of the following main steps: strategy formulation, idea generation and screening, product concept development, business analysis, product design and prototype testing, process design and testing, final business analysis, full production, commercialization, and customer use and feedback or evaluation (Booz *et al.* 1982; Cooper 1983).

These models have been categorized by Saren (1984), who distinguished between five different types of product development models:

1 departmental-stage model;
2 activity-stage models;
3 decision-stage models;
4 conversion process models;
5 response models.

Departmental-stage models view the development process as a series of stages that are connected with a specific function or department (Saren 1984). The idea moves from one department to the next until it merges into a new product and is introduced in the market. These models pay little attention to the actual activities in the development process, but merely provide some insight in the departments that are usually involved in the development process.

Activity-stage models focus on the actual development activities that are carried out in the process. The process is broken down into a number of activities that are conducted sequentially. Several different activity-stage models have been proposed in the literature that all focus on different types of activities that vary in the amount of time and effort spent on each stage (see, for instance, Cooper 1983; Saren 1984). One of the most influential activity-stage models has been introduced by Booz *et al.* (1982), who distinguished six stages: idea generation, screening, commercial evaluation, technical development, testing and commercialization. The main advantage of these models over departmental-stage models is that they specify the tasks that need to be conducted (Saren 1984).

The third type of product development model is the decision-stage model. Instead of breaking down the innovation process into a series of activities, these models break down the process into a series of decisions or evaluation points (Hart and Baker 1996). The emphasis in these models is on the go/no go decision that has to be made after each stage.

The first three types of 'traditional' product development models reflected a linear sequence of the activities in the process. The linearity in these 'phase-review processes' (Griffin and Hauser 1996) models reflected the fact that the activities described above were, in practice, conducted sequentially. For every step in the process there was a functionally specialized department of the organization that would contribute its specific knowledge into the new product. This sequential method of product development led to major advantages of specialization, but it also meant that the product was 'thrown over the wall' from one department to another and that there was little communication and cooperation between functional areas. The result of the scarce communication and cooperation was that prototypes differed from the accepted design, the development process was very time-consuming, nobody was responsible for the new product because there was no clear ownership, and there was no feedback on the actual use of the product (Hart and Baker 1996).

Conversion process models provide a view of product development as the transformation of inputs (raw materials) into outputs (new products) (Twiss 1980). The advantage of these models is that they do not look at innovation processes as a logical sequence of activities, but emphasize that innovation processes are much more chaotic and less rational (Saren 1984). Schön (1967) does not describe innovation in terms of raw materials and new products (representing input and output), but argues that innovation is the conversion of uncertainty into risk. By taking this standpoint, Schön rejects the rational view of product development as portrayed in the three previous models.

The fifth group of models in Saren's classification are response models. These models are based on the fact that organizations respond to change in the environment. The four-stage process, based on the work of Becker and Whisler (1967 in Saren 1984), features perception, search, evaluation and response. Becker and Whisler (1967 in Saren 1984: 23) further specify the four stages as:

1 stimulus: on individuals in a firm to conceive a new idea;
2 conception: of the idea for an innovation;
3 proposal: by the inventor (or product champion or others) of a project for development;
4 adoption: (or rejection) of the innovation.

Both the response and conversion process models reflect product development approaches with more attention for human actors. Saren's classification, although sufficiently comprehensive (Hart and Baker 1996), has been extended by Buijs and Valkenburg (2000) who added two different models: learning models and integrated models. The learning models were a further development of the response models and focused on organizational learning. In the integrated models (as developed by Andreasen and Hein 1987) the development process is portrayed as a process of integrated interaction between market, product and production. The remainder of this section will elaborate on integrated product development.

Integrated product development

In the 1980s and early 1990s, the disadvantages of sequential product development were becoming increasingly noticeable. In their study of product development in the automotive industry, Clark and Fujimoto (1991) have pointed to several negative consequences of the sequential method, among them long development lead times, communication problems and increased costs. Integrating the various activities in the innovation process is one way to overcome these problems. In the late 1960s, Lawrence and Lorsch (1967) claimed that integration between functions was needed in order to facilitate coordination and communication. Recently, these thoughts have been explicitly applied to problems of product development in an increasingly competitive and quickly changing environment. New 'concepts' such as Quality Function Deployment (Griffin 1992), Concurrent Engineering (Berndes and Stanke 1996) and Integrated Product Development (Clark and Fujimoto 1991) have a common element: they all integrate development and design activities with other business processes.

The following excerpt is taken from a presentation by a special product design unit that was part of a large manufacturer in the light engineering industry. It illustrates what needs to be done when developing new products:

> the processes and stages through which a manufacturer has to pass his new products before they can be put on the market are of great complexity and rely on the ordered coordination and collaboration of a number of specialists. It is considered that the most flexible and satisfactory means of doing this is to link these departments together ... This Development Department must be staffed by individuals ... embracing marketing, sales, psychology, art (in its broadest sense), production planning, buying, estimating ... etc (Metal Box Company Limited 1947)

This excerpt refers to the integration of departments as described in the previous section. An interesting detail is that this presentation dates from 1947. It is possible that the method described failed in the end. At the time of the presentation the company had just started to work with this multidisciplinary department and the consequences of its implementation are not known. However, it is striking that 'new' approaches to product development (such as concurrent engineering, quality function deployment or integrated product development) are similar to this 'old' notion of innovation. To state that they are completely the same would not give enough credit to the groundbreaking work of several scholars, but to claim that integrated solutions to product development are new is also an overstatement. Maybe it is fair to speak of revised approaches of new product development, because there have been some very useful revisions to the old integrated development concept (see, for instance, Clark and Fujimoto 1991).

Integrated product development concepts aim at reducing communication problems, and thereby lead times and costs, by the early distribution of information between, and the involvement of, different functional areas (Clark and Fujimoto 1991; Wheelwright and Clark 1992; Pisano 1997). Because information is shared in an early stage of the innovation process, there is a reasonable chance that product characteristics can be better understood, which will avoid design errors. Clark and Fujimoto (1991) argue that integration of upstream and downstream functions leads to richer, more frequent, bilateral and early communication, which in turn leads to better manufacturability and quality.

The simultaneous conducting of activities is another essential variable of integrating functions, which means that the activities of later development phases (e.g. production engineering) are started before the earlier phases have finished (e.g. product design). The shortening of product development lead times depends heavily on the amount of overlapping activities in the innovation process. The level of integration that is needed for success depends on the stage of the project (Moenaert and Souder 1990). Earlier stages (such as idea generation, screening and concept development) that are more uncertain usually require more integration than the latter stages of the development process.

Individuals in organizations have to match their activities to realize a desired outcome. In order to perform a set of tasks these individuals need some kind of coordination. Coordination refers to the degree to which the activities of organizations' members are fitted and linked together in order to accomplish a collective set of tasks. The need for this coordination originates from the lack of knowledge of all relevant issues in a set of tasks. According to Hitt *et al.* (1993: 162), innovation processes can only be successful if large amounts of information from various disciplines are 'obtained, processed and interpreted'. Hitt *et al.* claim that the 'ability to communicate and integrate the divergent, but critical perspectives of engineering/production with management and other important business functions (e.g., purchasing, marketing) play a critical role in the design and commercialization of innovation' (1993: 163). Integrating information from multiple functions in the organization is thus necessary to develop new products. Therefore, it is essential to coordinate the functional specialists involved in the innovation process, because these specialists often do not have the necessary 'umbrella' view of the innovation process.

Coordination and simultaneity of activities are, to a large extent, interlaced with communication and cooperation. Communication is the exchange or sharing of information by one function with another through a process of transformation (Moenaert and Souder 1990). Because various functional specialists are involved in the development of new products, communication processes are often troublesome (see p. 76). Cooperation relates to the process of several people working together in order to create a new product (Kahn 1994). Communication and cooperation are closely related, but are distinct. Communication seems to be more related to the functioning of the organizational members, whilst cooperation depends more on the design of the organizational structure. A distinction between horizontal and vertical communication is probably necessary, for coordination and cooperation both depend on these types of communication. In the case of very effective and efficient coordination, the need for horizontal communication decreases, which can be seen when product champions are in control of an innovation process. However, when the focus is on cooperation there is less need for vertical communication, which happens when project teams are self-organizing.

Similarly, the (partial) parallelization of activities, as proposed by concurrent engineering aims at shortening product development lead times by means of improved communications between formerly strictly sequential activities (Berndes and Stanke 1996). Some of the most important elements of simultaneous or concurrent engineering involve cutting back departmental barriers, promoting interdepartmental cooperation and creating close links between customers and suppliers. Standardization lies at the core of the parallelization and integration concepts. Although this might appear paradoxical in a concept for innovation, standardization has to be considered a major leverage for innovation when it is related to 'procedural aspects as phases or structuring of operations' or 'to the organization of the structure such as interfaces between projects and departments' (Berndes and Stanke 1996: 21). By standardizing these aspects it is possible to improve communication and understanding between various disciplines.

One other important issue in the product development approach concerns the role of the customer. It has been argued that customers or users should be involved in the development process (von Hippel 1988). Quality Function Deployment (QFD) is a formal management process for product development that tries to capture and convert the 'voice of the customer' into new products (Griffin 1992). It is an integrated product development approach with explicit consideration for the customer. QFD 'manages *across* individual functional aspects of new product development ... providing mechanisms that weave the individual functional tasks into a coherent process' (Griffin 1992: 173). The 'house of quality' is the basic design tool in QFD and is founded on the belief that products should be designed to reflect customer desires. In order to achieve this, marketing people, engineers, and other parties involved in the product development process must work closely together from start to finish.

Teamwork

More and more companies believe that teams are a means to encounter the lack of communication between functional departments (Katzenbach and Smith 1993). They rely on such teams, especially in the field of product development (Pinto and Pinto 1990; Eisenhardt and Tabrizi 1995). Product development teams have been the object of study for a long time. Allen (1977) was one of the first to study communication between project team members. He argued that members should be closely connected and communicate accordingly in order to bring about a successful product development process. These multidisciplinary teams are also a 'logical means to generate more creative, less problem-riddled solutions, faster' (Donnellon 1993: 377). They are, however, different from self-organizing or self-managing teams in regular operations. The main difference between these teams and product development teams is the temporal involvement of team members in the latter type of teams. Once the project is completed, the team members return to their functional departments.

Product development teams are temporary teams consisting of representatives from the various departments involved in the development process. However, these team members often conduct their specialist activities in their regular work environment, usually the functional department they represent, because they are assigned to the project on a part-time basis. With respect to this type of teams Donnellon (1993) makes a distinction between 'team work' and 'teamwork'. The first represents a group of people that works as a team in name only. The team members are mainly representatives of their functional departments and try to contribute independently to the task of the team. They do not feel responsible for the entire development task. 'Teamwork' is very different from 'team work'. A team in this respect is 'a small number of people with complementary skills who are committed to a common purpose, performance goals, and approach for which they hold themselves mutually accountable' (Katzenbach and Smith 1993: 45). This definition of teams displays four necessities. First, a team needs the right mix of skills to do the job. The right mix of skills depends on functional expertise, problem-solving and decision-making skills, and interpersonal skills (Katzenbach and Smith 1993). The composition of a project team is therefore very important (Brown and Eisenhardt 1995). Team members must have technical skills as well as team player skills. Teams with more experienced and senior organizational members have more possibilities for dealing with problems. They know how the organization works and are often able to find 'shortcuts', meaning that formal procedures might be skipped in order to speed things up.

One of the main problems with project teams is that it takes time for the members to get acquainted and to trust each other. Therefore, team composition should also include having members on the team who already know each other, because teams in which the members previously worked together do not need to go through the process of 'getting to know each other'. Naturally it is neither possible nor desirable to have the same team members for every project. An additional element in team composition is the complementarity of team roles (Belbin 1993). If all team members have the tendency to be a 'plant' or 'chairman', the team will not function properly. Second, the team is committed to a common purpose and performance goals. The team needs a common, meaningful purpose that is related to the performance goals. This purpose provides the team with an identity that keeps conflicts constructive (Katzenbach and Smith 1993). The performance goals need to be an integral part of the team's purpose in order to maintain a clear and consistent focus. Third, the team needs to be committed to a common approach (how they will work together). The approach includes economic, administrative and social aspects of work. The team needs to decide who will do certain jobs, what targets and schedules to set and how decisions will be made (Katzenbach and Smith 1993). In other words, they have to agree on the specifics of work. Fourth, mutual accountability is also needed for a group to become a team. Only by being responsible as a team, can team members be committed to the team. Mutual accountability is all about promises and trust between team members (Brown and Eisenhardt 1995).

Teams and thought worlds

Despite the positive effects of teamwork, teams cannot be considered a panacea to all the shortcomings of a functional organization. Researchers point at continuing communication and cooperation problems between representatives from various departments inside multidisciplinary teams. In the background of these problems are 'sociocultural differences' between these functional areas (Gupta *et al.* 1986). These differences create barriers for working together actively and understanding the need for cooperation.

People differ in the way they perceive information and interpret situations. In their classic book on organizations, March and Simon (1958) claimed that specialization affects the information people receive. When organizational members conduct a specific task, it is likely that this will affect their frame of reference and the perception of their environment. Production managers see different problems than IT managers or marketing managers. People interpret situations in their own way, depending on their mental models or interpretive schemes. These models or schemes are developed over a long period of time and are influenced by a person's background (social and educational) and the direct environment of the individual (see, for instance, Daft and Weick 1984; Dougherty 1992). According to Lord and Foti (1986) these schemes are the knowledge bases by which individuals interpret information. Apparently, specialists from functional departments do not speak the same language and create little understanding for each other's activities. Dougherty (1992) argues that 'departmental thought worlds' are a major constraint for a shared understanding between representatives from different departments involved in the innovation process. Due to the different backgrounds of individuals from various departments, these individuals do not share the same understanding of various aspects in the development process. Individuals develop 'schemes' based on assumptions about their work, the organization and reality (Daft and Weick 1984). People in departments share their schemes to some extent, since they often have more or less similar backgrounds (in education for instance). Because of this, departments create an identity, or 'thought world', that separates them from other departments, meaning that communication and cooperation are increasingly difficult to achieve. This leads to an increase in time-to-market and costs and a substantial decrease in quality.

An important aspect of these thought worlds is that they include ideas of other individuals' behavior and actions, which are very difficult to change (Downey and Brief 1986). Implicit notions of organizational members lead to conclusions about events that are perceived in different ways, meaning that individuals react differently to the same phenomena. Especially in organizations with heterogeneous members who do not share the same values, this might be problematic. Developing new products often includes heterogeneity of organizational members, which makes it very difficult to 'bond' individuals. The concept of 'social bonding' implies that people with similar schemes will communicate and collaborate to a greater extent than people with different schemes (Downey and Brief 1986). The problem is obviously twofold. First, members in a new product development team with different schemes will have difficulty in communicating and collaborating, because of the heterogeneity between them. Second, these members will share their schemes with the functional departments they 'belong' to, which means that differentiation between team members might increase, leading to a more troublesome integration of functions.

Teams and language

A problem related to the differences in perceptions is that people in functional departments develop their own language. In 1938, Barnard pointed out the importance of communication and language in organizations. People that do not speak the same language will find it difficult to communicate. There are numerous examples of people from functional departments who do not speak similar languages, resulting in troublesome communication and cooperation (Crawford 1994; Gupta *et al.* 1986; Moenaert and Souder 1990). When new products are developed, several functional departments that speak different languages are involved, paving the development path with obstacles. Communication problems occur between representatives from various functional departments (Ruekert and Walker 1987), but in manufacturing industries the most important problem in the innovation process, in terms of interfaces, seems to be the R&D/marketing interface (see, for instance, Gupta *et al.* 1985; Souder 1987; Gupta and Wilemon 1990; Moenaert *et al.* 1994). The differences between engineers (R&D) and marketing specialists have been described in great detail, since the success of innovations depends heavily on the functioning of this interface (Souder 1987).

Most problems related to the R&D/marketing interface start with wrong perceptions of customer needs by R&D personnel. Marketing specialists transform their perceptions of customer needs into information about the new product that should be developed and transfer this information to the R&D department. The interpretation of this information by the R&D specialists is seldom without mistakes and misunderstandings. As a result, marketing specialists view R&D personnel as 'unresponsive, oversophisticated and overexuberant about impractical ideas' (Souder 1987: 161). R&D personnel, on the other hand, do not understand the haste of marketing people in getting products to market. In addition to this, they do not seem to understand why it is not possible for marketing to specify product features more accurately or predict customer needs (Souder 1987). The consequence of these mutual misunderstandings is a large number of iterations. The product concept goes back and forth between marketing and R&D due to a lack of understanding between the two (Moenaert and Souder 1990; Moenaert *et al.* 1994).

Results of the exploratory study

The exploration of the literature on product development points to the importance of project structures as a salient factor in innovation processes. These project structures have been created to combine the advantages of functional specialization with the need for lateral communication and coordination on a project basis. Recently, debate about the organization of product development has moved beyond these structures to emphasize integration and parallelization of specialist activities. Problems of communication between members of the resulting multidisciplinary project teams have received much attention (e.g. Ruekert and Walker 1987; Katzenbach and Smith 1993). Our study started with the assumption that some of these trends, concepts and problems, as found in the manufacturing-based literature, would also be visible in the financial services sector, especially now that product innovation is more important there too. The following empirical investigation has served the double purpose of surveying the product development landscape in financial services and testing the actual usefulness or accuracy of traditional, manufacturing-biased notions for this particular sector.

Project organization

The organizational structures of the financial companies investigated were predominantly functional in character, i.e. in many companies specialized departments were responsible for tasks in relation to all products of the company. However, there was a clear tendency to reorganize along product lines, with departments becoming responsible for all tasks in relation to a specific product (or customer) category. Several organizations indicated that they were functionally organized, but also had a project organization horizontally spread over the functional organization. The respondents from these organizations did not agree with the term 'matrix'. In their perception, a matrix organization was something different. Those organizations that did claim to have a matrix structure also indicated that the project managers had no formal authority. The latter is, however, a main feature of a matrix organization. It was, therefore, very clear that most organizations were still functionally oriented or were 'modified bureaucracies'.

Most organizations (thirty-two out of thirty-nine) did use project teams as a means to develop new products. The seven companies that did not form project teams were small or medium sized and had various reasons for not developing products in project teams: the size of the company did not 'allow' project teams, the scope of the development project (only some minor adjustments) or the nature of the product did not ask for teaming up. One company with a 'state-of-the-art' information system incorporated possibilities to develop new products on a modular basis in 'real-time', i.e. in close cooperation with the customer.

In the companies that did form project teams, several types of project teams were found: teams with a permanent composition; teams with a composition that was changing in the course of the development process (depending on specific activities needed in each phase of the project); informal project teams that were not officially organized; and a 'group of people' to support the initiator. The two types mentioned first formed the dominant design (in 80% of the companies that used teams) for project teams. However, most project teams were so-called 'lightweight team structures' (Wheelwright and Clark 1992).

Although most companies worked with project teams during the implementation phase, the project organization was not clearly defined in more than half of the companies. After the idea had been introduced to management, a first go/no go decision was taken. After this decision a project leader was assigned who had to gather some people for his/her project team. In smaller organizations, this was done in a more informal way because it was often very clear who would be in the team in these organizations. In the larger organizations, formal procedures were used. Project leaders had to contact heads of departments to ask for representatives from the departments concerned. In these larger organizations the project organization as a whole was much more formalized. Projects crossing functional boundaries tended to have the same hierarchical structure everywhere: a steering committee at the top, a core project team and, if needed, functional workgroups. The steering committee had mainly an advisory role, but on occasion also had the power to stop a project at specific times. The core project team consisted of the project leader and representatives of functional departments who acted as the leaders of the functional workgroups. These workgroups were mainly occupied with specialist activities, and the members of these workgroups rarely interacted with members of other workgroups. For smaller projects there usually was no steering committee but merely a high-ranked manager who was in charge of the project. The project leader had to consult with this high-ranked manager when decisions had to be made. There was little contact between this top manager and the other members of the project team. A 'heavy' project manager or product champion was not found in this study.

Thus, new service development is often conducted in project teams, but the members of these teams remain first and foremost representatives of their functional departments. They are involved in the project activities on a part-time basis and as such they often work on the project when it best suits their individual agendas, meaning that team members did not conduct project tasks at the same time. An interesting point was made by most IT managers, who claimed that the 'rest' of their organization had serious problems with project-based working. They confirmed that most team members in product development teams remained representatives of their functional departments. The IT managers also claimed that this was not the case for the IT representatives, since IT has a history of working in projects and IT employees always belong to a project instead of a functional department. This was clearly seen differently by the product managers who were interviewed. The section on teamwork (see p. 83–84) elaborates on the problematic effects of this 'functional' perspective of the team members.

Product development approach

The literature on new product development (and service development) indicates that innovation processes can, and indeed should, consist of a large number of consecutive activities. Most companies in this study distinguished four stages in the innovation process [idea stage, product specification stage, product building stage (which can also be a part of the implementation) and implementation stage]. Each of these stages consists of several activities. These activities correspond to a certain extent with the activities described in the manufacturing-based literature. The companies were asked to name the three activities that they paid most attention to. The activities that financial companies pay most attention to are the design of information systems (mentioned by twenty-two out of thirty-nine companies, i.e. 56 per cent), the accurate description and design of the product (42 per cent), the development of a clear concept on which management can base its decision (33 per cent), the preparations for selling the product (36 per cent), and the generation and screening of ideas (33 per cent). Whereas most product development models in the literature end with some kind of evaluation stage, little attention is paid to the regular and formal evaluation of the innovation process in the financial services sector. Only eight companies claim to evaluate the innovation process. The four stages that were distinguished by most companies will be discussed in the remainder of this section.

Idea stage

Various sources for new ideas were mentioned. However, almost half of the companies (eighteen) did not make a systematic effort to collect these ideas. The other twenty-one companies argued that they had a structured approach to gather ideas that 'float around' in the organization. About half of these twenty-one companies, however, claimed that people from various departments will spontaneously inform the department responsible for innovation about their ideas. This is, of course, difficult to verify, because it is impossible to prove that people did not share their ideas. It is well known that repeated rejection of ideas in the past can be a major reason for withholding new ideas. Given the traditional structure and bureaucratic culture of most organizations, rejection rates have probably been high in the past. The results from the interviews also showed that almost 40 per cent of the companies that claimed to structure the gathering of ideas, did not use the front and back office directly as a source for new ideas. Of the eighteen companies that lacked a structured approach, more than 60 per cent did not use front- or back-office employees other than for their process knowledge, which means that customer information is probably unused because customer information enters the organization both at the front- and back-office departments.

In the financial services sector, the screening of ideas is often based on a description of the characteristic features of the new product. The concept is then approved or rejected by management. Management in some companies still approve or reject new projects on the basis of an annual budgetary cycle, but in most companies this is considered a thing of the past. In order to speed up developments, more flexible arrangements have been devised. As noted above, in most companies it is only after the approval of a proposal by management that a project team will be formed.

Product specification stage

In most companies there are several decision moments where products can be stopped, but the most important is the first go/no go decision, after which a project team is formed. The marketing department often starts with the first description of the new product. The members of the project team will either individually or as a group conduct several activities to specify the product features. This results in an accurate description of what the product is and does. Specifying the product features (product design) is one of the activities that receives a lot of attention. This stage ends with a written description (sometimes consisting of more than 70 pages) of the product. Almost all companies (87 per cent) indicate that they make use of parallelization of development activities, especially after product specification has been completed. Two separate parallel flows are frequently initiated: an automation/administration flow and a marketing/communication flow. These two flows base their work on the extensive description of the product.

Product building stage

The automation/administration flow usually starts when the product specifications have been clearly described. The main task of the IT department is to prepare the administrative systems for the new product, but it may also include special software supporting the sales effort. The new product usually has to be fitted into the existing systems. Although most companies claim that IT is not determining what products will be developed, the incorporation of the new product into the existing information systems is the main bottleneck in the innovation process. It is difficult to describe the features of new products in clear terms for information technologists. The persons defining the products do not know the requirements of the IT system and the IT people lack feeling for the product. As a consequence, numerous iterations are needed to fit the new product in the system in such a way that it is satisfactory to all parties involved. These iterations slow down the innovation process and use the same technical and human resources several times, reinforcing the already existing shortage in human and technical capacities. Surprisingly, the IT department was, and often still is, not directly represented in the project teams of our thirty-nine companies. The interviews with the IT managers confirmed this state of affairs. They argued that the traditional practice of 'passing on the stick' to the next department was, at least until very recently, prevailing in their organizations. In their experience, product developers considered the IT part of new service development as something that could be simply 'outsourced'. As a result, the first time the IT department hears of the new product is frequently after detailed product specifications have been approved by management, which means that they have no influence on the product's features. And again, it often was not clear to information technologists what the product characteristics exactly implied. In order to solve some of these problems of mutual understanding, organizations are appointing a liaison person or integrator to the project teams. They are charged with translating the product specifications to the 'real' IT people who eventually design the systems. These liaison persons often have received special training for this task: they are either marketing people who have received additional training in IT or the other way around. Almost all project teams nowadays include such liaison persons, which has led to an earlier distribution of information between the different functional areas in both business and IT. In most organizations (thirty-three out of thirty-nine) a fundamental distinction is made between these liaison persons and the actual designers of the computer systems in the IT department. A final activity in this stage concerns testing. Although most organizations claim to pay some attention to this activity, the IT managers state unanimously that too little attention was paid to the testing process. However, accurately testing the new product often led to new insights in the shortcomings of the product specifications.

The marketing/communication flow in the building stage is led by the marketing department and includes packaging, brochure writing and finding an appropriate name. Whether a publicity campaign is undertaken to introduce the new product to the public depends on the level of novelty of the product concerned. Although marketing plays a major role in this stage, top management usually makes the final decisions (much more so than in the automation flow, which is usually less well understood by top management).

Implementation stage

After these parallel activities have been carried out, the innovation process converges in the final implementation stage. This involves the introduction of the product to the distribution channels and the instruction of personnel and intermediaries. The introduction of the product to the intermediaries and/or branch offices is mostly organized by special training sessions for a large number of agents. Some of these agents have been involved in the generation of ideas or have seen preliminary concepts of the product, but most agents do not know about the product before it is ready for sale. At these meetings, special attention is paid to the delivery of services to the customer and afterwards account managers will explain the product and the accompanying software in more detail to intermediaries and representatives of the branch offices. Direct writers will also be concerned with the instruction of call center personnel.

Parallelization can reduce the lead-time of financial products. This may be especially important because product imitation plays an important role in competition, and speed in imitation is an important determinant of the market share that can be captured with the new product. Most companies found it very difficult to indicate the average length of the overall process of product development. Several aspects were seen as contingent and therefore not always manageable:

- *The nature of the product* was probably the most important determinant for the length of the process. Adjustments of existing products took at most six to nine months, but in most companies these adjustments were carried out in less than three months or somewhere between three and six months.

- *Innovations that were perceived new* for the Netherlands as a country also needed more time to finish. An innovation that was perceived new by the organization averaged a development time of six to nine months in the medium and smaller sized companies, whereas the larger companies often needed nine to twelve months or between one and two years.

The main reasons for these differences, which were indicated in the interviews, were the 'weight of the past' in information systems (legacy systems) and the hierarchical decision-making processes.

Teamwork

A single department (marketing, product development or product management) that is charged with new product development usually carries out the early activities in the innovation process. Other functional departments are consulted, advise the developers, and provide information. After the product concept has been presented to the company management and management has approved the proposal, a project team was formed in thirty-two organizations.

In these project teams, various functional disciplines are represented, for example marketing and/or product development and/or product management, automation (indirectly through the IT liaisons or integrators), front and back office (occasionally), management, legal affairs, branch offices and intermediaries, and actuaries (when insurance products are developed). The members of these project teams conduct several specialist activities, mostly individually and occasionally with other team members, and take care of the communication with the departments concerned. The members of the project team frequently involve other members of their department (depending on the size and impact of the new product). Thus, most of the actual work is being done in mono-disciplinary work groups. The main communication flows in this situation are vertical and rarely horizontal. As was indicated earlier, two parallel activities are started after the product specifications have been consolidated. The translation of the specifications to information systems turns out to be very troublesome in all the companies in the survey. On the one hand, this is due to a lack of knowledge of insurance or banking matters on the part of information technologists and, on the other hand, to the lack of insight in the possibilities of IT on the part of other organizational members as well as the inflexibilities of the existing computer systems. Even the creation of IT liaisons has not always solved this translation problem.

Language and thought world problems appeared (expressed by nineteen organizations) between the representatives (especially marketing and IT) from the functional departments in the teams. Some companies (twelve out of thirty-nine) have trained their marketing employees to obtain more insight in information systems as a means to make sure that future innovations connect better with computer systems at an early stage and that product specifications can be described in 'IT language'. Other companies (three out of thirty-nine) have replaced part of their IT personnel with employees with more knowledge of organization and business administration to make sure that IT is more focused on the organization as a whole. A third solution (found in thirty companies) was the installation of a special unit or department, which operates as an intermediary between marketing and the actual system designers. These liaison persons are actively involved in the project team, but the system designers are not represented. They receive the information from these intermediaries and have no influence in the product specifications. These designers claim, however, that their contributions could be more valuable if they were included in the team, because they are able to tell if certain specifications are possible to design in the existing systems. For true innovators this might be the reason for not involving system designers in project teams.

Another important language and thought world problem was identified between actuaries and representatives from other departments in the insurance companies. More than half of the respondents in the insurance companies claimed that actuaries were an important source of problems in project teams. It seemed that the actuaries always disapproved of the ideas coming from marketing/product development. This had often resulted in frustration in the marketing/product development department, especially so because the actuaries have difficulties explaining why certain product specifications are not possible. Exactly what an actuary does is very difficult to comprehend for the rest of the team members, and actuaries are often not capable of explaining it in a 'normal' language.

Generally, it can be noted that the introduction of multidisciplinary project teams may reduce the coordination, communication and collaboration problems between departments, but they are certainly no guarantee for a successful cooperation between individuals in the team. The individual members of the teams usually see themselves as representatives of functional departments and they remain specialists in their field. The fact that they are members of one team does not immediately increase their capacity to collaborate with other specialists. Nineteen companies experienced serious communication problems (marketing/IT and actuary/project team) and considered them a major bottleneck in the innovation process. Although it was not explicitly referred to in the theoretical discussion, organizational culture seems of great importance here. Most organizations (thirty) indicated that the organization's culture could be defined as 'traditional' or 'departmental'. Day-to-day routine activities were often favored against developing or implementing new ideas, which were perceived as extra work instead of an opportunity. Departments, or heads of departments, are rewarded on the basis of departmental output. Sending personnel on an innovative journey means that they cannot contribute to the department's output. Since this leads to fewer rewards, incentives for innovation are not present and priority is given to routine work in the department.

Barriers for incremental product innovation

The exploratory study revealed four problematic aspects in the organization of product innovation processes:

1 type of project organization;
2 project-based working and utilization of NPD methods and tools;
3 communication and cooperation between people;
4 information systems.

Type of project organization

The dominant type of project organization in the exploratory survey was identified as a 'lightweight team structure'. In the banks and insurance companies that were studied this meant that representatives from functional departments were assigned to a project team on a part-time basis and the project leader did not have any formal authority. This caused two important problems. First, the team members work both on routine and non-routine tasks. Day-to-day work processes cover the routine activities, while the project organization requires non-routine activities. These two subsystems of the organization often have (perceived) incongruent goals. Day-to-day processes are concerned with routine activities that keep the organization running in the short term. The project organization serves mid- or long-term goals that are necessary for the viability of the organization as a whole. Resources are needed for both types of activities and because most companies in the financial services sector lack sufficient resources, a regular battle for resources is more rule than exception. Second, it appeared that most team members did not conduct their project activities at the same time. If one of the team members worked on the project and had some question regarding the work of one of the other team members who at that moment was not working on the project, this could easily lead to a lack of responsiveness on the part of the 'team member'.

Project-based working and utilization of NPD methods and tools

In the early 1990s, financial companies started to consider other ways of organizing their work processes. Project teams are a new type of organizational configuration in which work is divided between a few members who have to work closely together on a shared task. This new way of working (with employees from different disciplines) seems to be problematic in many financial institutions. Due to a lack of experience, team members find it difficult to work in a cross-functional project team. Besides the lack of experience of team members (and managers) with working in project teams, it appears that the financial services sector has not progressed very far in the practical application of insights derived from manufacturing practice. Process models and development manuals were developed, but it was not clear if these models and manuals were adequate. In many cases these models were not even used.

Integrated product development was not found in any of the organizations in this study. The product development approach was still mainly conducted sequentially and, to some extent, in parallel flows. Tools or methods to involve the customer or intermediaries (such as QFD) in the development process were also not discovered. More information is needed to uncover the reasons for the infrequent use of the NPD tools and methods.

Communication and cooperation between people

Creating a shared understanding between the members of a project team is often suggested to enhance communication and cooperation. Especially in product development situations, where people from different departments are involved, it seems necessary to establish some common ground. This means that there is a need for a shared understanding between the team members in order to prevent conflict situations. The exploratory study revealed several difficult relations between members from different departments, which led to serious communication and cooperation problems. Successful integration of team members is, however, a prerequisite for new product development. A lack of communication and cooperation will decrease the chances for integration, which in turn negatively affects the potential for innovation.

Information systems

It was mentioned above that the complexity of the information systems makes it difficult to develop new products. What this actually means is still hard to grasp. Apart from the notion about the complexity of the systems, more insight is needed to figure out if it is either not possible to make major adjustments to the information systems (as the IT employees sometimes claimed) or not in the interest of the IT department because it disturbs their daily activities (which was heard from some of the product developers/marketers).

Preliminary conclusions

In most financial companies the overall organizational structures are still mainly based on the traditional principle of functional specialization. Similar to Johne (1993), no purely team-based organizations or other 'new' structures were found. However, under the influence of such notions as Business Process Redesign (see Davenport 1993), several organizations are now moving toward process-based structures, focusing on product groups or customer groups. Still, the majority of organizations remain functionally departmentalized.

Multidisciplinary project teams are formed to develop new products, especially in the case of more radical product innovation. The members of these teams come from various functionally specialized departments. In most cases, team members act primarily as representatives of their department and the teams therefore rarely function as teams with a shared understanding of their mission. Project leadership is correspondingly weak. Heavy project managers or product champions are a rare species in the financial sector. Although the vocabulary of teamwork is used, the supposed advantages of teamwork are hardly realized. This becomes clear in the persistence of all sorts of communication and cooperation problems between disciplines, the solution of which, supposedly, was the main reason for creating multidisciplinary teams.

Product innovation processes are often described in terms of a number of more or less consecutive stages (Cooper 1983; Cooper and De Brentani 1991). Most companies in the financial services sector distinguish four stages in the innovation process: the idea generation stage, the product specification stage, the product building stage and the implementation stage. As mentioned above, the idea generation stage is mainly the task of a single department. The results of the survey suggest that financial companies tend to neglect some major potential sources of new ideas, especially front-office personnel who are in close contact with customers. Some companies, however, do arrange special meetings with various representatives of the front (and back) office in order to gather ideas or ask for advice. Direct involvement of customers appears to be extremely rare. This is particularly noticeable in view of the simultaneousness of production and consumption in services and the close interaction with customers, which would have to take place then. During the stages of further specification and building of software and marketing material, functional departments (or representatives from these departments) conduct 'their own' tasks. Little cooperation between these activities, let alone integration, seems to exist. Some activities are conducted in parallel, but not in the 'concurrent engineering' sense of close mutual support and mainly autonomously of each other. Integrated product development, as described by Clark and Fujimoto (1991), is not widespread in the financial services sector.

One could argue that the nature of the product makes such cooperation and integration unnecessary. However, all companies struggle with delays and failures in product development due to problems of communication and mutual understanding. Members of different functionally specialized departments, regardless of whether they were members of one team or not, have difficulties in understanding each other. The same is true for the proponents of a new product and the people working in the distribution channels (which can be intermediaries or branch offices). For the latter group of people, processes are changed and these actors in the distribution channels have to be convinced of the added value of the new product. In manufacturing, new products often take the place of existing ones, but new financial products usually do not replace existing ones and the sales force may be reluctant to sell an additional product if it feels that existing products are already providing sufficient business.

A closer look at the communication/understanding problems shows that in the financial services sector most communication problems tend to lie at the interface between marketing and information technology departments and (in insurance companies) between actuaries and the other project team members. It may be that the intangible character of these services makes it more difficult to come to a common understanding between persons with different backgrounds. Moreover, the fact that financial services are characteristically backed up by a complex administrative system, which in some cases has to be kept functioning for several decades, may easily lead to the perception that the supportive information systems are the essence of the product. If this perception prevails in the IT department, communications with marketing are greatly impeded.

Financial products used to have very long life cycles (30 years or more were no exception). Given the nature of services, all these products are always present in the organization's information systems. This means that these information systems very often dated back from the 1970s. To keep up with the latest developments, adjustments were made to the old systems or new parts were connected to them. This tangle of information systems is difficult to understand for lay persons, but in some cases also for IT personnel. Most IT employees have not been with these companies for more than five to ten years. Knowledge of the old systems has rarely been transferred to the new employees. Accurate knowledge of all the systems is scarce, which also makes it difficult to change the systems in new product development efforts.

The exploratory study shows that many of the concepts found in the literature on industrial product development can also be applied to service development. However, it appears that the financial services sector has not progressed very far in the practical application of insights derived from manufacturing practice. Only seldom do companies succeed in integrating functions and disciplines into a coherent product development system. To some extent, this may be due to the simple fact that, until recently, the financial market was quite stable, offering relatively limited opportunities for innovation. Increasing turbulence on the market and growing competition will force companies to improve their innovative performance. The specific features of services as opposed to physical products, however, also contribute to this state of affairs. The intangibility as well as the high information content of financial services appear to be at the basis of the substantial problems of communication and understanding arising in the product development process.

The exploratory study has revealed several problematic aspects in new service development. However, it must be noted that the findings of this study should be considered preliminary. Most information was derived from people responsible for product development. Additional information was collected in IT departments, but in new service development several other departments are considered important players. They might have different opinions concerning the organization of development processes. The next chapter presents the results of the in-depth case studies of several new service development processes that were conducted in three financial organizations. The specific features of services and the financial sector that might influence development processes will be examined more closely in the case studies. At this stage it seems premature to decide whether or not the preliminary expectations can be supported.

6 Organizing new service development

In the previous chapter we presented a first glimpse of what actually happens during new service development processes in banks and insurance companies. In order to gain a more in-depth understanding of the organization of innovation processes in these firms, three in-depth case studies have been conducted. This chapter merely describes the main issues related to the organization of new service development processes. The findings of the exploratory survey were used to structure this chapter. First, we briefly introduce 'the' financial firm according to its organizational structure. Next, we elaborate on how the project organization actually functions. Subsequently, the way integration between functions is handled is described, and conflicting interests as well as priorities between these functions are clarified. Finally, the use of NPD methods and tools are illustrated. The quotations in this section are extracted from the transcripts of the case study interviews.

Introducing financial firms

Most of the banks and insurance companies have undergone periods of restructuring in the last decade. The change towards matrix and process-based structure has not been an easy one and it is doubtful if real changes in the way people are working have occurred. According to internal documents in one of the firms in our study, the main reason for the change towards a matrix organization was: 'our organizational structure is not always adequate for carrying out changes and a temporary organizational form is a possibility to fight this.' The main feature of the matrix would be that employees of different departments would cooperate on projects with dual leadership; a project leader and a functional manager. The employees would remain in the functional organization and would only be able to spend a small amount of their time in the project organization.

One of the main problems, however, is that these firms have remained highly departmentalized. The departmentalization led to involvement in only a very small part of the development process. Representatives from a specific department only cared for their small piece of the pie.

> I was just a small module in that project. That is the way to look at it. The most important thing was that people accepted me as a module and the only thing I had to do was to act whenever it concerned my module. I would not interfere with the rest of the project. Why should I?
>
> (BanCo project team member)

> There were several serious problems in the project, but these were all related to technical issues so they did not concern me.
>
> (BanCo project team member)

> People are really occupied with their own little group and serving this little groups' interests. When something has to be solved, this is not something we do in a collaborative way, but it is always forwarded to some group that just has to solve it.
>
> (SureCo project team member)

Despite the structural changes, most respondents frequently referred to the organizational structure as still being traditional, meaning that work activities were concentrated in specialized departments according to functions. This division of labor has its reflection in the product development process. Project team members from different departments lack the overview of the entire development process. In many product development projects, the functional way of working still prevails. People look at the project with their departmental 'spectacles'. We found this to be the case in all the firms we studied, not only the firms that we used for our in-depth perspective on the organization of new service development processes as described in this chapter.

Project organization

New services are developed in some kind of project organization. These can be a part of ongoing business, or they can be separated from the functional departments. The project organization consists of several layers: a manager that provides the project assignment, a steering group, a project leader and a project team. The team members might also be leading a subproject team that is related to their functional expertise. This organization has been properly established in financial firms.

> My general idea is that projects are much better organized. We used to do something, but nobody knew what it was. Now we have a clear organization, subprojects are defined, the structure is plain and simple. In the old days you would have a project leader that went shopping for resources in the organization and he would come up with something. Now it is much more structured.
>
> (SureCo business-unit manager)

The majority of projects are conducted next to the daily activities. In order to embed these projects in the organization and provide them with a clear identity (distinguishing them from daily activities), project offices are created. These are mainly occupied with projects that involve more than one functional discipline and are carried out in a multidisciplinary fashion. One of the main goals of these project offices is to eliminate potential conflicting interests between participating departments. They often provide the project managers for the development teams.

> The project office is closely related to the regular (daily business) organization and is involved in projects in the daily organization that exceed departmental boundaries. This idea originated from the possible contradictory interests that needed to be eliminated. First the project organization was a unit next to the organization and we were seen as a violation on the daily organization. We thought that if we were a part of the daily organization the chances of acceptance would be higher.
>
> (BanCo project leader)

Project leaders from the office have no formal power, however, so they are often not entitled to make major decisions. They are assigned to facilitate the process and have little knowledge of the product's content.

> He had to make sure the product was introduced. Thus, he had to instruct people to do their tasks in the project. This was not always easy, because this was his first project.
>
> (BanCo project team member)

> He only had to direct the team members. That was the idea. He tried to do this, but he merely noted what needed to be done. He needed to be more directive instead of just looking what was going on.
>
> (BanCo project team member)

When the project leader does not come from the project office, the product manager is the project leader. However, managing projects requires skills other than managing a product. Since developing new products is not a routine job, many project leaders are relatively new to the job and have little experience to look back at. As a result, many recurring mistakes are being made in managing projects. Several respondents at SureCo argue that a project leader should be a process leader, thus a facilitator that makes sure that the projects run in to as few problems as possible. The process leader does not need content knowledge about the project, but must have the proper skills to guide the process. Management has recently decided that process leaders will be appointed for new product development projects:

> It has been decided that there will be a project leader for these kinds of projects with no knowledge about the product that is being developed. He only has to facilitate the process.
>
> (SureCo project team member)

> Fortunately there will be a project leader that will focus on guiding the process. Combining the product manager role with the project leader role has caused some problems.
>
> (SureCo project team member)

This means that the tasks of the project leader will change from focusing on the contents of the product to facilitating the development process, frequently communicating, and looking ahead for possible problems.

The project leaders are not able to 'hire' people on a full-time basis for their projects, which was to a large extent a result of the low priority of management (according to the project leaders). In general, department heads assign employees to the team. However, some projects had so-called 'heavy' project leaders that insisted on having people available full time for their projects. In one case, BanCo 2, the project leader 'threatened' to cancel the project. Since he was a senior and well-respected manager in the organization, he was able to do this.

For many projects, a steering committee with managers from the most important departments is established. They have to make sure that the project is kept in progress. A problem with the steering committees is that the team is often slowed down due to lengthy discussions in the committees. The project teams also consist of representatives from various departments. The departments that were involved in a large part of the development process have a representative in the core team (often there is a core team and a peripheral group of people less directly affected by the new service). Although the involvement of many departments is required, this increases the complexity of the projects considerably. The multiplicity of meanings and opinions regarding the new soon to be developed service often leads to a lack of clarity on what the new service should exactly look like. It also means that there can be major differences between the departments with respect to the need for the new service.

> Basically it is not clear what goal we have in mind for this product. There are people in the organization who claim that it can never be profitable, so that is one problem. Other people argue that it can be profitable but only if you can sell it in large quantities because of the low margins. These low margins are a second problem. And I know for sure that there is an undertow in the organization, for certain with the actuaries, who already know that this product is not good at all. So you

> have a lot of work convincing them, before you can even start developing this product.
>
> (FinCo product manager)

In most cases, team members are only available on a part-time basis for their projects. Internal documents clearly state that having full-time project leaders is something to strive for and the same should also be the case for team members whenever possible. In practice this was hardly the case and full-time project membership was found in only two projects.

The project team carries out most of the activities in the development process. The teams are often formed after the product specifications have been completed. The project leader establishes the team on the basis of the assigned capacity. The heads of departments decide who will be the departments' representative on the team. It appeared that there are no criteria present for selecting team members. People who have some time available are assigned to a project, while there is no attention paid to specific skills.

> They more or less assign people from the top. An assignment will be given and someone will be appointed. The project leader can hardly influence this. He could go to a department and ask for someone specific. But there are no criteria for people to work in a team. If you have the time, you can do it. There is no attention being paid to the skills of people.
>
> (SureCo project leader)

During the projects, the team members do not share the same location and most team members are not available full time. Working on a shared location is sometimes done, but only when this is considered necessary (in the case of problems and deadlines). The respondents seem to disagree about the use of a shared location.

> It is very difficult to start a project and have the team members share the same location, because there is no basis for talking about the project. So I don't think that it is a good idea to have ten team members in the same room in the beginning of the project.
>
> (SureCo project leader)

> In order to avoid these problems (that concerned the ambiguity of the product specifications, P.V./J.R.) people should cooperate more and share the same location. This is especially important to clarify what the product should look like and what everyone's perspectives are.
>
> (SureCo business-unit manager)

> The separation of people in multiple locations does not do the project much good. Then you also have a physical barrier between departments. You just don't know what happens everywhere.
>
> (SureCo project team member)

There are, however, some exceptions to what has been described above. In the next chapter we will explicitly address the key differences between the successful and unsuccessful projects we studied. Here, we mainly provide a more in-depth view of what happened in one of the successful projects to illustrate the difference with the general features of project organization described above. In the FinCo 2 project, management agreed with a project proposal from a brainstorm session (meaning that it was not very detailed), and a project team was appointed to develop this product. The next step was to crystallize the concept in product specifications. Goals had to be determined, an estimation of the costs and benefits had to be made and the project organization had to be set up. The project leader had very clear ideas about managing projects, and more specific, product development projects. He insisted on having a small team with dedicated people. In the brainstorm session, the project leader asked each of the future members whether they would be available full time for the entire process. Partly he required them to work on the product itself, but he insisted that all team members were ambassadors for the project in their functional departments. The team members were also liaisons between the team and the rest of the organization. Because of the impact of new product development for the organization, explicit attention was needed. The liaison task was to keep the organization informed. In other projects it was very common that all sorts of people wanted to know everything about a project and thus interfered with the project. The organization was, and still is, not used to working in projects and line managers were not fond of the idea of losing control over their employees. In order to avoid all sorts of problems and interference, the project leader was very clear: 'it is my project so mind your own business.' He was allowed to do this due to the support from top management and his own senior position in the organization. One FinCo team member describes the project leaders' role very nicely:

> His role can be described as 'guarding the project from the bureaucratic influences within FinCo'. He did this very well. Everybody in the organization who thought that he or she had something to say about the project was simply ignored or he replied 'none of your business, this is my project'. This meant that the team could move on without interference and that is the only way to be innovative.

With respect to the content of the product the project leader was certainly not an expert. Other people in the team focused on the content of the product. The team members claimed that this was never a problem, since the project leader always guarded the process and made sure that obstacles were removed. The product specifications were a product of joint effort between the team members. A team member would make a contribution from his functional background, which was always followed by consultation with the rest of the team. The team members agree that the meetings were very constructive, which eventually led to a product ready for introduction in five months. A huge advantage of this project was that while the specifications were still being developed, automation co-ordinators [full-time integrators between IT (programmers) and the 'business'] started working on the design of the administrative systems with programmers. They were able to work with the programmers literally at the same desk (see also the next section). At the same time, marketing was preparing an introduction campaign for which they hired an external marketing agency. Several other activities, such as 'branding' the new product, were also outsourced. According to the team members, these activities could be done in a much better way by external agencies that had the necessary expertise. Front- and back-office people were educating employees that had to sell the new product. This was all done within five months. The project reached its climax during the introduction session. Again the team hired external expertise to assist with the introduction. The introduction was unique.

> We had fireworks, audio and video equipment, laserbeams, you name it and it was there. It was a huge show. People applauded afterwards and told us this was something they had never seen before. I think that this session has been very good for the publicity of the product.
>
> (FinCo project leader)

Integration of departments

When working in project teams, various people from different departments have to cooperate. Developing new financial services means that multiple departments are involved. These people often have implicit images of what the 'end product' should look like. Naturally, these images are not always the same and this might lead to misunderstanding and miscommunication. Most of the time a large number of people is involved, meaning that it is not always possible to communicate intensively with everybody. This aspect needs much attention in project teams because of the risk of people losing their commitment to the team. Extensive communication at both horizontal and vertical levels of the organization is needed. Besides this, it is important to align different interests in the project team. A manager from FinCo stated the following:

> Someone might think this and then someone else thinks that. Communication is always tricky. You notice that it often leads to a confusion of tongues. Even if things are written down on paper, it is still very well

possible that people interpret the same things in a different way. That will always be very troublesome to manage.

There was little communication between team members in the development process. This was even worse when subgroups were involved in the project organization. Several respondents indicated that they initiated communication themselves in order to receive information from other workgroups. People in the subgroups were rarely informed on the activities in the other subgroups. Information provided by the steering group was also lacking. The steering group had a monthly meeting with the project leader and sub-project leaders. At this meeting, the problems and the overview of the project were discussed. The sub-project leaders rarely ever reported back from these meetings to the work teams. The following quotes all come from the BanCo 1 project team members.

> There was no horizontal communication, it was all top down. I have tried to work on having more intensive communication, but it was very difficult.

> I read many names from people who were working on this project, but I never saw any of them in real life.

> Formally there is no horizontal communication, it was arranged vertically via the steering committee, the project leader to the subproject leaders and the members of the teams. Informally you occasionally would go to members of other workgroups to get some information.

> What happened in the subgroups was not visible for the other subgroups. You should ask the subgroup leaders. Every workgroup would carry out their tasks.

The cooperation between the subgroups is also troublesome. Some people are involved in the project at a later stage and are not extensively informed. They hardly know what is expected of them and what they can expect from the other team members. Communication and cooperation are not optimal in many projects we studied. The development process of FinCo 2, however, had very few problems with respect to interfunctional communication, which was due to the very strict approach of the project leader and the cooperation of people from different departments in the first stages of development. Everybody knew what to expect and it was made very clear from the start what the results of the project would be if everybody cooperated. The project team had weekly meetings that were very well organized and documented. The project leader referred to the way of working as a 'semi-military operation', which also meant that there was little room for arguments outside the planned path. During a special kick-off session, where all the team members were present, the project leader made it perfectly clear that once someone agreed to his terms and conditions for managing the project, there was no way back. The project then needed highest priority from all involved and a 'no' or a 'but' was not accepted. According to the team members there was a 'chemical reaction' during the kick-off; therefore communication and cooperation were a lot easier. Everybody knew what was expected of him or her and promises were always kept. An advantage of this team was that the project leader selected the team members himself. As was mentioned before, he selected people with experience and credits in the organization, but an even more important aspect of the selection was that several people had already worked together in other projects. This was affirmed by some of the team members:

> All I can say is that I personally know him (pointing at organization chart) for a long time already. We did some training and projects and we trust each other blindly. So this relationship existed and the project leader 'borrowed' it for the team. And this guy (again pointing at organization chart), we also knew him already and he just fitted in as for his enthusiasm and his character.
>
> (FinCo project team member)

> We spoke each others language to a large extent which was the added value of this specific team. If you would have had people that had been in the company for only a short period of time or who hardly knew each other, than we might not have succeeded in this short period of time.
>
> (FinCo project team member)

Another very unique characteristic of this project was the shared location. The project leader insisted on having a special project location where team members could work on the project. A crucial activity in new financial services development is translating the product specifications into the companies' automation systems. Because of the shared location it was possible to cooperate very closely, and if problems arose, everyone was present to solve the problem together.

> These chaps were working with us at the same desk in room 10.14. This makes it very easy to ask questions or to ask someone for his opinion. If you don't work in the same room, maybe you will never ask that question and continue in the wrong direction.
>
> (FinCo project team member)

> We all agreed that we should have a group of people consisting of the programmers for the back and front office software, the automation coordinators, and the project leader. These people were in the same office, meaning that communication lines were very short and in case of a

problem we were able to present it to the person responsible. That was very pleasant.

(FinCo project leader)

Representatives from some departments have interesting opinions of other departments involved in product development. The problematic integration of the various departments involved in development processes is also caused by the negative image the departments have of other departments. In general, people always complain about IT (it takes too long and it costs too much). More interesting, however, were the remarks that were made about the marketing and product management departments. These department do not have a very good reputation. The remarks below comment on certain departments of the organization and were made by people from other departments.

> Mainly due to this way of working, throwing product specifications over their departmental wall into several other departments, a very skeptical attitude has developed with respect to marketing and the people who work there. Do we only pay attention to the commercial side or might there also be a little amount of attention for the technical side of these issues? Marketing does get the blame for the failure of many new products. It is like this every year; 'there is another marketing job, we know how it works by now'. This is the reaction in the whole organization.
>
> (BanCo marketing manager)

> There is absolutely no faith in the people from the marketing and product management departments. You can just stop anybody in this organization and ask him or her if their projects are delayed and they will all confirm this. The people from marketing are not really taken seriously by the rest of the organization because they never finish a project.
>
> (FinCo IT manager)

> You just have to look around and you will see that IT is always causing problems.
>
> (FinCo project team member)

> Where you often see conflicts is in the world of actuaries. What you see is that they would simply say 'this is how it is and there is no other way'. Well, that will often collide with plain horse-sense.
>
> (FinCo project team member)

The negative image of the marketing/product development department also affects product development projects. In general, all development projects are the responsibility of (and most of them are also initiated by) marketing/product development. The other departments are not responsible for product development at least their performance is not measured on the basis of new products or any form of contribution to new product development. Several managers confirmed these image problems of marketing/product development. It is obvious that this will raise the barriers to successful integration.

Another reason for the problematic integration was the lack of shared understanding in the project teams. People from the various departments did not speak each other's languages or had different visions.

> There were four main stakeholders in this project. I had the feeling that they did not speak each other's language at all. That was one of the reasons for the problems. Another reason was that in our organization they were not used to cooperate with each other. They had lived a separate existence until this project.
>
> (BanCo project leader)

> The language was not always the problem. It also had to do with the very distinct visions that arise at some point. For instance, marketing had a different interpretation of the product concept than the actuaries. So, it was not even the language, but the basic ideas about the foundation of the product.
>
> (FinCo project leader)

It seems that these problems are not merely communication problems due to differing languages. An important cause for communication problems in product development is the lack of understanding for other departments' interests and different visions of what the new product should look like.

> I think that when you look at the legal and marketing aspects that everything is relatively simple. It is legal or not, there is a customer demand or not. These things speak for themselves and as an individual you can comprehend that. But this actuarial stuff, for me too, is a lucky bag where you throw some things in and numbers come out and on the basis of these numbers you say if something is possible or not. That is rather complex.
>
> (BanCo business-unit manager)

> Well, to a large extent I think it is a lack of understanding, yes. But that has a lot to do with the complexity of his profession. I think that not all actuaries are capable to explain in plain understandable Dutch why something is not possible.
>
> (FinCo project leader)

Different languages, poor communication, negative image, a lack of understanding of the other persons' position and many discussions in the project team: all these aspects make integration in project teams more difficult to manage. We came across these problems frequently and they seem to resemble a reality that many projects suffer from.

Conflicting interests and priorities

Related to the problematic integration were the conflicting interests between departments and the priorities assigned to the development of new services. At BanCo, for instance, there were clear conflicts related to product development between the regular, daily business organization and the project organization. These have to do with different interests and priorities between the departments involved in product development. Most employees were not used to giving up the interests of the department for the broader common good of the company.

> To some extent this is caused by the priorities of the departments. They have a lot of daily business that is much more important for them. If they also need time to work on some creative new idea, they can not finish the daily workload.
>
> (BanCo project leader)

> There is a tension between the daily organization and the project organization. These two have different interests and priorities and these often conflict. Product developers have a constant fear of not being top priority, which means that the project will not be finished in time, or even, not at all.
>
> (BanCo business-unit manager)

People working in different departments at FinCo also appear to have conflicting interests when it comes to working on product development projects. For many departments, product development is something that 'also needs to be done', but only if there is some time left after the daily work is finished. Commitment to the project is not optimal in this situation. When choices have to be made whether to spend time on the project or on the daily tasks, daily tasks are prioritized. Several respondents realized that this way of working can be detrimental to new product development:

> It should not be possible that they (project members) have their daily activities and next to these their project tasks. Some things are bound to take over then and you could say that people are swayed by the issues of the day, which means that the daily activities take precedence of project activities. So, they should be freed from their daily activities otherwise it will not work.
>
> (FinCo project leader)

> It is also possible that people think 'I have done my share' and just hand it over to another department. Someone might then put it on another pile of work and waits until next week to continue working on it. But then another week has past.
>
> (FinCo project team member)

Project members rarely carry any responsibility for the outcome of the project. They all try to contribute in their departments' best interests, which is not always best for another department or the organization as a whole. Freeing people to work on product development projects is a management task. Project proposals are also approved on the basis of necessary (human) resources. Management decides how much time project members can devote to the project. Priority is therefore also needed at the top of the organization. Without priority from the top it will be much more difficult to develop a new product. One obvious reason for this tension is the output-based reviews for departments by management. Every department is rewarded on the basis of its daily activities. There are no possibilities for rewards based on collective efforts. Functional managers in the daily organization are therefore not really motivated to cooperate in product development projects, because this probably means a reduction in output and less rewards.

> This is caused by the control side of our organization. You get judged on the results of how well a certain group of products is doing. Management has decided upon this issue. So, when you are rewarded on the results of this group of products, you are going to act accordingly. Our management obviously sees the departments as parts. Although this is slowly changing, we still have a long way to go.
>
> (BanCo project leader)

The differences in priorities among the departments led to strong delays in the development process. According to many of our respondents the relative lack of interest in product development was caused by their dedication to another project.

> At the investment department a reorganization had top priority and as such most of the time was spent at this (reorganization) project. The other departments also had their own projects, which made it difficult to see that MGH was also important. Everybody saw the importance of this project, but there is a large gap between seeing the importance and acting accordingly.
>
> (BanCo project leader)

> One of the problems was that all the departments had big projects next to this one, which had a higher priority. This meant that they were very

busy. Most of the time people were only concerned with the interests of their departments and did not see the use of MGH for their department.
(BanCo project team member)

> Project FPP (another product development project) was also in progress at the same time. I think that because this was their (the department responsible for FPP) product, they were more interested in it than in a joined product. They often told us that they just did not have the time because they were testing something for FPP. Our project got delayed because of these things.
> (BanCo project team member)

One team member in the SureCo 1 project phrased the problem of conflicting interests and priorities in the following words:

> You can see that people from the different departments are only interested in their own patch. While they should be working for the organization as a whole. You notice that they try to influence product development from the perspective of their department, and this should not be the case. I think this goes for all departments; the product manager that wants the most innovative product, the marketer who wants to have the best introduction, the administrative organization (back office) who wants as little work as possible and IT who always gets the blame if something fails, which makes them react in a very defensive way by saying 'this is not possible in our system'. I really don't know how you can change this behavior.'

Due to these conflicting interests, many product development processes are not finished satisfactorily.

Use of new product development methods and tools

In the beginning of the new service development NSD process, new ideas are first developed into short notes on what may be a product. After the idea is approved by management, the product specifications are described by a product developer (a product manager) and a product specialist from the same department. The product manager defines the boundaries of the product and the specialist develops the specifications according to the boundaries. The product manager and the specialist rarely cooperate with other departments at this point, meaning that the product specifications (which serve as input for several subsequent activities) are often developed in a rather isolated way. The project team is formed after the product specifications have been described, and representatives from various departments are involved in this team. The commercial side of the organization (marketing, product development and product management) usually leads this first stage. Several respondents claim that they were involved in the process too late.

> From my point of view I was involved too late. I think I would have altered the product specifications and the planning of the project. There was some friction on these issues with the project leader (the product manager). In the end we managed to work it out, but we had a confrontation.
>
> (SureCo project team member)

> I got involved in the project in October. The first set of product specifications was already finished by then. You can hardly influence these specifications when you become involved this late.
>
> (SureCo project team member)

After completing the product specifications, most of the tasks are divided and the team members go back to their department to work on these tasks. The different sub-processes are conducted in parallel, but some activities are so intertwined that a lot of communication is necessary between the people in these subprocesses. There should be a lot of combined action between the disciplines, but this is easier said than done. Several projects provide illustrative evidence of the difficulties of combined action in product development:

> The way it happened, was that the specs were 'delivered' and we just started building. During the building phase there were a lot of functional modifications to the specs necessary. The creative stage is thus not completed adequately.
>
> (SureCo project leader)

> What you would see, is that people would deliver their work in phases because deadlines were not met by other parts. This is not communicated in any way. You would just receive a small part of what should have been finished and they would tell you 'the rest will follow next week'. You have to try to adapt to what you will be receiving, which is not the most efficient way to work.
>
> (SureCo project leader)

After the product specifications have been translated into business specifications, a test-team is called into action. However, testing is something that receives little attention.

> A lot of people think that testing is not part of our competencies and they are not being rewarded for testing. So, there is not a lot of priority and

> energy for testing. Because of the lack of priority for testing it can be very difficult to be motivated for these projects.
>
> (SureCo project leader)

> The announcement of the final deadline was not a very smart thing to do. You will be stuck to this date and you cannot change it anymore. This often leads to products that are introduced to the market that are not even finished or have been tested for a short time.
>
> (SureCo project team member)

The latter remark is one of the reasons for the tensions in the organization. According to marketeers and product developers the product was completed and ready for introduction, but the back-office departments were not able to administrate the product properly. The project organization, however, often stopped at this point.

> The product was introduced two weeks ago, but the systems are not ready for it. Not even a first release. The product has been introduced; they announced it so there was no way back. A week before introduction we heard that the administration could never be ready on the date of introduction. This happens too often in this organization.
>
> (SureCo back office employee)

> I have pointed at this several times in the project team. Why don't we introduce it one or two months later, so we can get it right this time. But you see that it does not work that way. Our customers will probably not be happy with this. Marketing keeps telling us that they focus on the customer, but all they care about is this fancy product which can be sold quickly.
>
> (SureCo project team member)

Thus, although the development process has not been completed the project organization dissolves, which means that there is no more overview of the activities that still have to be done. According to the respondents this is caused by the marketing department, which has the responsibility for introducing new products on the market but does not care about the administrative requirements of new products. This leads to tensions between the departments and between the team members from these departments, especially for the administrative side of the organization:

> The product is by no means completed. The front end is finished and that looks really nice for the customer. Some of my colleagues, who were previously involved in product development projects, said that the guys from marketing have already ordered the party hats and are leaning back now. But in the back office this is completely different. Here we

> panic. These problems have just been thrown over the fence. So from the outside it looks nice, but from the inside it is a mess.
>
> (SureCo back office manager)

Many financial companies have developed a structured approach to product development in order to speed up the time to market. According to internal documents we studied, these approaches are structured ways of working that assure a short as possible development time from the birth of a new idea for a new product or service until introducing it into the market. Since most of these approaches are more or less similar, we will look at one specific method identified in one of the organizations we studied. Within the company, the approach is called SPEED and it consists of several stages.

- stage one: origination, recording/documenting and submitting of an idea;
- stage two: quick scan; quick scan and broad check of the idea and first go/no go decision by management;
- stage three: project proposal; developing ideas into more concrete product specifi-cations and second go/no go decision by management;
- stage four: execution of project; developing the idea into a new innovative product or service, testing, introducing the product and evaluating the process.

In short, this is the standard way that has to be followed when a new product is being developed. Each of these stages is described extensively in a 'project manual'. The activities that have to be carried out, the people responsible in each stage, and a time schedule are listed in the manual. Several contradictory remarks were made by different BanCo project team members about SPEED:

> A problem in the use of SPEED is that the ideas on this concept differ in our organization. Here at BanCo there is no unequivocal way of talking about SPEED.

> SPEED is mainly an advantage in time, to enter a new market very rapidly, but does by no means lead to lower costs or improved performance. Due to shifting priorities the last activities are carried out a bit sloppy.

> In a way it is a major improvement. However, our information systems are not adapted to SPEED. The slightest little change, and you have to test for three months, which slows things down.

> Well, I don't know if we can do anything about it, but when I think of SPEED, I say 'quick and dirty'. All the products that have been developed this way are not very nice products. They are dirty on the backside, are not finished, and require a huge amount of manual labor.

> Perfect. I think it is a really good structure. The main advantage of SPEED is that during the early stages you really have to think of what you are doing. SPEED forces you to think.

The opinions of the respondents differed on several aspects of SPEED, but on the whole most people were positively critical towards SPEED. They were positive because it seems to be a huge improvement on the way things were done previously, but also critical because the development process can be improved on several aspects. An interesting aspect from the SPEED manual was that the focus is on the first three stages. Management closely follows these three stages, whereas the actual execution of the project receives much less attention. Several project members considered this to be problematic:

> The stage after the project proposal has been approved is hardly paid any attention to by management. The entire organization falls apart at that stage. There is a project organization with a project leader, but he really has to put up a fight to keep the project going. Even if the project has been approved it is definitely not the case that everyone will be on your side.

The several stages of the SPEED process will be described in more detail below. Table 6.1 lists the activities and serves to illustrate the amount of attention the various activities receive in the manual. A distinction is made between initiation (stages one, two and three) and implementation (stage four).

Table 6.1 Number of pages related to core SPEED activities

Initiation		*Implementation*	
Idea	4 pages	Project execution	5 pages
Quickscan	10 pages	Testing	5 pages
Project proposal	21 pages	Introduction	7 pages
		Evaluation	4 pages
Total	35 pages	Total	21 pages

Stage one: origination, recording/documenting, and submitting of an idea

Everybody at BanCo can submit an idea for a new product at the 'project office'. The submission of ideas is thus formalized in order to make it clear for all employees where and how to submit ideas. Another goal of the project office is to have a central desk that serves as a means to pass on ideas and decide quickly. However, this philosophy is not yet functioning optimally:

> We tried to create a process for generating ideas. I don't think that we really established something on this part, but there are more ideas generated. However, most ideas still originate from the product development department, which should not be the case.
>
> (BanCo business-unit manager)

The first stage is mainly concerned with documenting the idea (using a standardized form) and submitting it to the project office. The project office distributes the ideas to the 'right' people who will react to the idea. Employees that submit an idea often have informal contact with people from other departments and may have already asked for a first quick response to the idea.

Stage two: quick scan; quick and broad check of the idea and first go/no go decision by management

After submitting an idea, management can decide for a quick scan to be conducted by the initiator. The quick scan is a first rough check of the attractiveness of the product to be developed. During this stage, several departments will examine the product idea for its feasibility. At least two departments have to look at the idea from their perspective. This leads to two short reports on the basis of which management makes the first go/no go decision. The initiator of the SWK project mentioned that it sometimes was necessary to overstate the expected profits of the product in this stage in order to get approval for the next stage.

Stage three: project proposal; developing ideas into more concrete product specifications and second go/no go decision by management

After the quick scan has been approved, the next stage is concerned with the project proposal. The importance of the project proposal is indicated in the SPEED manual by the number of pages dedicated to this subject. In this proposal, attention has to be paid to the purpose of the new product, the costs and benefits (the former in terms of both people and machines) and the expected development time. The project proposal is a rather extensive document on the basis of which management decides to continue or cancel the project. The initiator is expected to consult people from several departments, especially with respect to the costs and benefits of the new product. The management team that decides whether to continue or cancel projects has some hundred projects under consideration continuously. The management team will review all ideas that surface in the organization. Several of the respondents have criticized this management team:

> It has to be decided in the management team. There has to be some kind of unity. The available resources are distributed over projects in the management team. One problem is that they can accept a proposal but often don't know what is happening at the lower levels of the organization.
>
> (BanCo business-unit manager)

> It was the intention that the members of the management team were given a management summary and that the division manager (where the product is most closely related to) was given the full report. He was able to read all the details and should then be able to answer all possible questions from the rest of the management team. It does not seem to work this way. The entire team receives the full report and what I hear is that everybody keeps interfering with everything, with all the details. This means that time to market increases due to a lengthy decision process.
>
> (BanCo project leader)

Many of the comments related to the functioning of the management team are concerned with the allocation of resources. In the project proposal it should be mentioned who is going to be on the project team, or at least how many people are needed. Especially with respect to IT personnel, this is very important. When the management team approves the proposal, the resources that are needed according to the proposal are also approved. However, there seems to be a gap between the allocation and the availability of resources. Several respondents, in both projects, argued that promises were made that could not be realized. People that were allocated to a project were often busy working on other projects or did not have time for the project due to their 'daily' activities.

> Management can even approve a project without the needed capacity being secured. In a way it didn't really matter whether you had sufficient resources, because when a new, more interesting project was prioritized, they (human resources) were moved to the new project.
>
> (BanCo project leader)

Stage four: execution of project; developing the idea into a new innovative product or service, testing, introducing the product and evaluating the process

In the product development manual, this last stage receives only limited attention. Most attention is paid to the first stages. Once a decision has been made to develop a new product, management more or less leaves it up to the project leader. As will be argued below, it is necessary for management to be more involved in the execution of the project. The last stage is divided into five smaller stages: execution, testing, introduction, evaluation and 'second phase development'.

Execution

After management approves the proposal, the next step is to execute the project. The first part of the execution stage is a joint effort. All people involved in the project work on the description of product specifications. Everyone does so from their own perspective, meaning that a lot of time is spent on discussion and clarification. What seems most interesting is that the various development activities are split up into several separate routes after the product specifications have been completed. There is usually a commercial route and a technical route. The former consists of marketing activities, such as designing brochures and labeling the product. The latter consists mainly of actuarial (depending on the nature of the product) and IT activities. The hardest part is often the technical route because several adaptations have to be made to either the existing information systems or the product specifications. It was made clear during the interviews that it is very difficult to describe the specifications exactly in terms of information systems. When the product is built (transforming the specifications into the information systems), IT personnel are often confronted with unexpected obstacles in the form of specifications that cannot be incorporated in the system. After the two routes have been completed the product needs to be tested. Both market and technical tests might be conducted.

Testing

BanCo does not pay a lot of attention to market testing. Testing new products is mainly related to technical testing, which is only relevant when information systems are adjusted. There are several tests that a new product will be confronted with: a unit (integration) test, a system test and a user acceptation test. Technical testing has received increased attention, which has led to the implementation of a test laboratory. The test laboratory tries to objectively judge the product and provides the feedback to the project leader and the team.

> We even have a special test laboratory where we try to find out if the product can be released in the market. We did not use to have any such thing.
>
> (BanCo project team member)

Introduction

The introduction consists of delivering the product to the branches and training and educating personnel. Very often, new products mean adaptations to the information systems with respect to administrative tasks as well as front-office (sales) activities. Personnel have to be trained and educated in order to deliver the appropriate service to the customers. A special 'Introduction Platform' has been installed to guide new product introductions.

Evaluation

The last step of the SPEED process receives very little attention in the manual. The main goal of an evaluation is to learn from previous experiences and to share them with other organizational members. The evaluation is also used as a formal closure of the project. It might be a coincidence, but in the two reviewed projects this final step received no attention at all. Neither of the two projects was subjected to an evaluation.

> We try to do this very cautiously. It has to grow into our organization. Today we hardly do this. Nothing is documented when it comes to the execution of the development process. You don't know when a project is finished, they just end into nothing.
>
> (BanCo project leader)

Second phase development

Normally the development process ends with the evaluation. However, it was often said at BanCo that products are not finished when they are introduced to the market, the so-called '80–20 rule'. Eighty per cent of the product has to be completed at introduction. The other 20 per cent will be done in the second development phase, which is not an official part of SPEED. As a result a lot of problems occur during the completion of this 20 per cent. Both attention and resources have been redistributed to other projects, so there is little time and leadership available.

Conclusion

This chapter provided an in-depth view of what actually happens during NSD processes in financial services firms. We included data from product innovation efforts of three organizations. The results show that the firms in our study struggle with managing the project organization and that the collaboration between the departments involved in these projects is problematic. They speak different languages, do not have a shared understanding of what needs to be developed, and even claim to have different interests and priorities. This makes it extremely difficult to successfully develop new services in a short time. Many firms (also those in the exploratory survey) have expressed that they use product development manuals. There are, however, many respondents who claimed that they did not know about the existence of such manuals, or they did acknowledge the existence but claimed that it was only scarcely used. The next chapter offers an institutional perspective on the persistence of problems that affect these organizations in their product innovation efforts and uses data from twenty-four innovation projects in twelve companies.

7 An institutional perspective on persistent innovation problems

The previous chapter presented the case study results and provided some in-depth information concerning the organization of new service development. It was shown how three financial companies organize their product innovation processes. In Chapter 5, four problematic aspects related to product innovation were briefly described. The main goal of this chapter is to develop more generalized insights into the problem areas in the banks and insurance companies. In order to structure our analysis, we used the theoretical framework presented in Chapter 2. Hence, we make a distinction between regulatory, normative and cultural-cognitive institutional forces that affect the development of new financial services. We take into account institutional forces at the organizational (macro) and intra-organizational (micro) level. The macro data were collected at the organizational level, whereas the micro data were collected at the business unit and project level. Therefore, we will distinguish between successful and unsuccessful projects, as explained in Chapter 4, only for the intra-organizational-level forces. We will start this chapter with the organizational forces and then turn to the intraorganizational forces.

Organizational institutional forces

The organizational institutional forces identified in our data worked similarly in all the firms included in this study. We have used exemplary quotes to further illustrate some of the key findings. These are listed in Table 7.1

Regulative forces

The Dutch government has traditionally imposed strict regulations on the collaboration between banks and insurance companies by means of the structure policy. The Dutch Central Bank (DNB), responsible for the banking sector, habitually objected to these collaborations, but in the early 1980s this policy was altered. Due to the liberalization of the Dutch 'structure policy' in 1986, however, it was possible for banks and insurance

Table 7.1 Organizational institutional forces

Organizational institutional forces	*Exemplary quotes*	*Number of respondents showing strong evidence*
Regulative	'The government still doesn't allow us to fully integrate with the insurance companies. Although I expect that this will happen soon, it is not yet the case. The liberalization of the structure policy has opened up numerous possibilities for the financial sector, but there are still some reservations on the part of the government.'	3 CEO 3 BU managers 5 Product managers 4 Project leaders 10 Team members
	'I think that one of the major players in our innovative behaviour is the government. They decide what we can and cannot do and set the boundaries for us. So, we may think of really innovative ideas, but it is then uncertain if these are accepted by regulation.'	
Normative	'Can you name two customers that are really waiting for a new financial product? I can't. They don't expect banks and insurance companies to be innovative. So, why should we care? Innovation has to be demand driven and this is not the case. This makes it easier for us.'	2 CEOs 4 BU managers 3 Project leaders 9 Product managers 11 Team members
	'I think that the recent problems with some financial products (referring to investment funds) and all the negative publicity that accompanied these problems, have seriously damaged the industry. Customers always expected that their money was safe. This was not the case. We have an obligation towards our customers to be careful. Innovation is not part of that strategy.'	
Cultural-cognitive	'We need to be able to react to our competitors. Whatever new product they launch, we must be able to develop that product within months. Otherwise our customers might leave us. So we must allocate the necessary resources to these projects. This is not always easy because we have a huge number of projects in our portfolio. That is why some of these projects take quite a long time to finish. There is just too much activity in our competitive environment.'	4 CEOs 4 BU managers 6 Product managers 7 Project leaders 14 Team members

companies to tighten their commercial relations. Changing EU regulations in 1992 allowed the removal of important boundaries between the banks and insurance companies (Flier *et al.* 2001). Because the Dutch government implemented the EU regulation immediately from 1992 onwards, banks and insurance companies were allowed to introduce a completely new range of financial products. Before the 1990s, issues such as marketing, innovation and product development were almost unheard of in the financial sector.

Despite the positive influence on the possibilities for product innovation on the part of the Dutch government, bank and insurance activities may legally still not be integrated. Hesitation with regard to full integration of banks and insurance companies therefore remains. Several bank managers interviewed claimed that their products could be more innovative if a full integration with insurance activities was no longer restricted. Although the Dutch government is currently highly in favor of innovation, this has not yet resulted in concrete policies to further liberate the financial markets (Flier *et al.* 2001). Perhaps the nature of the sector concerning possible negative impacts and security considerations causes the government to be extremely cautious regarding further integration.

During the analysis it became clear that most project leaders were more reluctant to experiment. They strictly followed the rules from the government and did not try to deviate from this path.

> The government is pulling our strings. We have very little room to innovate. So, what can we do? In my opinion, there is not too much we can do to be more innovative. Perhaps in a few years time when the government has loosened some of its grip on the sector. Personally, I don't bother too much with innovative experiments. It just takes too much time to figure out everything. And then you often end up with something that is not allowed anyway.
>
> (CashCo product manager)

In some firms we found a different way of reasoning. Here, it was often expressed that the government was indeed trying to restrict the opportunities for innovation and that some departments would follow these restrictions. However, these project leaders were more daring in terms of taking risks and experimenting. Although they acknowledged that the government has been a major obstacle with respect to the development of new innovative products, they let the regulatory forces influence their idea generation only to a small extent.

> I really think that we could be more innovative if the government would allow us to. There is still something that keeps it from opening up the financial market. It happens all too often that somebody from the legal department kills a project because apparently the government will not approve of it. That is really frustrating. However, I try not to let them

> control my ideas. I always look for the boundaries. There are always flaws in the governmental regulation and these are often the main sources of really cool new products.
>
> (SureCo business-unit manager)

Normative forces

Normative forces are external influences that come from the society at large. In the context of this research, this points to customer expectations as a major force. Financial services are difficult to understand for most customers. Two important reasons for customers to 'buy' financial products are trust and confidence. They expect that banks and insurance companies will take care of their money, i.e. they trust these organizations. Most consumers do not expect that banks and insurance companies will take risks with their money. For the banks and insurance companies, this means that there is no real incentive from society to be innovative and take risks. The reputation as a 'risk-taker' will probably have a negative impact on a company's performance. The CEO of FinCo stated in this regard:

> I don't think that we have to be the most innovative company in the business. We just have to make sure that we don't end up in the 'loser' category. We need products that are compatible, but we don't have to be leading the field. We have seen several examples of financial companies that took unnecessary risks with new investment products, which eventually led to a stream of negative publicity. Our customers also don't expect us to be innovative. They just want to be able to trust us with their money.

The effects of negative publicity are not directly visible, but it seems obvious that this should not occur too often, otherwise consumers could consider other financial services providers. Although there had been a change in consumer mentality (from saving to investing), taking risks was acceptable only under some conditions. The stock exchange had been growing rapidly and most people benefited from this growth. However, recently the stock exchange declined and many people went back to saving instead of investing. Trust and confidence are two very important factors in the societal expectations that prevent the banks and insurance companies from experimenting with combi-products. LifeCo's senior marketing manager expressed this in the following words:

> Of course we need to be careful with our innovative activities. Our customers don't ask for these products [referring to the latest combi-product]. What they want from a bank is a trustworthy relation. That is why we need to optimize our service levels and have excellent operational procedures. New products may be a part of that, but we have

> learned that operational performance is the main discriminator for the performance of banks and insurance companies. Therefore, we need to be sure that we do everything right before we start spending money on new products.

Many of the banks and insurance companies in this study claimed that customers are not interested in new products, but instead only value superior operational performance and high service levels. This is the main reason for these firms to focus on these activities. Surprisingly, many respondents talked about new product development as 'spending money' instead of investing in the future.

Cultural-cognitive force

The most important cultural-cognitive force in this study is operationalized as the imitative behavior of firms. During the panel sessions in the early stages of this research project, it was mentioned several times by experts in the panel that 'the banks and insurance companies in the Netherlands all imitate each other'. The results of the case studies clearly underlined the isomorphic behavior of financial companies. As explained above, organizations try to behave in a similar manner as competitors to avoid the risk of being different. Most product innovations are copied from successful competitors, which becomes even more evident when examining product portfolios in various companies. The larger financial organizations in particular seem to think that they need to have every product a competitor introduces to the market (see Table 7.1).

Once again we found that the opinions of top management differ from department managers and the team members involved in the development processes. Whereas many executives that were interviewed responded in line with statements from the annual reports supporting innovation (as mentioned in the Introduction), most project team members did not seem to agree with them. They were not convinced of the need for innovation. Departmental managers were mainly interested in projects that concerned their own department, as was already illustrated by some of the quotes above. However, most top managers indicated that new products are a way to generate money, commit customers to the company and increase the viability of the firm over time. For these managers, incremental product innovation was a valuable means to achieve this, because these innovations were in line with existing business activities and already familiar to many customers. The CEO of CreditCo stated that:

> It is rather easy for firms like this to develop new products. The current focus on combi-products allows frequent updates of existing products. In theory, this does not cost that much and in many cases our time-to-market is relatively short. Of course, we experience problems in

Table 7.2 Intraorganizational regulative forces

Intraorganizational regulative forces	*Exemplary quotes*	*Number of respondents showing strong evidence*
Organizational structure	'Working with other departments can be difficult. Since we are not used to that, we are still a rather hierarchical functional organization; we do not know how to avoid the rules and procedures. This bureaucracy often gets in the way of our innovative activities because here we constantly have to cross departmental borders.'	1 CEO 2 BU managers 3 Product Managers 6 Project leaders 15 Team members
	'We have revised our organizational structure to support innovative activities. Yet, at the end of the day it is only the really big infrastructure projects that are supported. Most of the product development projects are small projects and those get little attention in our organization. This is mainly due to the daily activities that our organization supports. You cannot tell this by looking at the organization chart, but this is the way we work around here.'	
Project management structure	'Our organization has been able to adjust rapidly to the introduction of the Internet. I think we were one of the first banks in this country to fully implement this new distribution channel. We basically follow a standard procedure in these radical projects. However, what I do feel is that we struggle with the smaller projects. When it comes to developing the newest generation of combi-products we experience major problems. This just takes too long. Our latest introduction took us almost ten months, while this was only an improvement to what we already had. It seems like the organization becomes paralysed after a period of radical change or that nobody realizes that these incremental improvements are absolutely necessary for the company.'	2 CEOs 4 BU managers 5 Project leaders 5 Product managers 14 Team members
	'Trying to keep everybody out the door, except those really needed to make this project a success. That is what we need to manage. However, this is very difficult in an organization where there are too many bosses. We constantly fight over this issue. Managing projects in an efficient way is tough here.'	

Table 7.2 Intraorganizational regulative forces

Intraorganizational regulative forces	*Exemplary quotes*	*Number of respondents showing strong evidence*
IT systems	'Of course you can't expect us to change our systems every time someone has a new idea. There are many new ideas in this organization and if I had my people work on all these ideas, they wouldn't have the time to do what they are actually paid to do: making sure that our information systems run properly. There is nothing on innovation in that description!'	3 IT managers 8 IT project members 7 Project leaders

> developing these products, but so do our competitors. I think we have been able to earn some 10 to 15 million Euros from our latest version of this specific combi-product (CreditCo 1 project). We need these products because if we don't offer them our competitors will, and customers will leave us. The traditional life cycles of our products have decreased tremendously, which means that customers are more frequently interested in buying new products or renewing the old ones.

However, mimetic behavior was not aimed at innovation. Most product innovations that are developed are modifications of existing products at most. The following quote came from one of the panel sessions. One of the members, a senior executive of a large financial corporation (not one of the case organizations) argued that there was no need for the financial sector to be innovative. He was supported by seven out of ten panel members when he said:

> Why should we be innovative as a sector? Nobody is asking for that. We make a lot of money with the way things are going. Our profits have been at a maximum for years, without being innovative. So we don't really need innovation to survive. Most of our competitors have been around for ages and they probably will be around for several more. All this innovation stuff is just not something we should do. Let other industries be creative and innovative. We will just make money the way we have always done it.

Intraorganizational regulative forces

Intraorganizational regulative forces are relatively easy to identify. These forces are highly influential in organizations due to their 'power to set rules, monitor activity, and enforce compliance' (Wicks 2001). The case studies revealed that most financial companies tried to change their formal structure. The divisionalized form has emerged as well as business-unit structures. The organization charts of Dutch financial incumbents have, therefore, changed substantially over the past two decades. In order to improve the potential for product innovation, these structures have often been modified into matrix- or project-based organizations that should encourage cross-functional cooperation. However, we identified strong differences between the procedures and structures in various business units. In Table 7.2 we included some exemplary quotes that were shared across a large number of respondents.

Unsuccessful projects

The organizations in our study demonstrated that the new structures did not function as they were supposed to at the shop-floor level. Individual actions that were aimed at avoiding the old departmentalized structure were in some cases sanctioned. Exchanging information between departments was experienced as being difficult and at times not even desired. The removal of a PayCo project leader illustrates the coercive force that flows from the organizational structure and its accompanying rules and procedures. Formal rules and procedures dictate organizational behavior in many business units in the financial services sector. Although these rules are often meant to improve the efficiency and effectiveness of organizations, they may also affect organizations negatively. This was clearly the case in the unsuccessful projects in our study.

> 'I always thought that informal communication was a good means for doing these projects. However, people did not like it when I did this. The procedures in our manual also do not mention this informal way of working. Everything has to go by the book in this part of the organization, it always has. It is suffocating. They even removed me from one of the projects because I did not use the normal procedures.
>
> (PayCo project leader)

Furthermore, people in a specialized department did not bother about other departments and it appeared that they only cared about their own activities and interests. Members of project teams at BanCo, and subsequently FinCo, phrased the utilitarian logic behind this way of thinking and behaving:

> 'I was just a small module in that project. That is the way to look at it. The most important thing was that people accepted me as a module and the only thing I had to do was to act whenever it concerned my module. I would not interfere with the rest of the project. Why should I?'

There were several serious problems in the project, but these were all

> related to technical issues so they did not concern me. Why should I spend my energy on issues that do not really concern me?

This kind of thinking is enforced by the perceived departmentalized structure that does not allow for horizontal linkages between the departments. In this way, people rarely integrate, do not talk with other departments, and have no clear insight of other departments' contributions to the organization as a whole or to the product development process. Interdepartmental linkages are not allowed and therefore people do not look beyond the domain of their own department. The CEO of FinCo claimed that tensions between various parts of the organization have often resulted in several conflicts in product development and other innovative activities. Furthermore, product developers that originate from the commercial side of the organization often have limited insights into the organization's technological capabilities. This lack of market-technology linking (see Burgelman 1983) in the development process leads to several iterations between commercial and technical departments. In addition to these limited insights into each other's activities, the various subsystems of the organization seemed to have incongruent goals. In thirty-one of the thirty-nine organizations studied during the exploratory interviews, was mentioned that the representatives of the functional departments were trying to defend their own interests, which even led to conflict situations. A senior manager at HypCo formulated it in the following words:

> There is a strong tension between the various parts of our organization that are involved in innovative projects. These have different priorities, which often leads to conflicts in the project teams. Every one of those individuals involved in the project is still a member of a functional department and is not really bothered about the value of the new project for the organization as a whole. When you look at our organization chart, you think that we left the functional structure behind and became more flexible. In practice, however, everybody just tries to satisfy his or her own needs, that is, their departments' needs.

Thus, although the formal structures have changed in favor of flexibility and innovation, informal structures have a strong regulative impact on the actual day-to-day activities. It is these informal structures that obstruct incremental product innovation.

Whereas employees in banks and insurance companies used to be appraised and rewarded for the number of policies processed, in the new structures this had not changed. Especially for smaller projects, this has had a detrimental effect. Team members often do little work on these projects, because they fear that they will be sanctioned if the departments' targets are not met. The functional heads of departments were therefore not very willing to free some of their employees to work on new product development projects. It is interesting that radical innovation ('big') projects are not disturbed by these sanctioning mechanisms. This is largely due to the fact that these concern the organization as a whole and are often directly enforced by top management. For example, most banks and insurance companies have adjusted rapidly to the introduction of the Internet. Many resources were made available for these projects, whereas this is one of the major problems in the smaller projects. As a result, incremental projects sometimes take up to 24 months to be completed (see also Table 4.5). Many firms in our study do not seem to realize how important these projects are; little attention is paid to them and they are the first to be cancelled when resources are scarce.

> Our organizational structure is set up to support innovation. However, this only applies to big projects. When smaller projects are involved the misery begins. Team members hardly work on these projects, because they will be sanctioned if they do not reach the targets for the department they normally work for. So, the functional team leaders are not really interested in letting people go to work on new product development and start harassing my project members about targets that should be reached. How are you supposed to run a project if this is constantly slowing down the development process?
>
> (BanCo project leader)

This clinging to formal rules and procedures had a strong inhibitive impact on the product development activities. In seven of the business units where we studied unsuccessful attempts at incremental product innovation, we were able to identify some kind of sanctioning mechanism used to keep in line with the standard procedures.

The existing information systems are also an important regulative force, which set hard boundaries for new products yet to be developed. Due to the changes in legislation, banks and insurance companies were allowed to offer combined components. When developing these 'combi-products', this also meant that information systems that traditionally only administrated mortgage products now had to combine insurance products and investment products as well. Because these systems were developed separately, a lot of energy has to be spent on integrating the various systems. Most of these systems, however, date from the 1970s or 1980s and carry a huge weight of the past. They are not easily adapted, let alone combined with other systems.

> When you follow the market closely you will see that it is all about combi-products. This will probably continue for several years, because we can come up with the strangest combinations. The only problem is that our systems have not grown with the latest developments. They are just too old-fashioned.
>
> (AssurCo IT manager)

> We had some serious problems with IT, which was caused by the complexity of our systems. This product had affected the administrative systems of three units. All sorts of connections were needed and it was not easy. In the end we had to make some concessions to the product.
>
> (CashCo product manager)

In most cases, this meant that the product concept was less innovative than it was originally intended, and therefore the information systems inhibited the development of new innovative products. Most of the times the product concept would be adjusted in line with IT possibilities, because it was considered impossible to change the information systems. A highly experienced IT project member (working on his eighth product development project) at BanCo pointed out the following:

> Well, these marketing guys think they can just develop anything. But their ideas always involve something radical, which means that we have to alter our systems. You just can't expect that we change our systems every time they come up with a good idea. It just doesn't work that way. If they want something new, it better fit the system.

Because of the complexity of the information systems it is not possible for people outside the IT department to judge whether adjustments to the systems can be made or not. It was frequently mentioned that IT personnel were not really interested in product development and often claimed that something was not possible. Most new products are still IT driven or at least guided by the state of IT. For the project team members or the project leader it would then be very difficult to disagree. Most of the times the product concept would be adjusted.

> I don't know what it is with IT, but whenever you talk to someone from IT you just don't know what they are talking about. It is really complex and you don't have a lot of understanding in these matters. Whenever they say that something is not possible or that it costs this much or takes this amount of time to finish, you more or less take it for granted. In the end it is always more expensive and more time consuming.
>
> (RiskCo business-unit manager)

> There is always something wrong with IT. They (IT personnel) always start a meeting by saying that something is just not possible. I know that they had a lot of work with the EURO and Millennium projects, but they don't seem to be interested in product development. Of course it means additional work for them, but it should not be this easy for them to say that something is not possible.
>
> (Banco project leader)

Product developers in all twelve failed projects complained that the IT department often claimed that when some new product was being developed the adaptations needed in the system were not possible. This necessitated adjustments in the product concept. In all twelve cases, this meant that the product concept was less innovative than was originally intended, and therefore the information systems inhibited the development of new products. A complicating factor is that it is not possible for people outside the IT department to judge whether adjustments to the systems are possible or not. One of the IT managers (from RiskCo) expressed this way of thinking:

> We tell our product managers time and again that our systems cannot handle these new products. But they keep coming up with silly ideas. When my people are finished with designing the processes the original concept needs to be adapted to our standards. Personally I don't really like that my people waste their time on these activities ... It just doesn't make sense to spend all our money on some minor extension of products that we already have. I still don't understand why we do this.

The current information systems in many banks and insurance companies are indeed a major barrier to innovation. The necessary integration of different administrative systems is especially problematic. Since banks and insurance companies started to combine their products into 'combi-products' they also had to integrate the administrative systems. These systems, however, date from the 1970s and 1980s and are not easily adapted, let alone combined with other systems. This means that in many organizations these so-called legacy systems actually determine if innovation is possible or not. These systems are the core of financial companies and have been developed to support individual functions. This means that they are focused on enabling local efficiency instead of enhanced integrative performance.

Successful projects

One of the key features of the successful projects is their separation from the regular organization, not leaving room for 'outside' interference. The bureaucratic influences from the organization were successfully kept away from these projects, meaning that the team members could concentrate on their project tasks without being bothered with routine day-to-day activities. Several respondents claimed that the only way to avoid the excessive rules and procedures in their organizations was to isolate their projects. In these situations, separate structures were designed to shelter the new product from the standing organization. Furthermore, in the successful projects the team members were reluctant to use formal rules and procedures, such as product development manuals. The business units that were able to develop successful new products used a different set of rules and procedures.

> When I was transferred to the Business Unit Pensions, I was immediately asked to forget all the procedures used in the rest of the organization. I knew this was a rather strange bunch of cowboys, but in the first development project I was involved in, I immediately understood what they were doing and why they were doing it. These guys almost made me swear not to look into any manual. They claimed that that would restrict our creative capabilities. I must admit, we pulled it off in only four months.
>
> (CreditCo marketing manager)

Key to all the successful projects in our study was the idea of 'letting go'. Several business-unit managers claimed that every innovation project required a different approach. They did acknowledge the fact that the process consisted of several well-known stages, but they argued that, because of the high degree of iteration needed in the process, it was not really appropriate to force innovation projects into a straightjacket. Instead, they stressed the importance of creativity and freedom to manoeuver. These managers also proactively anticipated incremental improvements in the information systems. These improvements were used in combination with the development of new incremental combi-products.

Although the information systems in many firms were restrictive to the development of new financial services, some business units radically redesigned their systems to fit a new product. This was the case in the FinCo 1 project, for example, where a new IT system had to be designed from scratch and subsequently connected to the existing systems. Together with the IT developers, the project team discussed the specific product characteristics. The entire team (including IT personnel) was working in the same room during this crucial stage. As mentioned by one of the team members, the physical distance between the various project members was less than 20 feet, meaning that communication lines were always short in case of unclarities.

> This is probably one of the few examples in the industry where the concept of the new product was really leading instead of IT. We were allowed to design a new system that could then be added to the existing system. So, for us, IT was not a barrier at all. These guys really liked designing a new system, so everybody was happy in this project.
>
> (FinCo project team member)

It is obvious that this rarely happens when incremental innovations are involved. The impact of these innovations is often not big enough for firms to really invest in IT systems. In this case, the new product was foreseen to play an important role in the future of the company. And although the government did not yet allow for its full potential, FinCo envisioned a future for more advanced types of these products. Hence, they decided to invest in a new system that could accommodate for a future generation of new related services.

Intraorganizational normative forces

Normative aspects of institutions are often found in notions of appropriate behavior (March and Olson 1989). The emphasis of normative forces is on 'prescriptive, evaluative and obligatory dimensions' of social life (Scott 2001: 54). In this research project, intraorganizational normative forces refer to existing norms, values and expectations in the financial companies that participated. In Table 7.3 we included some exemplary quotes concerning the normative forces that were shared across a large number of respondents.

Unsuccessful projects

These were without exception associated with ruling values and norms directed at the avoidance of risks and the reduction of uncertainty. Several examples from the data are used to illustrate this. Traditionally, product innovation processes were divided into two main stages: initiation and implementation (e.g. Rogers 1995). The front-end stage was labeled 'fuzzy', allowing for creativity and loose coupling between organizational units. However, the business-unit managers in our study did not favor loose coupling in the initiation of innovative activities. Instead, close monitoring of the activities at this stage seems to be widespread in financial companies, not allowing for a lot of creativity. The CEO of FinCo claimed that:

> Our functional managers want to know every little detail of each and every idea that is being suggested before they approve of anything. Because there are many ideas floating around in this organization, the time between the actual submission of an idea and approval by management can be months. In product development this is far too long. Often this is even increased, because they want additional information. They want to be so sure of an idea, that they completely forget that in innovation there are always risks involved. But they try to reduce risks to below zero. So creativity is also reduced to a minimum, because everything needs to be controlled, checked and double-checked. How can you be innovative with an attitude like this? This does not only happen in the major projects that we do, but also in minor product development projects.

There is a clear attitude of risk avoidance displayed in the business units

Table 7.3 Intraorganizational normative forces

Intraorganizational normative forces	*Exemplary quotes*	*Number of respondents showing strong evidence*
Risk avoidance attitude	'Managers are too much involved with the nitty-gritty details of projects. This means that they are overwhelmed with work. They have to read all these proposals for new projects. So before we even get our approval, this may take a long time. And then we have to report back too often about the progress, further delaying the process. Even small projects need to be checked and double-checked. It probably has to do with the nature of our business. People do not want to gamble with our products.'	2 CEOs 3 BU managers 12 Project leaders 16 Team members
	'This organization does not breath innovation. Previously I worked in a different industry and there innovation was really important. People dared to take risks. Here it is also considered important, but only when the outcome is certain. This is not the idea of being innovative. Risks are part of the innovation game.'	
Expectancy gap	'These guys really expect us to innovate. At least that is what they see during the new years' speech. But if you knock on their door for money because you have this really cool idea, then nobody's home. So, I don't really see how we should do it. I think that it is not really needed, but it sounds nice to say something like this.'	4 BU managers 6 Project leaders 14 Team members
	'We have absolutely nothing that rewards innovation. I know that our CEO wrote this one-liner in our annual report expressing the need for new products, but our organization is not ready for it. How can you expect people to actually work on new products when they are getting paid for optimizing operational activities? Nobody in the project team receives any kind of incentive when the new product is developed and implemented in a really short time. So, these projects are often delayed. People would rather work on what they are paid for, what is expected of them. In our case, processing policies.'	

Continued overleaf

Table 7.3 Intraorganizational normative forces

Intraorganizational normative forces	*Exemplary quotes*	*Number of respondents showing strong evidence*
Social obligation	'My main frustration is that our managers do not stick to their decisions. Once a project has been approved you expect that you can finish it. But this is hardly ever the case. They start reshuffling employees as soon as a new project proposal is launched. To me this is very demotivating and I know that many of the team members feel the same way. I really think that quite a few of them don't spend as much time on a project as they are supposed to do. But, you can't blame them, because before they know it they are reassigned to a different project. They are not given an idea that their efforts on a certain project are valued.' 'Some of the people that used to work on this project actively tried to switch to another project that they liked better. I do not know exactly why we allow this, but they are probably capable of convincing their team leaders that they should be transferred. There is no loyalty for these incremental projects.'	14 Project leaders 12 Team members

we studied. Many of our respondents claimed that managers constantly think they should reduce any risk involved with innovative projects. Furthermore, the data clearly showed that this type of attitude is mainly related to projects that involve product innovation, which means, for instance, that the banks and insurance companies we studied are not resistant to change in general. Several product managers argued that their employees did come up with suggestions for further improving the operational performance.

> My team leaders are always involved in trying to improve daily activities. They keep coming up with initiatives, small and large, to further streamline our core business. But when it comes to initiatives for combi-products they freeze. Perhaps there is too much risk involved, or they just don't have an overview of the possibilities.
>
> (HypCo product manager)

This kind of risk-avoiding behavior is reflected in much of the innovative activities of the firms in our study and is closely related to the formal rules and procedures. The product development manuals, for instance, clearly describe what type of initial scans are needed before a decision is taken to actually develop a new product. The actual number of pages related to these initial stages, before a go/no-go, is often twice the number of pages spent on the execution and implementation. The formal rules and procedures (including the manuals) are often used as straightjackets that inhibit innovative behavior, and they also lead to expectations of appropriate behavior.

The results from our case studies also showed that there is a gap between the expectations from management regarding the necessity of incremental product innovation and the perception of these expectations by the employees. This frequently meant that employees did not understand that innovation was highly valued, or at least claimed to be highly valued, by top management. The annual reports of the banks and insurance companies all make statements about the importance of innovation. Some of these explicitly mention the development of new products to be of crucial importance. However, we found that both business-unit managers and subsequently 'shop-floor' employees not only had little interest in new products, they also did not see these activities to be very relevant for their organization. Moreover, for shop-floor level workers new products mean more work in terms of the development activities to be undertaken and the hours of training needed to understand the new product and its functioning in the IT systems. In addition, new products usually mean an extension of the already broad product portfolios. Another reason frequently identified in our case organizations is related to ambiguity of the organizational goals. The project leaders particularly experienced this. They claimed that many projects are completed in a very different team composition compared with the 'starting line-up'.

Although CEOs were rather surprised about the lack of innovative behavior, there is at least one logical explanation for the lack of innovative behavior observed in all the case study organizations. Employees of banks and insurance companies are not aware of the fact that they are expected to innovate. Several of our respondents claimed that their managers did not emphasize the development of new products. Furthermore, they were sometimes sanctioned for not reaching operational targets (for instance in terms of policies processed) and as a result did not value innovation. The following quote from a senior RealCo product manager serves as an illustration:

> 'We have absolutely nothing that rewards innovation. I know that our CEO wrote this one-liner in our annual report expressing the need for new products, but our organization is not ready for it. How can you expect people to actually work on new products when they are getting paid for optimizing operational activities? Nobody in the project team receives any kind of incentive when the new product is developed and implemented in a really short time. So, these projects are often delayed. People would rather work on what they are paid for, what is expected of them. In our case, processing policies.

The reward systems are still very much in line with traditional values of processing. This means that the employees experience their organization as a 'processing factory'. They acknowledge that top managers are always looking for ways to optimize the operational activities, which is considered relevant by most respondents. However, the expectations for innovation in this environment are considered very low. This is closely related to the lack of (social) obligation to incremental product innovation. The project leaders particularly experienced this. They claimed that many projects are completed in a very different team composition compared with the 'starting line-up'. Apparently, somewhere during the development process priorities shift to projects related to the daily activities, and team members are reallocated by their superiors who feel no obligation to finish the projects the team members were originally assigned to. Due to the high frequency with which this happens, the project leaders (and some of the team members) feel as if their projects are of little relevance. There was hardly any obligation for team members to finish their project activities. Their team leaders often did not expect them to spend too much time on product development. There were also team members who asked to be transferred to more interesting, at least from their functional perspective, projects and who felt little obligation to finish their prior activities. When they were able to present a solid argument to their superior, they were easily transferred to another project.

Successful projects

In the business-units with successful projects we identified a different set of normative forces, in particular ruling norms and values related to risk and mutual expectations, which were clearly directed to enabling incremental innovation. What was most striking in the interviews with respondents from these business units was the absence of 'risk' in their stories. Only when directly asked for aspects concerning risks did they talk about potential risks of innovation. Although these people were often referred to as 'cowboys', they were not reckless in any way. They merely considered risk to be an essential part of every innovation project, incremental or radical, but did not bother too much with avoiding it. One business-unit manager from CreditCo claimed:

> We borrowed Nike's slogan; Just do it. This is how it works. If you start wondering or recalculating everything too long there will be no new products launched or you launch them too late. This is even worse than an occasional failure. I know we are about the only ones in this company who do it like this, but it really works for us. And as long as they (referring to top management) let us, why should I start worrying about possible problems. We do our homework, but do not drown in it.

This quote illustrates the main differences in the perception and way of handling risk between the successful and unsuccessful projects. Whereas the unsuccessful projects spend the majority of their time on avoiding any potential risk, the successful projects are much faster at deciding whether or not to develop the new product. As a result, the development times were much shorter in these latter projects. Remarkably, this way of thinking is reinforced by the way these business units deal with formal rules and procedures. In the previous section it was explained that 'letting go' was considered essential for innovation. The idea of 'just do it' seems to be closely related to the rejection of using development manuals and other organizational procedures.

The successful projects also benefited from the clear expectations set by business-unit management. Even within the same firm there were major differences between the studied business units. Whether this was due to the functional background of the business-unit managers is not clear, although most unsuccessful projects came from units led by more 'traditional' management with a background in actuary or legal affairs. The more innovative business units were often (nine out of twelve) led by people from marketing who believed in innovation. They expected their employees to behave similarly. One of the marketing managers, on the board of the business unit, from ChipCo argued:

> We need to develop new products. That is our main discriminator. We are able to reap profits for six months then competitors have copied our product. So we must act fast. Our CEO understands this and has also expressed this in our annual report. I believe him and I expect my employees to behave accordingly. I know that some of the more traditional departments in our unit do not always agree with me, but fortunately quite a few of them 'have seen the light'. They know what I expect from them. If everybody realizes the importance of new products, we will outrun our competition.

The expectancy gap between top management and business unit, as it appeared in the unsuccessful projects, did not appear in the successful projects. The expectations from the board were aligned with the actual behavior in the successful projects. Again, this speeded up the development process and led to less iteration, especially since the team members fully realized that they needed to spend as much time as possible on these projects. The importance of this was clear to them and they acted accordingly. Most of the team members were fully devoted to the innovative projects they were working on and some considered it to be an honor.

> I was asked by my boss (marketing manager) to participate in this project. We designed a new version of [name of combi-product] that allowed us to better serve our customers. The CEO himself expressed the

> importance of this product and our business-unit manager was able to get a group of people that really wanted to make this a success. My team leader was not always happy with me, because I probably spend more hours working on the new project than on my other responsibilities. But he never really complained and let me finish.
>
> (LifeCo team member)

The successful projects all benefited from clear expectations set by management and the subsequent devotion from team members. According to many of the respondents in the successful projects there was a need for innovation, but they expressed that they enjoyed working on it because of the contribution to the company goals. The alignment of expectations between all levels of the firm has been a key success factor in these business units.

Intraorganizational cultural-cognitive forces

The cultural-cognitive emphasis of institutions resembles 'shared conceptions that constitute the nature of social reality and the frames through which meaning is made' (Scott 2001: 57). In this study, intraorganizational cultural-cognitive forces are shared conceptions and frames of reference belonging to distinct professional identities. Table 7.4 illustrates some of these cultural-cognitive forces by exemplary quotes from our respondents. These were shared across a large number of respondents.

Unsuccessful projects

Although the banks and insurance companies have changed their organizational structures (as described on p. 90–91), there is still a considerable degree of departmentalization. As a result of this departmentalization, the various professional disciplines involved in innovation processes have developed different systems of meaning over time. The departments in the case companies seemed to have their own way of working (accompanied by specific jargon or language and even dress codes) and their own vision of the path the organization should follow. The specialists from different disciplines did not speak the same language and created little understanding for each other's activities.

Difficulties arise when non-routine activities are implemented that involve other professional disciplines. This was clearly the case in the unsuccessful projects in this study. Project team members represented their functional department. This led to difficulties in creating a common understanding of the aims, properties and process-requirements of a new product. It often involved aspects, such as different languages and visions, that resulted in lower levels of cooperation in the project teams. Most of these problems manifested themselves on the interface between marketing and IT departments and (in the case

Table 7.4 Intraorganizational cultural-cognitive forces

Intraorganizational cultural-cognitive forces	*Exemplary quotes*	*Number of respondents showing strong evidence*
Shared systems of meaning	'The problem is that we have too many departments involved in these projects and they do not understand each other at all. They do not speak each other's language very well to put it mildly. So this creates problems in every project that crosses a departmental boundary.' 'What you will typically see is that these departments have developed their own way of thinking and acting. They have grown into this organization in a specific way and it is very difficult to change that in these projects. The problem this generates is that everybody involved in the project thinks in terms of 'we' and 'they'. And they all think that the other one should not benefit more than them. This does make it more complicated as a project manager.'	3 CEOs 3 BU managers 8 Project leaders 10 Team members
Dominant identities	'I think that it is clear who is in charge in this organization. There are a bunch of departments that block most of the innovative activities. Even when management has approved, somewhere later in the process someone will step up and argue that the product needs to be adjusted because some part of it is not possible. Often this relates to the information systems, but also the legal and actuarial departments tend to reduce the innovative potential of new products.' 'We have too many people that claim that something is not possible, not allowed or not profitable. Because insurance products are highly complex, these people are very powerful. I normally don't really understand what they are exactly talking about. So, then it becomes a matter of trust. And then the question is do you trust the one who is in charge? Probably not, but we still have to work with them. For innovation this is killing.'	1 BU manager 6 Product managers 11 Project leaders 17 Team members

of insurance products) between actuaries and the other team members. According to a senior product manager at SureCo, this kind of behavior has developed over the years and is an illustration of the existence of professional disciplines with their own specific identity.

> I think it has to do with the fact that the departments involved in the development process have developed a certain way of thinking over the years. They have created a kind of special identity. There are strong 'we/they' feelings in this organization. This makes it difficult when you have to work on innovative projects that need to combine these different identities.

Eventually, the most dominant identities decided what happened. In the unsuccessful projects these were often actors from the actuarial, legal and IT departments. These departments had a limited interest in exploring new opportunities, and instead focus on exploiting the companies' existing practices.

In addition to the potential problem of different identities, there is always the risk of one of these identities becoming dominant and preferring the exploitation of current competencies. In the banks and insurance companies studied, this dominance was, not surprisingly, found in the more traditional parts of the organization, such as actuaries and legal departments. A BanCo marketing manager experienced these problems, but also more or less gave in to the dominance of the more traditional professional disciplines:

> Our main 'problems' are the actuarial, legal and IT departments. They always say that something is not possible, not allowed or not profitable, which means that we have to adjust the product concept and make it less innovative. I really regret this way of working, but I have learned from experience that this is the way it works in this organization. And because of the complexity of the issues that they raise, we don't have a clue whether they are right. What is really annoying is that they hardly come up with acceptable alternatives. So in fact, these departments are leading in product development, yet nobody admits it.

Successful projects

The successful projects in our sample show that different meaning systems do not necessarily have to lead to conflict situations. In four of the successful projects, project leaders focused on team building and creating a shared understanding before the team actually started working on the project. A special kick-off session was organized in which the team members quickly discovered that they could cooperate together despite their differences. These projects were, however, given the opportunity (in terms of funding and top management support) to actually invest in team building. Instead of these project teams being dominated by different identities, they converged into groups with a shared identity. Again, the organization of these projects, while still representing an improvement to existing combi-products, resembled some of the organizational characteristics of radical innovation projects (as described by Veryzer 1998; De Brentani 2001; McDermott and Colarelli O'Connor 2002).

> What we actually do is more or less pretend that these projects are major breakthrough innovations. We set up the entire organization, as if it were a radical project. We separate it from the regular organization, away from all the rules and procedures, because otherwise our daily operations will interfere. We have people who are almost fully dedicated (in time) to the project and they all work in the same room. Only if we set it up like this the rest of the organization realizes that this is important for the entire organization, which creates a better position for the project when it needs to be implemented.
>
> (SureCo business-unit manager)

In eight of the successful projects we were able to identify similar attempts to frame the image of incremental innovation projects as radical innovation projects. For many business units this seemed to be the only way of managing incremental projects. Some of the business-unit managers claimed that increasing the importance of their projects for the whole organization gave them a better position in bargaining for resources. It was also acknowledged, however, that this is not possible for all projects.

8 Towards an institutional theory of innovation

Introduction

The innovation literature emphasizes that incremental innovations do not differ much from existing product portfolios and therefore routine procedures and capabilities are sufficient to instigate this type of innovation (Colarelli O'Connor 1998; McDermott and Colarelli O'Connor 2002). However, many incumbent firms still struggle with incremental product innovation efforts despite the numerous studies suggesting solutions to overcome potential barriers (Cooper 1999; Benders and Vermeulen 2002). Occasionally, they are capable of successfully developing incremental innovations, which means that the innovation is developed and launched onto the market rapidly and smoothly. The main reason for this variation in success is not only due to a superior organization of projects or a more sophisticated use of the available tools to develop new products, as has often been suggested by the new product development literature (e.g. Cooper 1999; Belliveau *et al.* 2004; Kahn 2004). We have argued that institutional forces have a strong impact on the innovative efforts of incumbent firms. We claim that an institutional perspective has the potential to complement the existing innovation literature, because it uncovers some of the underlying reasons for the (lack of) innovative behavior of organizations. In this chapter we develop a framework of innovation in which the institutional components enable or obstruct innovation. In line with Greenwood and Hinings (1996) we also believe that institutional theory holds much promise for explaining change and innovation. The innovation literature can benefit from the valuable insights developed in the institutional literature. The model we develop below is aimed at explaining the occurrence or lack of innovation in established firms. We build our explanation in two parts. First, we briefly revisit the institutional forces that were described in Chapter 7. We demonstrate their impact and highlight the interaction between various forces that has a reinforcing effect on the potential for innovation. Second, we use a set of institutional components that work as precipitating or enabling dynamics (cf. Greenwood and Hinings 1996). Together these components provide an indication of the

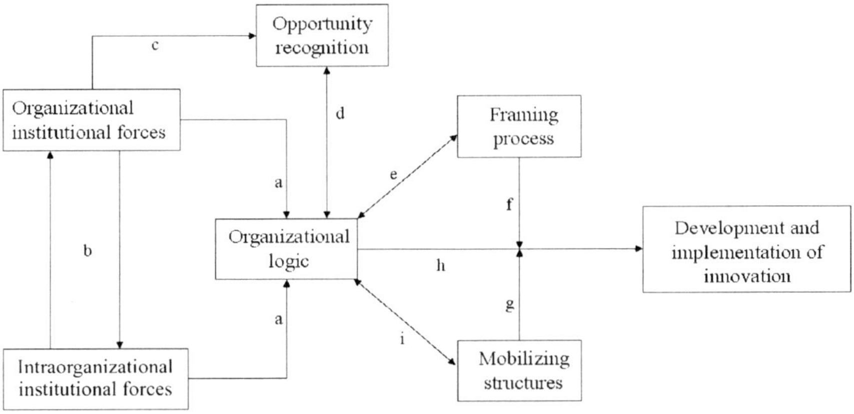

Figure 8.1 An institutional framework for innovation

potential for innovation in established firms. For these firms it is most likely possible to develop a new product every once in a while, but to reach a level of sustained innovation will be a daunting task.

A model for innovation

In developing our model we acknowledge that organizations are infused with value and have a strong degree of taken-for-grantedness in which actors accept the ruling norms and values as appropriate. Over time this causes stability and inertia (Tolbert and Zucker 1983). This emphasis on inertia results in the continuous reproduction and reinforcement of these norms and values, which can only lead to convergent change. Whereas radical change is considered problematic, convergent change is considered the more normal occurrence (Greenwood and Hinings 1996). We have demonstrated, however, that innovations that lead to convergent change in an organization can still be problematic. In order to elaborate our model we first explain the functioning of institutional forces and how these affect the central component of the model, i.e. organizational logics. At this stage, the model is at a level of abstraction that does not warrant formulating propositions. We rather regard it as an analytical framework that might help to analyse innovation from an institutional perspective and might guide further research efforts in this area.

Institutional forces

In Chapter 2 we distinguished between regulatory, normative and cognitive forces that could be identified at two levels: organizational and intra-organizational. These forces have a direct influence on the development of organizational logics over time (line a in the model). Regulatory forces at the intraorganizational level, for instance, primarily deal with facilitating or obstructing exchanges among members of an organization (cf. Zucker 1988). Rules and standard operating procedures, but also organizational systems, act as formal authority systems (March *et al.* 2000) that facilitate or hinder exchanges between organizational members. They regulate flows of information and resources within the organization. However, internal structures exhibit 'the social permanence of institutions'. When the degree of internal institutionalization in incumbent firms increases over time, similarity with other organizations, including the degree of codification and interdependence, will make it more difficult for incumbent firms to change these structures (Zucker 1988:35). At the organizational level, regulatory agencies, such as the national government and professional associations, have been identified as dominant forces in the process of institutionalization (Hoffman 1999; Greenwood *et al.* 2002). These forces also have an effect on the recognition of opportunities for innovation (line c). Dobbin and Dowd (1997) argued that policy has a direct effect on organizations, which causes firms to think about new practices. Likewise, professional associations have been identified as a means for recognizing opportunities for innovation. Greenwood *et al.* (2002) illustrate the role of professional associations in the accounting industry in which prevailing logics were redefined; this created new opportunities for change.

Normative forces also affect the organizational logic. These forces introduce a prescriptive dimension into social life, by which people in specific organizational roles are expected to fulfil certain obligations (March and Olson 1989). These expectations become ingrained in the dominant organizational logic that focuses the attention of individuals on those issues in line with expectations (cf. Thornton 2002). Uncertainty reduction and risk avoidance are key normative components that strongly determine the ruling logic within an organization. At the organizational level, organizations look for legitimacy to find congruence between organizational values and wider societal values. An active external orientation to understand customer values and needs is crucial for the success of new products (Cooper 1999; Ulwick 2002). Hence, recognizing true customer values should be incorporated in the organizational logic and offer new opportunities (line c).

Cultural-cognitive forces include different systems of meaning and dominant identities. The shared systems of meaning are negotiated over time in interaction processes between organizational actors (Scott 2001). These taken-for-granted patterns are the core of social action (Zucker 1987) and are maintained for long periods of time without further justification. They lead to the development of strong organizational logics that are inherently difficult to change. At the organizational level, mimetic mechanisms lead to modeling behavior of organizations that copy successful peers in order to become legitimate (DiMaggio and Powell 1983). Not only will these mimetic mechanisms affect the dominant logics within organizations, but copying the actions of successful firms will lead to new opportunities for innovation (line c). Front-runners may lead the pack into a rat-race of developing new products. We have seen this in the financial industry time and time again. When one of the more innovative firms launched a new product that proved to be highly successful, the other firms in the industry would introduce a slightly improved version of this product as soon as possible.

In institutional research the emphasis on process dimensions or interaction dynamics is limited (Tolbert and Zucker 1996). Institutional theorists have argued that different institutional forces compete with each other in complex situations (Meyer and Scott 1983; Scott 2001). However, it has also been argued that the three pillars of institutions may be analytically distinctive but are intertwined and interconnected in practice (Hirsch 1997; Hoffman and Ventresca 1999). Few empirical studies demonstrated that multiple institutional forces can simultaneously exert pressures on organizations (Ruef and Scott 1998; Hoffman 1999; D'Aunno *et al.* 2000; Scott *et al.* 2000; Wicks 2001). Although we tried to describe the forces separate from each other, the forces are clearly interwoven with each other. The rules and procedures that drive organizational behavior seem to interact with perceived expectations. Normative forces closely interacted with the meaning systems of different professional disciplines, which in turn interacted with the regulatory forces. The interaction between forces (line b) further enforces their impact on the organizational logic. In this research context we found indications that the institutional forces do not compete with each other, but instead are complementary and reinforce each other in favor of either more stability or more innovation.

Precipitating dynamics

In our study of the development and implementation of complex incremental product innovation projects, we have provided evidence that intra-organizational and organizational institutional forces had a strong impact on the innovative efforts of established financial firms. Central to our notion of innovation are two concepts that precipitate any potential innovation: *opportunity recognition* and *organizational logics*. In order for organizations to engage in innovative work, opportunities have to be recognized. This is strongly dependent on the degree of institutionalization of an organization and multiplicity, i.e. the openness of the organization to external practices (Dorado 2005) on the one hand, and the presence of 'bricoleurs' (Lévi-Strauss 1966) on the other hand. The notion of logics points at taken-for-granted organizing principles that strongly direct individuals within organizations (Friedland and Alford 1991). There may be several logics present within an organization at the same time. Powerful groups impose their preferred logics (Brint and Karabel 1991: 355), but insurgent logics are contained within less advantaged players. Hence, we see different combinations of logics that have different outcomes for the innovative attempts of firms. We elaborate on both concepts.

The institutional forces develop over time and have led to the development of distinct *organizational logics* (cf. Friedland and Alford 1991). These logics are sets of material practices and symbolic constructions that constitute the organizing principles of an organization and are available to the individual members (Friedland and Alford 1991: 248). They guide individual actors in their behavior and function as cognitive maps. Logics are built up through experience and specify what goals and values the organization adheres to. Furthermore, logics guide the allocation of resources, define the playing field in terms of organizational politics, and establish routines and capabilities that may either obstruct or facilitate innovation and change (Washington and Ventresca 2004: 84). The prevailing logic in an organization at a certain moment in time directs the constituents in the same direction. New entrants need to comply with this logic or need sufficient power to reframe it (Beckert 1999). Besides a dominant logic, there may also be secondary or repressed logics that represent the interests of less powerful players in the organization. Scott *et al.* (2000) argue that these may become more influential over time and can even act as triggers for institutional change.

Essential to explaining the possibilities for innovation is that organizational logics focus the attention of organizational members on issues and solutions that are consistent with the prevailing logic (cf. Thornton 2004). Logics not only determine which issues and problems organizations attend to, but also determine what answers are available and appropriate. Furthermore, they legitimate certain strategic choices (Thornton 2004) by structuring the cognition of actors in organizations and providing a collective understanding of how strategic interests and decisions are formulated (Thornton 2002: 82).

We distinguish between three sets of logics:

1 Routine logics, in which all groups demonstrate a strict adherence to prevailing rules and procedures. Risk avoidance is highly valued and there is a strong focus on the day-to-day practices. The potential for innovation in this logic is low, yet firms that operate in this logic do occasionally innovate. Pressures from the wider institutional context may lead to recognized opportunities and trigger ad hoc innovation that is supported by the powerful groups in the organization. Mimetic mechanisms are most likely to cause firms adhering to a routine logic to engage in innovative behavior. Most firms in our sample demonstrated a routine logic.
2 Dual logics, in which some groups support the routine logic and some groups support the innovation logic. The potential for innovation in this logic depends strongly on the position of the powerful groups. Dominant groups are more likely to follow routine logics that will hinder the potential for innovation. Their position may be altered by opportunities

that are recognized as potentially beneficial to the powerful groups. There were some firms in our sample (LifeCo and SureCo) in which dual logics were present.

3 Innovation logics, in which all groups recognize the importance of innovation and wilfully engage in experimentation and continuous alterations of existing products and processes. In the financial services firms we did not discover firms that adhered to this logic, but one can think of firms like Apple, TomTom and firms in the high-tech industries. Key to these organizations is the continuous exploration of new opportunities. These firms may suffer from poor exploitation results because the next interesting project is already initiated, but their innovative potential is extremely high.

The ruling logics within an organization provide an indication of the innovative potential of organizations. The more restrictive the rules and procedures in an organization, the more risk averse the norms and values, and the more organizational actors are responsive to daily practices, the more likely it is that the innovative potential of the firm will be relatively low due to the adherence to a strict routine logic. When such firms do occasionally engage in innovative behavior, they will most likely encounter serious problems in the development process. Firms that are open to deviate from existing rules and norms and encourage experimental behavior from its employees are more likely to have a higher innovation potential.

Although institutionalized logics are inherently difficult to change, there are *opportunities* for deviation. We argue that logics, when taken for granted, may leave room for alteration when interesting opportunities are recognized by decision makers (line d). New opportunities can be recognized only if the logics focus the attention of decision makers on a limited set of opportunities that are consistent with the prevailing logic (Thornton 2002). The potential for recognizing opportunities is dependent on the multiplicity and the degree of institutionalization (Dorado 2005). Multiplicity is related to the openness to other influences outside the organization (cf. Greenwood and Hinings 1996). The more open an organization, the more it is exposed to external influences and the more likely it will facilitate innovative behavior. The openness of organizations allows for the generation of tensions that will stimulate the development of new practices (Seo and Creed 2002). When new opportunities arise that are beyond the scope of the ruling logics, tensions within the organization will increase. There will be actors that recognize opportunities at an early stage, which will initiate tensions between different groups. Organizations that are characterized by their closed nature will lack such tensions and have less potential for innovation. Besides multiplicity, the degree of institutionalization is an important indicator for the recognition of opportunities. Organizations that are highly institutionalized are typified by behavioral patterns that are taken for granted (cf. Berger and Luckmann 1967). In these situations it is unlikely that organizations will engage in innovative activities since these are unthinkable. There may be room for incremental innovation that builds on routine behaviors, but these can only gain ground through slow accumulation. Based on these two components, multiplicity and degree of institutionalization, Dorado (2005: 394) makes a distinction between three types of opportunity recognition forms. Organizations can be 'opportunity opaque', which means that the organization will be highly isolated and/or highly institutionalized. There is little room for opportunities in such organizations because they cannot be identified and resources will not be available to support them. 'Opportunity transparent' organizations are substantially institutionalized, which means that there are possibilities to recognize opportunities and act upon them. The third type is called 'opportunity hazy'. In these situations there is a high degree of unpredictability because the numerous opportunities that can potentially be recognized create complexity. It is difficult for organizations to make sense of such a situation.

This leaves us with an intriguing question. Who will recognize the opportunities? If organizational actors are blinded by the organizational logic, who will be able to first spot possibilities that ultimately lead to innovation. In the innovation literature it has frequently been argued that product champions are needed to safeguard innovation projects from all sorts of disturbances. Product champions are individuals who support new initiatives, and can help to overcome delays and difficulties in the innovation process (Markham and Griffin 1998). These individuals are often found in senior positions, are prepared to support new service initiatives, can ensure commitment to projects in terms of time and money, are able to overcome delays and difficulties in the innovation process (Chakrabarti 1974; Shane 1994) and play a critical role in successful innovations. Champions are also crucial in initiating and stimulating an overall climate for innovation (Martin and Horne 1993; Markham and Griffin 1998). The absence of such champions often results in major problems for innovation projects. However, the champion comes into play once opportunities are recognized. The champion does not have to be the same individual that has recognized the opportunity.

Recently the literature on agency within institutional theory is increasingly converging upon the notion of institutional entrepreneurship (DiMaggio 1988, Rao *et al.* 2000; Garud *et al.* 2002; Maguire *et al.* 2004). Institutional entrepreneurs have the ability to identify opportunities, create new systems of meaning, mobilize resources, and raise collective action among field members for projects they value highly (Fligstein 1997). They are thus capable of deinstitutionalizing existing and introducing new institutional logics. We use the idea of bricolage (Lévi-Strauss 1966) to illustrate which individuals are most likely to recognize innovative potential. The bricoleur is an 'amateur craftsman who turns the broken clock into a pipe rack, the broken table into an umbrella stand, the umbrella stand into a lamp, and anything into something else' (Douglas 1986: 66). In other words, the bricoleur uses whatever crosses his path to 'make transformations within a stock repertoire of furnishings' (Douglas 1986: 66). There are three reasons for using the idea of bricolage (Dorado 2006). First, it highlights a connection with past forms and path dependency. Second, it welcomes wilful and creative actors. Third, it acknowledges the constraints in which bricoleurs act. While Burt's (2005) notion of brokerage and brokers is related to the notion of bricolage and bricoleurs, we argue that bricoleurs do not necessarily bridge holes in networks, but have an opportunity to create novel combinations of existing components because they are positioned at the intersection of distinct thought worlds (Dougherty 1992). Dorado (2006) argued that the term bricolage has been related to the discovery of new purposes for old materials and objects, the development of new technology through extensive interactions and the combination of various components. At the heart of this concept is the notion of innovation as defined by Schumpeter (1939), in which he explicitly refers to innovation as the outcome of new combinations of existing elements. Bricoleurs find themselves in positions where different elements come together.

Enabling dynamics

The possibilities for innovation derive from the organizational logics that dominate the organization and the potential for recognizing opportunities. Exactly how these develop is a function of institutional forces at the intraorganizational and organizational level. In line with Greenwood and Hinings (1996), who indicated that radical change can only come about in conjunction with enabling dynamics, we argue that logics and opportunity recognition are not sufficient conditions for innovation. The two enabling dynamics that we deem crucial for innovation are *framing processes* and *mobilizing structures*.

It is commonly accepted that institutional structures are socially constructed (Berger and Luckman 1967) by its constituents. The emergence of such collective understandings is typified by 'battles over meaning' and is constantly under challenge (Hargrave and van de Ven 2006). Scholars in the social movement area have specifically addressed this issue of *framing processes* or meaning construction (e.g. McAdam et al. 1996; Zald 1996; Benford and Snow 2000). A frame enables individuals to make sense of their environment. It 'helps to render events or occurrences meaningful and thereby function to organize experience and guide action' (Benford and Snow 2000: 614). Information has to be consistent with these frames or it will be repressed or ignored (Garud and Rappa 1994). Kaplan (2003) argued that framing is a political and self-conscious process in which meaning is negotiated between groups of individuals. This means that the frame that appeals to one group within the organization may not appeal to another group that has a different system of meaning. Hence, framing becomes a contest between different organizational groups (Hargrave and van de Ven 2006).

The construction of framing involves three core tasks (Benford and Snow 2000: 616–617): diagnostic framing, which concerns problem definition and focuses on blame or responsibility; prognostic framing, which involves the articulation of solutions and the strategies to carry these out; motivational framing, which provides a 'call to arms' or rationale for engaging in collective action. For institutional scholars, framing offers interesting opportunities, because it can demonstrate how institutional arrangements frame issues to become reproduced and maintained and how framing serves the goal of avoiding institutional disruption (Clemens and Cook 1999). There are three overlapping processes that provide insight into how frames are developed over time: discursive, strategic and contested (Benford and Snow 2000). Discursive processes refer to the articulation and amplification of issues, events or experiences that assemble a picture of reality that is more salient than others. Strategic processes are deliberative and utilitarian processes in which frames are developed for a specific purpose. This points at the essential idea that the interests and interpretive frames of constituents are aligned. Contested processes resemble the true nature of much framing. There are multiple parties involved in framing processes and each party brings its own frame. Through a process of extensive negotiation, shared frames may eventually arise. Underlying these framing processes are rhetorical strategies of legitimacy (Suddaby and Greenwood 2005). Frames will only be shared when they are considered legitimate by multiple actors. The strategic use of language, talk and conversation is aimed at bridging differences between constituents in order to align their frames.

Figure 8.1 illustrates a reciprocal relationship between framing processes and the organizational logic (line e). McAdam and Scott (2005) argued that these two concepts are closely connected, since both refer to belief systems providing direction and meaning to individuals. Logics, however, are much more about the power of dominant groups that hold certain ideologies, whereas framing emphasizes challenges for innovation. We argue that the outcome of the framing process will strongly depend on the ruling organizational logic. Those individuals that are aware of this relation and understand its embeddedness can benefit when initiating the framing process. Innovations in organizations under a routine logic, for example, are destined to be considered illegitimate. The new products, processes or practices that are to be developed are likely to go beyond the current domain of the organization. However, individual actors that initiate these attempts to alter the organizational path have an opportunity to mindfully deviate from the existing structures (Garud and Karnøe 2001). This may even create inefficiencies in the short term, but such steps are considered essential for future success. Garud and Karnøe (2001) illustrate the notion of mindful deviation by using the development of the Post-it® notes. They describe the development process as one in which Spence Silver (the scientist who discovered the weak glue) deliberately deviated from existing ways of mixing molecules. In order to arouse any passion for his invention he had to disembed current beliefs about glue and try to reframe the potential for such a product in the terms and language of existing institutions. Hargadon and Douglas (2001: 478) use a similar explanation for the success of entrepreneurial minds like Edison, who also was able to present the meaning and value of his innovations (including the novel features) in line with the existing institutions 'by giving them the appearance of familiar ideas'.

In our study, product champions in the successful projects engaged in a process of mindful deviation. They tried to frame projects in a slightly more radical way to arouse some excitement in the organization, while at the same time framing it in understandable ways. Although the true nature of most of these innovative attempts can be labeled 'mindful deviations' (Garud and Karnøe 2001), some were framed in a very deviant way (in firms under a dual logic). However, as Garud and Karnøe (2001) argued, this degree of deviance should not be too large for this will generate illegitimacy. Especially when the organization adheres to a routine logic, it is hardly possible to deviate too much from the logic. Thus, even in the case of competence-enhancing innovations it may be extremely difficult to find acceptance from established players and key stakeholders. To be accepted, product champions need to frame their new products in well-established arrangements that deviate from current products yet arouse enough interest to stimulate development. This process of mindful deviation or social embeddedness (Hargadon and Douglas, 2001) requires innovators to walk a fine line between exploration and exploitation (March 1991). Framing processes ultimately enable or constrain the possibilities for innovation (line f), which is partly dependent on the ability of the actor to carefully align this framing attempt with the ruling logics. We have explained that framing is not only about creating an understanding of an innovation, but also about understanding the political and social processes in which the innovation is and will be embedded. Actors need to realize that innovations are represented not by complete, distinct or sweeping shifts of existing logics, but rather a layering of logics (e.g. Cooper *et al.* 1996; Pinnington and Morris 2003) that is the outcome of a negotiation process (Thelen 2003). Awareness of the sediments, which refers to the persistent values, ideas and practices (Cooper *et al.* 1996: 624), 'involves the partial renegotiation of some elements of a given set of institutions while leaving others in place' (Thelen 2003: 225). Moreover, it requires an awareness of the interests and belief systems of different groups in the organization. Again we see an important role for the bricoleur.

The second enabling dynamic, *mobilizing structures*, has received ample attention in the literature. Mobilizing structures are 'collective vehicles, informal as well as formal, through which people mobilize and engage in collective action' (McAdam *et al.* 1996: 3). According to Campbell (2005), the formal and informal networks of individual actors are the foundation of mobilizing structures. Out of these networks innovations emerge. It follows then that innovation requires the collective action of multiple actors (cf. Colomy 1998). By crystallizing broad symbolic orientations in new ways and articulating specific goals, groups work to persuade other players to adopt the innovation. This once more illustrates the requirement of embedding innovations within shared frames that are understandable to many actors. We assume that change agents will not invent totally new frames in order for them to mobilize initial support and resources from powerful actors (Seo and Creed 2002). Still, innovation can be portrayed as a type of institution creation. Formating new institutions can be achieved by a number of practices through which actors engage in specific activities. Lawrence and Suddaby (2006) provide an excellent overview of different types of institutional work. Some of these actions are directly linked to innovation. Advocacy, for instance, refers to the 'mobilization of political and regulatory support through direct and deliberate techniques of social suasion' (2006: 221) and defining is concerned with the construction of parameters of future practices. Whereas many of the forms of institutional work are especially relevant for revolutionary change involving the turnaround of institutional practices, they are also valuable for understanding evolutionary changes (such as more incremental innovations) that have a strong impact on the organization. Their pace may be slower, but the impact of such alterations is not to be underestimated.

Although collective action will not always result in innovation, the potential for innovation is positively affected by mobilized structures that try to collectively bring about the desired change (line g in our model). However, the success of the mobilization effort is partly dependent on the organizational logic (line i in our model). The powerful groups can easily try to disrupt mobilization attempts by relocating entrepreneurial individuals in order for them to become marginalized. Marginalized actors who find themselves misaligned with the ruling logics will find it extremely difficult to suggest changes. Although these actors have been identified as potential change agents (Seo and Creed 2002), their lack of power will make their tasks even more daunting. This highlights the crucial role of social skills (Fligstein 2001). Mobilizing actors require social skills to be able to motivate cooperation from other actors. Social skill is defined as 'the ability to motivate cooperation in other actors by providing those actors with common meanings and identities in which actions can be undertaken and justified' (Fligstein 1997: 398). This means that actors need to engage in strategic behavior in order to persuade others to join forces or at least support them openly. They understand the difficulties and complexities in their organization and know what opportunities there are to be successful. Fligstein (1997) has described a set of tactics that these individuals may use, including maintaining ambiguity, wheeling and annealing, aggregating interests and networking with outliers. When individuals are able to combine these traits they are capable of disrupting or creating new institutions. Since the bricoleurs we described above are at the intersection of different thought worlds they may be well positioned to bring together different groups of people within the organization.

We argue that our framework holds different implications for incremental or radical innovation. Incremental innovations have a high likelihood of being framed within the ruling logics. These innovations are competence-enhancing and as such should be understandable for organizational actors. This does not mean that these are easy to develop, but at least they can generate a sufficient degree of passion in the organization. For radical innovations this will be much more complicated. Hence, we argue that especially radical innovations require effective mobilizing structures in order to gain sufficient support for the new ideas.

Concluding remarks

In this chapter we have presented an analytical framework for understanding innovation from an institutional perspective. Our model is not intended to discard the valuable work that has been done in the field of innovation management. We try to complement this literature by offering insights from institutional theory in order to explain the persistent problems with innovation many firms experience. Central to our model is the concept of logics. We claim that this is a crucial factor in the potential for firms to innovate, since it is closely related to the other precipitating and enabling dynamics. We believe that this set of components holds great promise to better understand the failed innovative attempts of established organizations. For students of innovation there are a number of lessons to be learned from our model. First, organizational logics are developed over time as a result of combinatory institutional forces. Second, organizational logics are central to the possibilities that firms have to innovate. Third, organizational logics are the nexus between the recognition of opportunities, framing processes and mobilizing structures. Fourth, innovators use existing institutional components to frame their task. Finally, they need to mobilize for collective action in order to enable innovative activities.

9 Conclusion

Introduction

Our goal in this book was to find an answer to the question, how organizational and intraorganizational institutional forces affect the development and implementation of incremental product innovations in financial services firms. We attempted to answer this question on the basis of interviews with 175 employees from various banks and insurance companies in the Netherlands using a grounded theory approach. The interviewees represented different hierarchical levels as well as functional areas such as marketing, IT services, product development, actuary, etc. After an exploratory stage, we performed a comparative case study analysis of twelve financial services companies that were active in the banking and insurance business.

Developing new financial services

Previous studies on incremental innovation focused primarily on product innovation in the manufacturing industry (e.g. Clark and Fujimoto 1991; Wheelright and Clark 1992; Banbury and Mitchell 1995; Pisano 1997). However, several developments common to many OECD countries in the last three decades, suggested that one should pay more attention to innovation in the service sector and especially the financial sector. First, during the last three decades services have moved to the center of economic activities in modern societies and in many OECD countries the added value created in the service sector now exceeds manufacturing. In the course of this growth process, many of these industries have changed beyond recognition. Second, in the financial services sector, the rapid development of IT has not only enabled an enormous increase in transactions per employee, but also created numerous opportunities for the development and marketization of new processes and products. Third, the financial sector in the Netherlands underwent dramatic changes in the last three decades. These changes were triggered by changing governmental policies both on the European as well as the national level. In general, policies on both levels were geared towards deregulation and liberalization of financial markets receiving an additional boost through the introduction of a single European currency in January 2002, which led to increased competition during the 1990s. In addition, the changes in the European welfare system, especially the pension system, increased the need for private retirement savings also in the Netherlands, which made it necessary for financial companies to come up with new products that would combine savings and (life-) insurance elements, the so-called 'combi-products'. Both the developments on the supply as well as the demand side contributed to the blurring of the boundaries between banks and insurance companies in terms of product innovation and, as a consequence, to increased competition.

However, given the general conservative nature of the banking and insurance sector, the long product life cycles, the need for security on the one hand and complex products on the other hand, financial companies primarily engaged in incremental product innovation, i.e. slightly changed existing products over time. Such a strategy minimizes the risk if compared to the introduction of radically new products. Since established insurance companies and banks have traditionally been characterized as rather risk averse (Vermeulen 2005) this kind of strategy does not come as a surprise. The question therefore arises of how the incremental innovation in these established companies takes place and how it is organized. The descriptive analysis showed that in most financial companies the overall organizational structures are still mainly based on the traditional principle of functional specialization. Similar to Johne (1993), we did not find a purely team-based organization or other 'new' structures. However, under the influence of such notions as Business Process Redesign (see Davenport 1993), several organizations are now moving toward process-based structures, focusing on product groups or customer groups. Still, the majority of organizations remain functionally departmentalized.

In most organizations, multidisciplinary project teams are formed to develop new products, especially in the case of more radical product innovation. The members of these teams come from various functionally specialized departments. In most cases, team members act primarily as representatives of their departments and the teams therefore rarely function as teams with a shared understanding of their mission. Project leadership is correspondingly weak. Heavy project managers or product champions are a rare species in the financial sector, although, in most of the successful cases, teams had a senior manager with considerable importance and the full backing of the top management. This allowed him or her to insulate the team from the bureaucratic routine tasks and limit the influence of functional departments in the innovation process.

Although the word 'teamwork' is readily used in almost all companies surveyed, the supposed advantages of teamwork are hardly realized. This becomes clear from the persistence of all sorts of communication and cooperation problems between disciplines, the solution of which, supposedly, was the main reason for creating multidisciplinary teams. Moreover, in most companies in the financial services sector, the idea generation stage is mainly the task of a single department. The results of this study suggest that financial companies tend to neglect some major potential sources of new ideas, especially front-office personnel who are in close contact with customers. During the stages of further specification and building of software and marketing material, functional departments (or representatives from these departments) conduct 'their own' tasks. Little cooperation between these activities, let alone integration, seems to exist. Some activities are conducted in parallel, not in the 'concurrent engineering' sense of close mutual support but mainly autonomously of each other. Integrated product development, as described by Clark and Fujimoto (1991), is not yet common in the financial services sector.

One could argue that the nature of the product makes such cooperation and integration unnecessary. However, all companies surveyed struggled with delays and failures in product development due to problems of communication and mutual understanding. Members of different functionally specialized departments, regardless of whether they were members of one team or not, have difficulties in understanding each other. The same is true for the proponents of a new product and the people working in the distribution channels (which can be intermediaries or branch offices). For the latter group of people, processes are changed and these actors in the distribution channels have to be convinced of the added value of the new product. In manufacturing, new products often take the place of existing ones, but new financial products usually do not replace existing ones and the sales force may be reluctant to sell an additional product if it feels that existing products are already providing sufficient business.

A closer look at the communication/understanding problems shows that, in the financial services sector, most communication problems tend to lie at the interface between marketing and IT departments and (in insurance companies) between actuaries and the other project team members. It may be that the intangible character of these services makes it more difficult to come to a common understanding between persons with different backgrounds. Moreover, the fact that financial services are characteristically backed up by a complex administrative system that in some cases has to be kept functioning for several decades, may easily lead to the perception that the supportive information systems are the essence of the product. If this perception prevails in the IT department, communications with marketing are greatly impeded.

The impact of institutional forces

Concerning the impact of institutional forces on incremental innovation, the study produced the following results. The regulatory forces, for instance, primarily deal with facilitating or obstructing exchanges among members of an organization (cf. Zucker 1988). This not only refers to the organizational rules and standard operating procedures, but also to the IT systems. For any innovation project in which multiple departments are involved (which is the case in complex incremental innovation projects), facilitating exchanges between representatives from these departments is crucial. However, internal structures exhibit 'the social permanence of institutions'. When the degree of internal institutionalization in incumbent firms increases over time, similarity with other organizations, including the degree of codification and interdependence, will make it more difficult for incumbent firms to change these structures (Zucker 1988: 35). The unsuccessful projects in our study clearly suffered from these regulatory institutional forces. In the successful projects we also were able to identify some kind of regulatory forces. These were, however, very much directed towards enhancing creativity. The rules that guide the actions of individuals in these projects were mostly informal, were clearly communicated and deviations were rarely accepted. Furthermore, the opportunities for developing more innovative versions of combi-products, in which banking and insurance activities are joined, are restricted by the government. Hence, there are few incentives to innovate from a regulatory perspective.

The normative forces in our study also affected incremental innovation. Managers in the unsuccessful projects displayed a strong risk-avoiding attitude on the one hand, whereas on the other hand they felt little obligation towards completing projects on time. The internalization of this kind of behavior generates expectations that guide the actions of other organizational members (Scott 2001). In our case, this meant that not only managers, but also team members, lacked social obligation. Furthermore, there were clear distinctions regarding the perceptions on the need for incremental innovation between various actors in the organizations studied; different perceptions of top managers, business-unit managers and lower level managers and employees directly involved in executing incremental product innovation projects in particular contributed negatively to the success of these projects. The unsuccessful projects in our study seem to be lacking institutional concurrence (Dougherty and Cohen 1995), which indicates that there is no alignment between what headquarters is thinking and doing and what employees are thinking and doing. In the business units that did manage to successfully develop incremental innovations, we found a different logic. Not only were the expectations clear and consistent in various layers of the organization, the perception of risk was quite different. Risk was valued as being 'part of the game' and could not be reduced completely. On the organizational (macro) level, normative forces do not contribute to increased legitimacy of incremental product innovation because customers are mainly interested in trustworthy financial partners instead of innovative players. Furthermore, customers have only limited interest in financial products or are unable to explicitly ask for new products. Whether this is actually true or not is of minor importance in this study. More important is that because of this perceived lack of interest from customers, there are few incentives for financial services companies to invest in incremental product innovations. Although we expected that customer expectations would be favorable to incremental product innovation, our respondents did not feel that there were strong incentives from customers to invest in these types of innovation.

Cultural-cognitive forces include different systems of meaning and dominant identities. When powerful actors in the organizations were opposed to innovation (cf. Greenwood and Hinings 1996), few resources were made available. The shared systems of meaning are negotiated over time in interaction processes between organizational actors (Scott 2001). The more time individuals spend interacting with identity-like individuals, the stronger the degree of segmentation in an organization (cf. Trice 1993). Again, we found strong differences between the successful and unsuccessful cases. The successful projects were almost all framed as radical projects in order to obtain and maintain the necessary resources and to be able to escape from the rules and procedures from the standing organization. With respect to the organizational-level forces, we noticed that all the firms in our study struggle with incremental product innovation, meaning that there are few available 'role models' to be imitated. We found similar approaches to dealing with incremental product innovation, which led us to believe that when a firm is successful (in terms of developing a steady stream of new products successfully), its practices may be copied.

Our data also provided empirical evidence for the existence of interactions between various institutional forces that reinforced their impact. The regulatory forces in our study clearly interacted with normative forces. The rules and procedures that drive organizational behavior seem to interact with the perceived expectations of employees regarding the core activities of their organizations. If employees are sanctioned for not reaching set targets (e.g. number of policies processed), while simultaneously not being rewarded for efforts in NPD projects, they may experience a lack of legitimacy for incremental product innovation. This way of working becomes normatively valued over time and then taken for granted. Furthermore, the business units that embraced incremental innovation created an atmosphere of 'letting go' of the formal rules and procedures, which simultaneously led to a 'just do it' mentality. The prevailing idea in these units was that incremental innovation always carries a certain amount of risk, but this should not stop or delay the development process. The latter normative force (risk avoidance) closely interacted with the meaning systems of different professional disciplines (intraorganizational), which in turn interacted with regulatory forces. A final example of interaction in this study was the framing of incremental projects as if they were 'radical' projects. These projects were separated from the regular organization and managed to escape the formal rules and procedures. The institutional logic in the business units that framed their projects in more 'radical' terms clearly differed from the more traditional business units in our study. Thus, in this research context we found indications that the institutional forces do not compete with each other, but instead are complementary and reinforce each other in favor of either more stability or more innovation.

Contributions

We have sought to make a contribution and extend our knowledge of innovation in the following areas. First, the financial services sector is one of the industries driving economic growth in most developed countries (Quinn *et al.* 1997; Alic 2001). Yet, the innovation literature is still dominated by examples from manufacturing (e.g. Clark and Fujimoto 1991). Our study demonstrated that many of the concepts found in the literature on industrial product development can also be applied to service development. However, it appears that the financial services sector has not progressed very far in the practical application of insights derived from manufacturing practice. Companies rarely succeed in integrating functions and disciplines into a coherent product development system. To some extent this may be due to the simple fact that, until recently, the financial market was quite stable, offering relatively limited opportunities for innovation. Increasing turbulence on the market and growing competition will force companies to improve their innovative performance. The specific features of services as opposed to physical products, however, also contribute to this state of affairs. The intangibility as well as the high information content of financial services appear to be at the basis of the substantial problems of communication and understanding arising in the product development process.

Second, up to now a large part of the innovation literature was based on describing innovation processes in the form of formal steps or procedures (e.g. Booz *et al.* 1982; Cooper 1983). This type of literature has a predominantly prescriptive nature and is oriented on how these steps should be taken. It pays less attention to what actually happens in innovation processes and the agents involved in the process. The present study tries to enhance our understanding of the underlying mechanisms that inhibit the innovative performance of incumbent firms and adds a distinctively analytical perspective to the literature on innovation.

Third, past research on product innovation in both manufacturing and service industries has taken a predominantly rational perspective and focused on key determinants that lead to successful product innovation. This large body of literature has examined what the development process looks like, what steps firms must carry out and what models could support the development process (Cooper 1983, 1984; Cooper and Kleinschmidt 1987; Cooper *et al.* 2002). Furthermore, product factors that separate winners from losers have been identified, such as a clear product definition, a differentiated product with unique customer benefits, and sufficient market knowledge (Thwaites 1992; Cooper 1999; De Brentani 2001). However, these determinants had not been able to fully explain the persistence of problematic innovation efforts. We broadened that view on incremental product innovation by using Scott's framework of the three institutional pillars to explain incremental product innovation, thus adding a complementary perspective. We illustrated how intraorganizational and organizational institutional forces come to shape the interests, priorities and behavior of organizational members (cf. Selznick 1957; Meyer and Rowan 1977; Zucker 1983, 1987; Scott 2001) in the development and implementation of incremental product innovation.

Fourth, the present study further integrates the literature of two fields of research, which previously had rarely talked to each other: innovation and neo-institutional theory. Innovations, especially competence-destroying innovations, cause major problems for established firms in mature populations and thus lack initial legitimacy. While competence-enhancing innovations tend to reinforce competitive positions, competence-destroying innovations go beyond current organizational competencies and create new opportunities. Although the financial innovations in our study are not competence-destroying innovations, also here two social forces collide: one that stimulates stability and the other that stimulates change (Hargadon and Douglas 2001: 476). Our study points out that the acceptance even of incremental or competence-enhancing innovations is problematic, because, although incremental innovations can be labeled 'familiar' (to all parties in an organization) and have therefore stayed on well-traveled paths, actors that try to champion these products do not always succeed in acquiring the necessary legitimacy for their product. In order to further understand the persistence of innovation problems, we developed an analytical framework based on institutional theory that should aid our understanding of these problems. By presenting our framework we did not intend to discard the literature on innovation management. We tried to complement and extend this literature by offering insights from institutional theory in order to explain the persistence of problems that firms experience. Central to the framework is the concept of organizational logics. We claim that this is a crucial factor in the potential for firms to innovate, since it is closely related to the other precipitating and enabling dynamics. Together we believe that this set of components holds great promise to better understand the failed innovative attempts of established organizations.

Limitations and future research

Although large parts of the data collection took part at the end of the 1990s and during the early 2000s, ongoing contacts with the field lead us to believe that the results are still valid and have a great deal of practical relevance. Many of the banks in our sample are still experiencing similar problems to the ones described in this book. One of the authors recently experienced this during a workshop with managers from two large financial companies. The results from the present study were acknowledged by the participants who admitted that they continue to struggle with innovation projects.

Furthermore, the institutional forces were studied in isolation, whereas several scholars have argued that these forces interact. Although we did find some evidence for this interaction, we did not study this explicitly. Finally, we used our framework to study a specific type of innovation: incremental product innovation. Radical innovations may follow a different trajectory and may be more legitimate because they are frame-bending. More research on these issues is needed.

Three directions for future research are proposed. First, scholars studying incremental innovation should also take institutional forces into account in their attempts to explain success. Special attention is needed for the interaction dynamics between the forces at different levels. As was argued earlier, institutional research has rarely focused on the interaction between various forces. Further research is needed to uncover the dynamics of interaction to fully understand (a) which institutional forces interact, (b) how these forces interact, and (c) how the interaction of forces affects the legitimacy of innovation. To shed more light on these interaction dynamics, detailed comparative case studies are required for at least two reasons (cf. Greenwood and Hinings 1996). First, understanding dynamics requires in-depth knowledge of the actual functioning of the studied phenomenon. Second, innovation processes are highly oscillatory and iterative. The interaction of various forces does not seem to resemble a linear path. These interactions are likely to be highly dynamic and to iterate on various occasions.

Second, empirical research is needed in other industries and in the financial services sector of other (EU) countries to investigate (a) the value of our framework in non-financial services firms and (b) the impact of nationally different macro institutional forces (Flier *et al.* 2001) on the legitimacy of incremental product innovation. It has been argued in the innovation literature that innovation differs across industries and countries. In some countries, innovation may prove to be more legitimate as the national government provides an environment that is conducive to innovation (Afuah 1998). Previous research has indicated that the national regulatory environment is related to the innovative behavior of firms (Volberda *et al.* 2001). The interaction between institutional forces at different levels may, therefore, contribute to a more positive relation between institutional forces and the legitimacy of product innovation. The analytical framework proposed in this book might be of help in this endeavor. We realize, however, that the analytical framework presented here is still on a very abstract level and has to be further developed into a model that allows for the operationalization and testing of hypotheses. Furthermore, there are more relations present between the elements than are currently displayed in our model.

Third, radical innovation should be studied using a similar conceptual framework in order to increase the understanding of the conditions under which managers can escape the identified institutional forces. In this book we focused on incremental innovation. Do radical innovation projects suffer from similar problems? If so, what are the specific conditions under which this happens? Both qualitative and quantitative research is needed to increase the understanding of radical innovation in the financial services sector. Case study research is needed to ascertain the influence of institutional forces on radical innovation. Large-scale quantitative studies are necessary to establish the relationship between the forces and the degree of product innovation in a firm (e.g. do firms with a more decentralized/centralized organizational structure develop more revolutionary new products).

Notes

1 The Structure Policy regulates the way in which collaboration between banks and insurance companies is approved of.

2 Several of these studies do not explicitly mention the degree of newness of the products studied. However, authors that studied radical innovation pointed out that most of these studies in product innovation were implicitly involved with incremental innovation (see for instance Colarelli O'Connor 1998; Veryzer 1998; McDermott and Colarelli O'Connor 2002).

3 See also the specialized innovation journals such as *Journal of Product Innovation Management*, *R&D Management* and *International Journal of Innovation Management*.

4 This section draws heavily on a working paper by Patrick Vermeulen and Jeroen de Jong entitled 'Innovation Research: what do we study? An Overview of Innovation Literature in the Last Decade (1994–2003)'.

5 This is in line with an overview of studies on services that are compared using the specific characteristics of services presented by Zeithaml *et al.* (1985). This overview clearly shows that intangibility is the only feature that was explicitly referred to as a service feature in all studies.

6 The top-ranked management journals in this study were *Academy of Management Journal*, *Administrative Science Quarterly*, *Organization Science*, and *Strategic Management Journal*.

7 According to Lee (1999), the same holds for quantitative research. There are not many agreed upon – definitions, which makes it difficult to compare it with qualitative research. Often, the differences are oversimplified into 'research with numbers versus research with no numbers'. The present study will not elaborate on the differences between qualitative and quantitative research. This chapter elaborates on the research strategy used for this study and therefore has no intent of discussing the distinctions between the two types of research. For those who are interested in the qualitative-quantitative debate, we would like to refer to Creswell (1994), Cassell and Symon (1994), Miles and Huberman (1994) and Denzin and Lincoln (1998).

8 It should be noted that empirical materials are not the same as data. Empirical materials are not ordered in any way, whereas data is material that has been ordered in order to analysen it.

9 The origins of grounded theory can be traced back to Glaser and Strauss's book *The Discovery of Grounded Theory: strategies for qualitative research*, which was published in 1967. Their book has had a strong impact on researchers in the social sciences and business studies. As a result, academics involved in exploratory research have tried to ignore any existing theory. These academics literally followed Glaser and Strauss's advice to 'ignore the literature of theory and fact on the area under study, in order to assure that the emergence of categories will not be contaminated' (1967: 37). However, both Glaser and Strauss continued to develop grounded theory, which resulted in a very complex and

difficult-to-read book by Glaser in 1978 entitled *Theoretical Sensitivity* and a much more accessible book by Strauss in 1987 entitled *Qualitative Analysis for Social Scientists.* Grounded theory 'gained a wider audience, a new spokesperson, and more disciples' when Strauss's 1990 coauthored book with Juliet Corbin appeared (Charmaz 2000: 512). Yet, not everybody was pleased with this book. Former colleague Barney Glaser was not able to accept the 'changes' (especially with respect to the use of theory) made to the initial grounded theory ideas. In the introduction of his 1992 book *Basics of Grounded Theory Analysis: emergence vs. forcing*, Glaser requests that Strauss 'pull the book' because it 'distorts and misconceives grounded theory' (1992: 2). One of the last comments Glaser raises in his introductory chapter is that Strauss and Corbin 'wrote a whole different method, so why call it "grounded theory"?' (1992: 2). Glaser might be right on this latter issue. Eisenhardt describes 'the process of inducting theory using case studies' (1989: 532) and clearly states that 'it is impossible to achieve this ideal of a clean theoretical slate' (1989: 536). She continues to argue that researchers 'should formulate a research problem and possibly specify some potentially important variables, with some reference to extant literature. However, they should avoid thinking about specific relationships between variables and theories as much as possible' (1989: 536). Strauss and Corbin's conception of grounded theory seems to be more in line with Eisenhardt's ideas of specifying some important variables in inductive case study research. Both Eisenhardt and Strauss and Corbin agree on the notion that it is impossible for researchers to enter the research field without any prior knowledge. The main reason for proceeding with Strauss and Corbin's work is their extensive treatment of coding procedures required for the analysis of empirical material. Although the words 'grounded theory' will be used in the course of this book, it should be stressed that we follow Strauss and Corbin's conception of grounded theory.

10 The banks in this survey represented over 95 per cent of the total Dutch market for consumer products, whereas the insurance companies accounted for over 75 per cent of the total life insurance market in the Netherlands (in premiums paid). The remaining 25 per cent are covered by more than seventy companies with market shares varying from 0.1 per cent to 0.5 per cent (Source: AM Statis Disk 1998, Assurance Magazine Statistical Disk).

References

Adams M.E., Day G.S. and Dougherty D. (1998) 'Enhancing New Product Development Performance: An Organizational Learning Perspective', *Journal of Product Innovation Management*, 15: 403–422.

Afuah A. (1998) *Innovation Management. Strategies, Implementation, and Profits*. New York: Oxford University Press.

Afuah A. (2003) 'Redefining Firm Boundaries in the Face of the Internet: Are Firms Really Shrinking?', *The Academy of Management Review*, 28(1):34–53.

Aldrich H. (1999) *Organizations Evolving*. London: Sage.

Aldrich H. and Fiol C.M. (1994) 'Fools Rush In? The Institutional Context of Industry Creation', *Academy of Management Review*, 19(4): 645–670.

Alic J.A. (2001) 'Postindustrial Technology Policy', *Research Policy*, 30(6): 873–889.

Allen T.J. (1977) *Managing the Flow of Technology*, Cambridge: MIT Press.

Ancona D. and Caldwell D.F. (1997) 'Making Teamwork Work: Boundary Management in Product Development Teams', in Tushman M.L. and Anderson P. (eds), *Managing Strategic Innovation and Change*. New York: Oxford University Press, pp. 433–442.

Andreasen M.M. and Hein L. (1987) *Integrated Product Development*. Berlin: Spring-Verlag.

Archibugi D. and Sirilli G. (2001) 'The Direct Measurement of Technological Innovation in Business', in Thuriaux B. *et al.* (ed.), *Innovation and Enterprise Creation*, Sophia Antipolis, November 2000, pp. 38–49.

Ashforth B.E. and Gibbs B.W. (1990) 'The Double Edge of Organiationa Legitimation', *Organization Science* 1: 177–194.

Atkinson P. and Hammersley M. (1998) 'Ethnography and Participant Observation', in Denzin N.K. and Lincoln Y.S. (eds.), *Strategies of Qualitative Research*, Thousand Oaks: Sage, pp. 110–136.

Avlonitis G.J., Papastahopoulou P.G. and Gounaris S.P. (2001) 'An Empirically-based Typology of Product Innovativeness for New Financial Services: Success and Failure Scenarios', *Journal of Product Innovation Management*, 18(5): 324–342.

Banbury C.M. and Mitchell W. (1995) 'The Effect of Introducing Important Incremental Innovations on Market Share and Business Survival'. *Strategic Management Journal*, 16: 161–182.

Bateson J.E.G. (1977) 'Do We Need Service Marketing', in *Marketing Consumer Services: New Insights*. Marketing Science Institute, pp. 77–115.

Baum J.A.C. (2002) *Companion to Organizations*. Oxford: Blackwell Publishers.

Beckert J. (1999) 'Agency, Entrepreneurs, and Institutional Change. The Role of Strategic Choice and Institutionalized Practices in Organizations', *Organization Studies*, 20(5): 777–799.

Belbin R.M. (1993) *Team Roles at Work*. Butterworth-Heinemann: London.

Belliveau P., Griffin A. and Somermeyer S. (2004) *The PDMA ToolBook 2 for New Product Development*, New York: Wiley.

Benders J. and Vermeulen P. (2002) 'Too Many Tools? On Problem Solving in NPD Projects', *International Journal of Innovation Management*, 6(2): 163–185.

Benford R.D. and Snow D.A. (2000) 'Framing Processes and Social Movements: An Overview and Assessment', *Annual Review of Sociology*, 26: 611–639.

Berger P.L. and Luckman T. (1967) *The Social Construction of Reality. A Treatise in the Sociology of Knowledge*. New York: Anchor Books.

Berndes S. and Stanke A. (1996) 'A Concept for Revitalisation of Product Development', in Bullinger H.J. and Warschat J. (eds.) *Concurrent Simultaneous Engineering Systems*. London: Springer Verlag, pp. 7–56.

Berry L.L. (1980) 'Services Marketing is Different', *Business Week*, May-June: 24–29.

Berry L.L. and Hensal J.S. (1973) 'Why do Some New Bank Products Fail?', *Bankers Monthly*, 40: 26–3.

Block Z. and MacMillan I.C. (1993) *Corporate Venturing. Creating New Business Within the Firm*. Boston: Harvard Business School Press.

Booz, Allen and Hamilton (1982) *New Product Management for the 1980's*. New York: Booz, Allen and Hamilton.

Bozeman B. (2000) 'Technology Transfer and Public Policy: A Review of Research and Theory', *Research Policy*, 29: 627–655.

Brint S. and Karabel J. (1991) 'Institutional Origins and Transformations: The Case of American Community Colleges', in *The New Institutionalism in Organizational Analysis*, Powell W.W. and DiMaggio P.J. (eds). Chicago: University of Chicago Press, pp.337–360.

Brown S.L. and Eisenhardt K.M. (1995) 'Product Development: Past Research, Present Findings, and Future Directions', *Academy of Management Review*, 20(2): 343–378.

Burgelman R.A. (1983) 'A Model of the Interaction of Strategic Behavior, Corporate Context, and the Concept of Strategy', *Academy of Management Review*, 8(1): 61–70.

Burgelman R.A. and Sayles L.R. (1986) *Inside Corporate Innovation*. New York: The Free Press.

Burns, T. and Stalker G.M. (1961), *The Management of Innovation*. London: Tavistock Publications.

Burt R.S. (2005) *Brokerage and Closure. An Introduction to Social Capital*. Oxford: Oxford University Press.

Buijs J. and Valkenburg R. (2000) *Integrale Productontwikkeling*. Utrecht: Lemma.

Campbell J.L. (2005) 'Where Do We Stand? Common Mechanisms in Organizations and Social Movements Research', in Davis G.F., McAdam D., Scott W.R. and Zald M.N. (eds), *Social Movements and Organization Theory*, Cambridge: Cambridge University Press, pp. 41–68.

Cassell C. and Symon G. (1994) *Qualitative Methods in Research: A Practical Guide*, London: Sage.

Chakrabarti A.K. (1974) 'The Role of Champion in Product Innovation', *California Management Review*, 17: 58–62.

Charmaz K. (2000) 'Grounded Theory. Objectivist and Constructivist Methods', in Denzin N.K. and Lincoln Y.S. (eds), *Handbook of Qualitative Research*, 2nd edn. Thousand Oaks: Sage, pp. 509–535.

Christensen C.M. (1997) *The Innovator's Dilemma. When New Technologies Cause Great Firms to Fail.* New York: Harper Collins.

Clark K.B. and Fujimoto T. (1991) *Product Development Performance.* Harvard Business School Press: Boston.

Clark J. and Guy K (1998) 'Innovation and Competitiveness: A Review', *Technology Analysis & Strategic Management*, 10: 363–395.

Clemens E.S. and Cook J.M. (1999) 'Politics and Institutionalism: Explaining Durability and Change', *Annual Review of Sociology*, 25: 441–466.

Colarelli O'Connor G. (1998) 'Market Learning and Radical Innovation: A Cross Case Comparison of Eight Radical Innovation Projects', *Journal of Product Innovation Management*, 15: 151–166.

Colomy P. (1998) 'Neofunctionalism and Neoinstitutionalism: Human Agency and Interest in Institutional Change', *Sociological Forum*, 13: 265–300.

Cooper D.J., Hinings C.R., Greenwood R. and Brown J.L. (1996) 'Sedimentation and Transformation in Organizational Change: The Case of Canadian Law Firms', *Organization Studies*, 17: 623–647.

Cooper R.G. (1983) 'The New Product Process: An Empirically-Based Classification Scheme', *R&D Management*, 13(1): 1–13.

Cooper R.G. (1984) 'New Product Strategies: What Distinguishes the Top Performers?', *Journal of Product Innovation Management*, 2: 151–164.

Cooper R.G. (1999) 'From Experience. The Invisible Success Factors in Product Innovation', *Journal of Product Innovation Management*, 16: 115–133.

Cooper R.G. and Kleinschmidt E.J. (1987) 'New Products: What Separates Winners from Losers?', *Journal of Product Innovation Management*, 4(2): 169–184.

Cooper R.G. and Kleinschmidt E.J. (1990) 'New Product Success Factors: A Comparison of 'Kills' versus Successes and Failures', *R&D Management*, 2(1): 47–63.

Cooper R.G. and De Brentani U. (1991) 'New Industrial Financial Services: What Distinguishes the Winners', *Journal of Product Innovation Management*, 8(2): 75–90.

Cooper R.G., Easingwood C.J., Edgett S., Kleinschmidt E.J. and Storey C. (1994) 'What Distinguishes the Top Performing New Products in Financial Services', *Journal of Product Innovation Management*, 11(4): 281–299.

Cooper R.G., Edgett S. and Kleinschmidt E. (2002) 'Optimizing the Stage-Gate Process: What Best-Practice Companies Do-I', *Research Technology Management* 45(5): 21–27.

Crawford C.M. (1994) *New Products Development.* 2nd edn. Burr Ridge: Irwin.

Creswell J.D. (1994) *Research Design: Qualitative and Quantitative Approaches.* London: Sage.

Cumming B.S. (1998) 'Innovation Overview and Future Challenges', *European Journal of Innovation Management*, 1: 21–29.

Dacin T., Goodstein J. and Scott W.R. (2002) 'Institutional Theory and Institutional Change: Introduction to the Special Research Forum', *Academy of Management Journal*, 45: 45–57.

Daft R.L. (1978) 'A Dual-Core Model of Organizational Innovation', *Academy of Management Journal*, 21(2): 193–210.
Daft R.L. (1995) *Organization Theory and Design*, 5th edn. St. Paul: West Publishing Company.
Daft R.L. and Weick K.E. (1984) 'Toward a Model of Organizations as Interpretive Systems', *Academy of Management Review*, 9(1): 43–66.
Da Silveira G. (2001) 'Innovation Diffusion: Research Agenda for Developing Economies', *Technovation*, 21: 767–773.
D'Aunno T., Succi M. and Alexander J.A. (2000) 'The Role of Institutional and Market Forces in Divergent Organizational Change', *Administrative Science Quarterly*, 45: 679–703.
Davenport T.H. (1993) *Process Innovation. Reengineering Work through Information Technology*. Boston: Harvard Business School Press.
De Brentani U. (1989) 'Success and Failure in New Industrial Services', *Journal of Product Innovation Management*, 6(3): 239–258.
De Brentani U. (1991) 'Success Factors in Developing New Business Services', *European Journal of Marketing*, 25(2): 33–59.
De Brentani U. (2001) 'Innovative Versus Incremental New Business Services: Different Keys for Achieving Success', *Journal of Product Innovation Management*, 18(3), 169–187.
De Jong J. and Vermeulen P.A.M. (2003) 'Organizing Successful New Service Development. A Literature Review', *Management Decision*, 41(9): 844–858.
De Jong J. And Vermeulen P.A.M. (2006) 'Determinants of Product Innovation in Small Firms: A Comparison Across Industries', *International Small Business Journal*, 24(6): 587–609.
Deephouse D. (1999) 'To be Different, or to be the Same? It's a Question (and Theory) of Strategic Balance', *Strategic Management Journal*, 20(2): 147–166.
Denzin N.K. and Lincoln Y.S. (1998) 'Introduction. Entering the Field of Qualitative Research', in Denzin N.K. and Lincoln Y.S. (eds), *Strategies of Qualitative Research*. Thousand Oaks: Sage, pp. 1–34.
Dewar R.D. and Dutton J.E. (1986) 'The Adoption of Radical and Incremental Innovations: An Empirical Analysis', *Management Science*, 32(11): 1422.
Dijksterhuis M.S., Van den Bosch F.A.J. and Volberda W.H. (1999) 'Where Do New Organizational Forms Come From? Management Logics as a Source of Coevolution', *Organization Science*, 10: 569–582.
DiMaggio P. (1988) 'Interest and Agency in Institutional Theory', in Zucker, L.G. (ed.), *Institutional Patterns and Organizations. Culture and Environment*. Cambridge, MA: Ballinger, pp. 3–21.
DiMaggio P.J. and Powell W.W. (1983) 'The Iron Cage Revisited: Institutional Isomorphism and Collective Rationality in Organisational Fields', *American Sociological Review*, 48: 147–160.
DiMaggio P.J. and Powell W.W. (1991) 'Introduction', in Powell, W. and DiMaggio P. (eds), *The New Institutionalism in Organizational Analysis*. Chicago: University Press, pp. 1–38.
Dobbin F. and Dowd T. (1997) 'How Policy Shapes Competition: Early Railroad Foundings in Massachusetts', *Administrative Science Quarterly*, 42: 501–529.
Donnellon A. (1993) 'Crossfunctional Teams in Product Development: Accommodating the Structure to the Process', *Journal of Product Innovation Management*, 10(5): 377–392.

Dorado S. (2005) 'Institutional Entrepreneurship, Partaking, and Convening', *Organization Studies*, 26(3): 385–414.

Dorado S. (2006) 'Negotiated Bricolage: a Model for the Formation of New Organizational Forms Inspired in a Study of Two Organizations that Pioneered Commercial Microfinance', paper presented at the 22nd Egos Colloquium, Bergen, Norway, 6–8 July.

Dougherty D. (1990) 'Understanding New Markets for New Products', *Strategic Management Journal*, 11(5): 59.

Dougherty D. (1992) 'Interpretive Barriers to Successful Product Innovation in Large Firms', *Organisation Science*, 3(2): 179–202.

Dougherty D. (1999) 'Organizing for Innovation', in Clegg S.R., Hardy C. and Nord W.R. (eds), *Managing Organizations. Current Issues*. Thousand Oaks: Sage, pp. 174–189.

Dougherty D. and Heller T. (1994) 'The Illegitimacy of Successful Product Innovation in Established Firms', *Organization Science*, 5: 200–218.

Dougherty D. and Cohen M.A (1995) 'Product Innovation in Mature Firms', in Bowman E. and Kogut B. (eds), *Redesigning the Firm*. New York: Oxford University Press, pp. 87–115.

Dougherty D. and Hardy C. (1996) 'Sustained Product Innovation in Large, Mature Organisations: Overcoming Innovation-to-Organisation Problems', *Academy of Management Journal*, 39(5): 1120–1153.

Douglas M. (1986) *How Institutions Think*. Syracuse: Syracuse University Press.

Downey H.K. and Brief A.P. (1986) 'How Cognitive Structures Affect Organizational Design: Implicit Theories of Organizing', in Sims H.P., Gioia D.A. and Associates (eds), *The Thinking Organization: Dynamics of Organizational Social Cognition* .Jossey-Bass: San Francisco, pp. 165–190.

Drew S. (1995) 'Accelerating Innovation in Financial Services', *Long Range Planning*, 28(4): 11–21.

Easingwood C.J. (1986) 'New Product Development for Service Companies', *Journal of Product Innovation Management*, 3(4): 264–275.

Easingwood C.J. and Storey C.D. (1993) 'Marketplace Success Factors for New Financial Services', *Journal of Services Marketing*, 7(1): 41–54.

Edgett S. (1993) 'Developing New Financial Services within UK Building Societies', *International Journal of Bank Marketing*, 11(3): 35–43.

Edgett S. (1994) 'The Traits of Successful New Service Development', *Journal of Services Marketing*, 8(3): 40–49.

Edgett S. (1996) 'The New Product Development Process for Commercial Financial Services', *Industrial Marketing Management*, 25(6): 507–515.

Edgett S. and Parkinson S. (1994) 'The Development of New Financial Services. Identifying Determinants of Success and Failure', *International Journal of Service Industry Management*, 5(4): 24–38.

Edvardsson B. (1997) 'Quality in New Service Development: Key Concepts and a Frame of Reference', *International Journal of Production Economics*, 52(1): 31–46.

Edvardsson B. and Olsson J. (1996) 'Key Concepts for New Service Development', *The Service Industries Journal*, 16(2): 140–164.

Edvardsson B., Haglund L. and Mattsson J. (1995) 'Analysis, planning, improvisation and control in the development of new services', *International Journal of Service Industry Management*, 6(2): 24–35.

Eisenhardt K.M. (1989) 'Building Theories from Case Study Research', *Academy of Management Review*, 14(4): 532–550.
Eisenhardt K.M. and Tabrizi B. (1995) 'Accelerating Adaptive Processes: Product Innovation in the Global Computer Industry', *Administrative Science Quarterly*, 40(1): 84–110.
Elsbach K.D. (2002) 'Intraorganizational Institutions', in Baum J.A.C. (eds), *Companion to Organizations*. Oxford: Blackwell, pp. 37–56.
Ennew C., Wong P. and Wright M. (1992) 'Organisational Structures and the Boundaries of the Firm: Acquisition and Divestment in Financial Services', *The Service Industries Journal*, 12(4): 478–497.
Ettlie J.E., Bridges W.P. and O'Keefe R.D. (1984) 'Organization Strategy and Structural Differences for Radical Versus Incremental Innovation', *Management Science*, 30: 682–695.
Fiss P.C. and Zajac E.J. (2004) 'The Diffusion of Ideas over Contested Terrain: The (Non)adoption of a Shareholder Value Orientation among German Firms', *Administrative Science Quarterly*, 49(4): 501–534.
Flier B., van den Bosch F.A.J., Volberda H.W., Carnevale C.A., Tomkin N., Melin L., Quélin B.V. and Kriger M.P. (2001) 'The Changing Landscape of the European Financial Services Sector', *Long Range Planning*, 34(2): 179–207.
Fligstein N. (1991) 'The Structural Transformation of American Industry: An Institutional Account of the Causes of Diversification in the Largest firms, 1919–1979', in Powell W.W. and DiMaggio P.J. (eds), *The New Institutionalism in Organizational Analuse*. Chicago: University of Chicago Press, pp. 311–336.
Fligstein N. (1997) 'Social Skill and Institutional Theory', *The American Behavioral Scientist*, 40: 397–405.
Fligstein N. (2001) 'Social Skill and the Theory of Fields', *Sociological Theory*, 19(2): 105–125.
Fligstein N. and Mara-Drita I. (1996) 'How to Make a Market: Reflections on the Attempt to Create a Single Market in the European Union', *American Journal of Sociology*, 102: 1–33.
Flipo J.P. (1987) 'On the Intangibility of Services', *The Service Industries Journal*, 7(2): 286–298.
Friedland R. and Alford R.R. (1991) 'Bringing Society Back In: Symbols, Practices, and Institutional Contradictions' in DiMaggio P.J. and Powell W.W. (eds), *The New Institutionalism in Organizational Analysis*. Chicago: The University of Chicago Press, pp. 232–263
Galakiewicz J. and Wasserman S. (1989) 'Mimetic and Normative Processes within an Interorganizational Field: An empirical Test', *Administrative Science Quarterly*, 34(3): 454–479.
Galbraith J.R. (1973) *Designing complex Organizations*. Reading: Addison Wesley.
Garcia R. and Calantone R. (2002) 'A Critical Look at Technological Innovation Typology and Innovativeness Terminology: A Literature Review', *Journal of Product Innovation Management*, 19(2): 110–132.
Garud R. and Nayyar P.R. (1994) 'Transformative Capacity: Continual Structuring by Intertemporal Technology Transfer', *Strategic Management Journal*, 15(5): 365–385.
Garud R. and Rappa M.A. (1994) 'A Socio-cognitive Model of Technology Evolution: The Case of Cochlear Implants', *Organization Science*, 5(3): 344–362.

Garud R. and Karnøe P. (2001) 'Path Creation as a Process of Mindful Deviation', in Garud, R. and Karnøe, P. (eds), *Path Dependence and Creation*. Mahwah, New Jersey: Lawrence Earlbaum Associates.
Garud R., Jain S. and Kumaraswamy A. (2002) 'Institutional Entrepreneurship in the Sponsorship of Common Technological Standards: the Case of Sun Microsystems and Java', *Academy of Management Journal*, 45: 196–214.
Geroski P. (1995) 'Entrepreneurship, Management and the Structure of Payoffs', *International Journal of Industrial Organization*, 13(2): 304.
Glaser B.G. (1978) *Theoretical Sensitivity*, Mill Valley: Sociology Press.
Glaser B.G. (1992) *Basics of Grounded Theory Analysis: Emergence vs. Forcing*, Mill Valley: Sociology Press.
Glaser B.G. and Strauss A.L. (1967) *The Discovery of Grounded Theory. Strategies for Qualitative Research*. Chicago: Aldine.
Goodrick E. and Salancik G.R. (1996) 'Organizational Discretion in Responding to Institutional Practices: Hospitals and Cesarean Births', *Administrative Science Quarterly*, 41(1): 1–28.
Goodstein J.D. (1994) 'Institutional Pressures and Strategic Responsiveness: Employer Involvement in Work-Family Issues', *Academy of Management Journal*, 37(2): 350–382.
Greenwood R. and Hinings C.R. (1996) 'Understanding Radical Organisational Change: Bringing Together the Old and New Institutionalism', *Academy of Management Review*, 21(4): 1022–1054.
Greenwood R. and Suddaby R. (2006) 'Institutional Rntrepreneurship in Mature Fields: the Big Five Accounting firms', *Academy of Management Journal*, 49(1): 27–48.
Greenwood R, Suddaby R., and Hinings C.R. (2002) 'Theorizing Change: the Role of Professional Associations in the Transformation of Institutionalized Fields', *Academy of Management Journal*, 45(1): 58–80.
Griffin A. (1992) 'Evaluating QFD's Use in U.S. Firms: a Process for Developing Products', *Journal of Product Innovation Management*, 9(3): 171–197.
Griffin A. (1997) 'PDMA Research on New Product Development Practices: Updating Trends and Benchmarking Best Practices', *Journal of Product Innovation Management*, 14(6): 429–458.
Griffin A. and Hauser J.R. (1996) 'Integrating R&D and Marketing: a Review and Analysis of the Literature', *Journal of Product Innovation Management*, 13(3): 191–215.
Grönroos C. (1990) *Service Management and Marketing. Managing the Moments of Truth in Service Competition*, Lexington: Lexington Books.
Gupta A.K. and Wilemon D. (1990) 'Improving R&D/Marketing Relations: R&D's Perspective', *R&D Management*, 20(4): 277–290.
Gupta A.K., Raj S.P. and Wilemon D. (1985) 'The R&D Marketing Interface in High-Technology Firms', *Journal of Product Innovation Management*, 2(1): 12–24.
Gupta A.K., Raj S.P. and Wilemon D. (1986) 'A Model for Studying R&D-Marketing Interface in the Product Innovation Process', *Journal of Marketing*, 50(2): 7–17.
Haaroff K. (1983) 'An Exercise in Product Development for the 1980s: International Cash Management Services', *International Journal of Bank Marketing*, 1(3): 56–68.

Hargadon A.B. and Douglas Y. (2001) 'When Innovations Meet Institutions: Edison and the Design of the Electric Light', *Administrative Science Quarterly*, 46(3): 476–501.

Hargrave T.J. and van de Ven A.H. (2006). 'A Collective Action Model of Institutional Innovation', *Academy of Management Review*, 31(4): 864–888.

Hart S.J. and Baker M.J. (1996) 'The Multiple Convergent Processing Model of New Product Development', in Hart S.J. (ed), *New Product Development. A Reader*. London: The Dryden Press, pp. 151–166.

Haveman H.A. (1993) 'Follow the Leader: Mimetic Isomorphism and Entry into New Markets', *Administrative Science Quarterly*, 38: 593–627.

Henderson R.M. and Clark K.B. (1990) 'Architectural Innovation: The Reconfiguration of Existing Product Technologies and the Failure of Established Firms', *Administrative Science Quarterly*, 35: 9–30.

Hertog F. den (1995) 'Entrepreneurship on the Shopfloor: Nationale Nederlanden', in Andreasen L.E., Coriat B., den Hertog F. and Kaplinsky R. (eds), *Europe's Next Step. Organizational Innovation, Competition and Employment*. Ilford: Frank Cass, pp. 197–209.

Hill C.W.L. and Rothaermel F.T. (2003) 'The Performance of Incumbent Firms in the Face of Radical Technological Innovation', *Academy of Management Review*, 28(2): 257–274.

Hippel E. von (1988) *The Sources of Innovation*. Oxford University Press: New York.

Hirsch P.M. (1997) 'Review Essay. Sociology Without Social Structure: Neoinstitutional Theory Meets Brave New World', *American Journal of Sociology* 102: 1702–1723.

Hitt M.A., Hoskisson R.E. and Nixon R.D. (1993) 'A Mid-range Theory of Interfunctional Integration, its Antecedents and Outcomes', *Journal of Engineering and Technology Management*, 10(1 and 2): 161–185.

Hoffman A.J. (1999) 'Institutional Evolution and Change: Environmentalism and the U.S. Chemical Industry', *Academy of Management Journal*, 42: 351–371.

Hoffman A.J. and Ventresca M.J. (1999) 'The Institutional Framing of Policy Debates', *American Behavioral Scientist*, 42: 1368–1392.

Hoffman K., Parejo M., Bessant J. and Perren L. (1998) 'Small Firms, R&D, Technology and Innovation in the UK: a Literature Review', *Technovation*, 18: 39–55.

Holstein J.A. and Gubrium J.F. (1998) 'Phenomenology, Ethnomethodology, and Interpretive Practice', in Denzin N.K. and Lincoln Y.S. (eds), *Strategies of Qualitative Research*. Thousand Oaks: Sage, pp. 137–157.

Jepperson R. (1991) 'Institutions, Institutional Effects, and Institutionalism', in Powell W. and DiMaggio P. (eds), *The New Institutionalism in Organizational Analysis*. Chicago: University of Chicago Press, pp. 143–163.

Johne F.A. (1993) 'Insurance Product Development: Managing the Changes', *International Journal of Bank Marketing*, 11(3): 5–14.

Johne A. and Harborne P. (1985) 'How Large Commercial Banks Manage Product Innovation', *International Journal of Bank Marketing*, 3(1): 54–70.

Johne A. and Pavlidis P. (1996) 'How Banks Apply Marketing Expertise to Develop New Derivatives', *Journal of Product Innovation Management*, 13(5): 440–452.

Johne A. and Storey C. (1998) 'New Service Development: a Review of the Literature and Annotated Bibliography', *European Journal of Marketing*, 32(3/4): 84–251.

Kahn K.B. (1994) *Marketing's Integration with Other Departments*, Dissertation, Virginia Polytechnic Institute and State University.

Kahn K.B. (2004) *The PDMA Handbook of New Product Development*, 2nd edn. New York: Wiley.

Kaplan S. (2003) 'Framing Contests: Micro Mechanisms of Strategy-Making in the face of Technical Change', working paper, MIT Sloan School of Management.

Katzenbach J.R. and Smith D.K. (1993) *The Wisdom of Teams: Creating the High-performance Organisation*. Boston: Harvard Business School Press.

Kostova T. and Roth K. (2002) 'Adoption of an Organizational Practice by Subsidiaries of Multinational Corporations: Institutional and Relational Effects', *Academy of Management Journal*, 45: 215–233.

Kotler P. (1994) *Marketing Management: Analysis, Planning, Implementation, and Control*. Englewood Cliffs, New Jersey: Prentice Hall.

Langeard E., Reffait P. and Eiglier P. (1986) 'Developing New Services', in Venkatesan M., Schmalensee D.M. and Marshall C. (eds), *Creativity in Services Marketing*. Chicago: American Marketing Association, pp. 120–123.

Larson E.W. and Gobeli D.H. (1988) 'Organizing for Product Development Projects', *Journal of Product Innovation Management*, 5(3): 180–190.

Lawrence P.R. and Lorsch J.W. (1967) *Organization and Environment*. Irwin: Homewood.

Lawrence T.B. (1999) 'Institutional Strategy', *Journal of Management*, 25(2): 161–188.

Lawrence T.B. and Suddaby R. (2006) 'Institutions and Institutional Work', in Clegg S., Hardy C., Nord W.R. and Lawrence T. (eds), *Handbook of Organization Studies*. London: Sage, pp. 215–254.

Lawrence T.B., Winn M. and Jennings P.D. (2001) 'The Temporal Dynamics of Institutionalization', *Academy of Management Review*, 26(4): 624–645.

Leblebici H., Salancik G.R., Copay A. and King T. (1991) 'Institutional Change and the Transformation of Interorganizational Fields: an Organizational History of the U.S. Radio Broadcasting Industry'. *Administrative Science Quarterly*, 36(3): 333–363.

Lee T.W. (1999) *Using Qualitative Methods in Organizational Research*. Thousand Oaks: Sage.

Leeuw J. de (1996) *Financiële conglomeraten in Nederland*. Amsterdam: NIBE.

Leonard D. (1998) *Wellsprings of Knowledge. Building and Sustaining the Sources of Innovation*. Boston: Harvard Business School Press.

Lévi-Strauss C. (1966) *The Savage Mind*. Chicago: University of Chicago Press.

Lievens A. (1996) *The Antecedents and the Role of Communication during the Innovation Process of New Financial Services*, Dissertation, Vrije Universiteit, Brussel.

Lievens A. and Moenaert R.K. (2000) 'Project Team Communication in Financial Service Innovation', *Journal of Management Studies*, 37(5): 733–766.

Lievens A., Moenaert R.K. and S'Jegers R. (1999) 'Linking Communication to Innovation Success in the Financial Services Industry: a Case Study Analysis', *International Journal of Service Industry Management*, 10(1): 23–47.

Linton J.D. (2002) 'Implementation Research: State of the Art and Future Directions', *Technovation*, 22: 65–79.

Lord R.G. and Foti R.J. (1986) 'Schema Theories, Information Processing, and Organizational Behaviour', in Sims H.P., Gioia D.A. and Associates (eds), *The Thinking Organization: Dynamics of Organizational Social Cognition*. Jossey-Bass: San Francisco, pp. 20–48.

Lounsbury M. (2001) 'Institutional Sources of Practice Variation: Staffing College and University Recycling Programs', *Administrative Science Quarterly*, 46(1): 29–56.
Lounsbury M. (2002) 'Institutional Transformation and Status Mobility: the Professionalization of the Field of Finance', *Academy of Management Journal*, 45(1): 255–266.
Lovelock C.H. (1983) 'Classifying Services to Gain Strategic Marketing Insights', *Journal of Marketing*, 47: 9–20.
Lovelock C.H. (1984) 'Developing and Implementing New Services', in George W.R. and Marshall C.E. (eds), *Developing New Services*. Chicago: American Marketing Association, pp. 44–64.
MacMillan I.C., McCaffery M.L. and van Wijk G.V. (1985) 'Competitors' response to easily imitated new products — exploring commercial banking product introduction', *Strategic Management Journal*, 6(1): 75–85.
Maguire S., Hardy C. and Lawrence T.B. (2004) 'Institutional Entrepreneurship in Emerging Fields: HIV/AIDS Treatment Advocacy in Canada', *Academy of Management Journal*, 47: 657–679.
Maidique M.A. (1980) 'Entrepreneurs, Champions and Technological Innovation', *Sloan Management Review*, winter: 59–76.
March J.G. (1991) 'Exploration and Exploitation in Organisational Learning', *Organisation Science*, 2(1): 71–87.
March J.G. and Simon H. (1958) *Organizations*. Wiley: New York.
March J.G. and Olsen J.P. (1989) *Rediscovering Institutions. The Organizational Basis of Politics*. New York: The Free Press.
March J.G., Schulz M. and Zhou X. (2000) *The Dynamics of Rules. Change in Written Organizational Codes*. Stanford: Stanford University Press.
Markham S.K. and Griffin A. (1998) 'The Breakfast of Champions: Associations Between Champions and Product Development Environments, Practices and Performance', *Journal of Product Innovation Management*, 15(5): 436–454.
Martin Jr, C.R. and Horne D.A. (1993) 'Services Innovation: Successful versus Unsuccessful Firms', *International Journal of Service Industry Management*, 4(1): 48–64.
Martin C.R. and Horne D.A. (1995) 'Level of Success Inputs for Service Innovations in the Same Firm', *International Journal of Service Industry Management*, 6(4): 40–56.
Maso I. and Smaling A. (1990) *Objectiviteit in kwalitatief onderzoek*. Meppel: Boom.
McAdam D. and Scott W.R. (2005) 'Organizations and Movements', in Davis G.F., McAdam D., Scott W.R. and Zald M.N. (eds), *Social Movements and Organization Theory*. Cambridge: Cambridge University Press, pp. 4–40.
McAdam D., McCarthy J.D. and Zald M.N. (1996) *Comparative Perspectives on Social Movements. Political Opportunities, Mobilizing Structures, and Cultural Framings*. Cambridge: Cambridge University Press.
McAdam R. and McClelland J. (2002) 'Individual and Team-based Idea Generation within Innovation Management: Organizational and Research Agendas', *European Journal of Innovation Management*, 5: 86–97.
McDermott C.M., and O'Connor G.C. (2002) 'Managing Radical Innovation: an Overview of Emergent Strategy Issues', *Journal of Product Innovation Management*, 19: 424–438.

McDonough E.F. (2000) 'Investigation of Factors Contributing to the Success of Cross-functional Teams', *Journal of Product Innovation Management*, 17: 221–235.

Meeus M.T.H. and Oerlemans L.A.G. (2000) 'Firm Behaviour and Innovative Performance. An Empirical Exploration of the Selection-Adaptive Debate', *Research Policy*, 29(1): 41–58.

Meidan A. (1996) *Marketing Financial Services*, London: MacMillan.

Metal Box Company Limited (1947) 'An Organisation for Development in Industry', *Proceedings of the Eighth International Management Congress*, Stockholm, pp. 375–383.

Meyer J.W. and Rowan B. (1977) 'Institutionalized Organizations: Formal Structure as Myth and Ceremony', *American Journal of Sociology*, 83: 340–363.

Meyer J.W. and Scott W.R. (1983) *Organizational Environments: Ritual and Rationality*. Beverly Hills: Sage.

Meyer A.D., Brooks G.R. and Goes J.B. (1990) 'Environmental Jolts and Industry Revolutions: Organizational Responses to Discontinuous Change', *Strategic Management Journal*, 11: 93–110.

Meyerson D.E. (1994) 'Interpretations of Stress in Institutions: the Cultural Production of Ambiguity and Burnout', *Administrative Science Quarterly*, 39(4): 628.

Miles M.B. and Huberman A.M. (1994) *Qualitative Data Analysis: an Expanded Sourcebook*, 2nd edn. Thousand Oaks: Sage.

Mintzberg H. (1979) *The Structuring of Organizations*, Englewood Cliffs, New Jersey: Prentice Hall.

Mintzberg H. (1983) *Structure in Fives: Designing Effective Organisations*. Englewood Cliffs, New Jersey: Prentice Hall.

Moenaert R.K. and Souder W.E. (1990) 'an Information Transfer Model for Integrating Marketing and R&D Personnel in New Product Development Projects', *Journal of Product Innovation Management*, 9(1): 91–107.

Moenaert R.K., Souder W.E., De Meyer A. and Deschoolmeester D. (1994) 'R&D-Marketing Integration Mechanisms, Communication Flows, and Innovation Success', *Journal of Product Innovation Management*, 11(1): 31–45.

Mumford M.D. (2000) 'Managing Creative People: Strategies and Tactics for Innovation', *Human Resources Management Review*, 10: 313–351.

Nelson C., Treichler P.A. and Grossberg L. (1992) 'Cultural Studies: an Introduction', in Grossberg L., Nelson C. and Treichler P.A. (eds), *Cultural Studies*. New York: Routledge, pp. 1–16.

Nelson R. and Winter S. (1982) *An Evolutionary Theory of Economic Change*. Harvard University Press: Cambridge.

Nijssen E.J., Hillebrand B., Vermeulen P.A.M. and Kemp R. (2006) 'Exploring Product and Service Innovation Similarities and Differences', *International Journal of Research in Marketing*, 23(3): 241–251.

Nonaka I. and Takeuchi H. (1995) *The Knowledge-Creating Company. How Japanese Companies Create the Dynamics of Innovation*. New York: Oxford University Press.

North D.C. (1990) *Institutions, Institutional Change and Economic Performance*. Cambridge: Cambridge University Press.

Oliver C. (1991) 'Strategic Responses to Institutional procesees', *Academy of management Review*, 16: 145–179.

Oliver, C. (1992) 'The Antecedents of Deinstitutionalization', *Organization Studies*, 13(4): 563–588.
Olson E.M., Walker O.C. and Ruekert R.W. (1995) 'Organizing for Effective New Product Development: the Moderating Role of Product Innovativeness', *Journal of Marketing*, 59(1): 48–62.
Olson E.M., Walker O.C., Ruekert R.W. and Bonner J.M. (2001) 'Patterns of Cooperation During New Product Development Among Marketing, Operations and R&D: Implications for Project Performance', *Journal of Product Innovation Management*, 18: 258–271.
Orrù M., Biggart N.W. and Hamilton G.G. (1991) 'Organizational Isomorphism in East Asia', in Powell W.W. and DiMaggio P.J. (eds), *The New Institutionalism in Organizational Analysis*. Chicago: University Press, pp. 361–390.
Palmer D.A. and Biggart N.W. (2002) 'Organizational Institutions', in Baum A.C. (ed.) *Companion to Organizations*. Oxford: Blackwell, pp. 259–280.
Perrow C. (1979) *Complex Organizations: a Critical Essay*. New York: McGraw-Hill.
Pettigrew A. (1985) *The Awakening Giant: Continuity and Change in ICI*. London: Basil Blackwell
Pierce J.L. and Delbecq A.L. (1977) 'Organization Structure, Individual Attitudes and Innovation', *Academy of Management Review*, 2(1): 27–37.
Pinnington A. and Morris T. (2003) 'Archetype Change in Professional Organizations: Survey Evidence from Large Law Firms', *British Journal of Management*, 14: 85–99.
Pinto M.B. and Pinto J.K. (1990) 'Project Team Communication and Cross-Functional Cooperation in New Program Development', *Journal of Product Innovation Management*, 7(3): 200–212.
Pisano G.P. (1997) *The Development Factory*. Boston: Harvard Business School Press.
Prahalad C.K. and Bettis R.A. (1986) 'The Dominant Logic: a New Linkage Between Diversity and Performance', *Strategic Management Journal*, 7(6): 485–501.
Quinn J.B. (1985) 'Managing Innovation: Controlled Chaos', *Harvard Business Review*, 63: 73–84.
Quinn J.B., Baruch J.J and Zien K.A. (1997) *Innovation Explosion. Using Intellect and Software to Revolutionize*, New York: The Free Press.
Rao H., Morrill C. and Zald M.N. (2000) 'Power Plays: How Social Movements and Collective Action Create New Organizational Forms', *Research in Organizational Behaviour*, 22: 239–282.
Reay T. and Hinings C.R. (2005) 'The Recomposition of an Organizational Field: Health Care in Alberta', *Organization Studies*, 26(3): 351–384.
Reidenbach R.E. and Moak D.L. (1986) 'Exploring Retail Bank Performance and New Product Development: a Profile of Industry Practices', *Journal of Product Innovation Management*, 3(3): 187–194.
Rickards T. (1991) 'Innovation and Creativity: Woods, Trees and Pathways', *R&D Management*, 21: 97–108.
Rogers E.M. (1962) *Diffusion of Innovations*. New York: The Free Press.
Rogers E.M. (1995) *Diffusion of Innovations*, 4th edn. New York: The Free Press.
Rothwell R. (1992) 'Successful Industrial Innovation: Critical Success Factors for the 1990s', *R&D Management*, 22(3): 221–239.
Ruef M. and Scott W.R. (1998) 'A Multidimensional Model of Organizational Legitimacy: Hospital Survival in Changing Institutional Environments', *Administrative Science Quarterly*, 43(4): 877–904.

Ruekert R.W. and Walker O.C. Jr (1987) 'Marketing's Interaction with Other Functional Units: a Conceptual Framework and Empirical Evidence', *Journal of Marketing*, 51(1): 1–19.

Saren M.A. (1984) 'A Classification and Review of Models of the Intra-firm Innovation Process', *R&D Management*, 14 (1): 11–24.

Schein E.H. (1997) *Organizational Culture and Leadership*, 2nd edn. San Francisco: Jossey-Bass.

Scheuing E.E. and Johnson E.M. (1989) 'A Proposed Model for New Service Development', *Journal of Services Marketing*, 3(2): 25–34.

Schön D.A. (1967) *Technology and Change: the New Heraclitus*. Oxford: Pergamon Press.

Schoonhoven C.B. and Jelinek M. (1997) 'Dynamic Tension in Innovative, High Technology Firms: Managing Rapid Technological Change Through Organizational Structure', in Tushman M.L. and Anderson P. (eds), *Managing Strategic Innovation and Change*. Oxford University Press: New York, pp. 233–254.

Schumpeter J.A. (1939) *Business Cycles: a Theoretical, Historical and Statistical Analysis of the Capitalist Process*. London: McGraw & Hill.

Schumpeter J.A. (1942) *Capitalism, Socialism and Democracy*. New York: Harper.

Schutz A. and Luckmann T. (1974) *The Structures of the Life World*. London: Heinemann.

Scott W.R. (1987) 'The Adolescence of Institutional Theory', *Administrative Science Quarterly*, 32: 493–511.

Scott W.R. (1994) 'Institutions and Organizations: Towards a Theoretical Synthesis', in Scott W.R. and Meyer J.M (eds), *Institutional Environments and Organizations: Structural Complexity and Individualism*. Thousand Oaks, CA: Sage pp. 55–80.

Scott W.R. (1995) *Institutions and Organizations*. Thousand Oaks: Sage.

Scott W.R. (1998) *Organizations. Rational, Natural, and Open Systems*. Upper Saddle River: Prentice Hall.

Scott W.R. (2001) *Institutions and Organizations*, 2nd edn. Thousand Oaks: Sage.

Scott W.R., Ruef M., Mendel P.J. and Caronna C. A. (2000) *Institutional Change and Healthcare Organizations. From Professional Dominance to Managed Care*. Chicago: The University of Chicago Press.

Selznick P. (1949) *TVA and the Grass Roots*. Berkeley: University of California Press.

Selznick P. (1957) *Leadership in Administration*. New York: Harper and Row.

Seo M. and Creed W.E.D (2002) 'Institutional Contradictions, Praxis, and Institutional Change: A Dialectical Perspective', *Academy of Management Review*, 27(2): 222–247.

Shane S.A. (1994) 'Are Champions Different from Non-champions', *Journal of Business Venturing*, 9: 397–421.

Shostack G.L. (1977) 'Breaking Free from Product Marketing', *Journal of Marketing*, 41(2): 73–80.

Shostack G.L. (1981) 'How to Design a Service', *European Journal of Marketing*, 16(1): 49–63.

Shostack G.L. (1984) 'Designing Services that Deliver', *Harvard Business Review*, January-February: 133–139.

Sijbrands S. and Eppink D.J. (1994) 'The Internationalization of Dutch Banks: a New Beginning?', *Long Range Planning*, 27(4): 35–47.

Singh, V. (1997) 'Systems Integration – Coping with Legacy Systems', *Integrated Manufacturing Systems*, 8(1): 24–28.

Song X.M. and Montoya-Weiss M.M. (1998) 'Critical Development Activities for Really New versus Incremental Products', *Journal of Product Innovation Management*, 13(2): 124–135.
Soni P.K., Lilien G.L. and Wilson D.T. (1993) 'Industrial Innovation and Firm Performance: a Reconceptualization and Structural Equation Analysis', *International Journal of Research in Marketing*, 10: 365–380.
Souder W.E. (1987) *Managing New Product Innovations*. New York: Lexington Books.
Storey C.D. and Easingwood C.J. (1993) 'The Impact of the New Product Development Project on the Success of Financial Services', *The Service Industries Journal*, 13(3): 40–54.
Strang D. and Sine W.D. (2002) 'Interorganizational Institutions', in Baum A.C. (ed.), *Companion to Organizations*. Oxford: Blackwell Publishers, pp. 497–519.
Strauss A.L. (1987) *Qualitative Analysis for Social Scientists*. New York: Cambridge University Press.
Strauss A.L. and Corbin J. (1990) *Basics of Qualitative Research. Grounded Theory Procedures and Techniques*. Sage: London.
Suchman M.C. (1995) 'Managing Legitimacy: Strategic and Institutional Approaches', *Academy of Management Review*, 20: 571–610.
Suddaby R. and Greenwood R. (2005) 'Rhetorical Strategies of Legitimacy', *Administrative Science Quarterly*, 50(1): 35–67.
Sundbo J. (1997) 'Management of Innovation in Services', *The Service Industries Journal*, 17(3): 432–455.
Terrill C.A. and Middlebrooks A.G. (1996) 'Service Development', in Rosenau M.D. *et al.* (eds), *The PDMA Handbook of New Product Development*. New York: Wiley, pp. 315–330.
Thelen K. (2003) 'How Institutions Evolve: Insights from Comparative-Historical Analysis', in Mahoney J. and Rueschemeyer D. (eds), *Comparative Historical Analysis in the Social Sciences*. Cambridge: Cambridge University Press, 208–240.
Thornton P.H. (2002) 'The Rise of the Corporation in a Craft Industry: Conflict and Conformity in Institutional Logics', *Academy of Management Journal*, 45(1): 81–101.
Thornton P.H. (2004) *Markets from Culture. Institutional Logics and Organizational Decisions in Higher Education Publishing*. Stanford: Stanford Business Books.
Thwaites D. (1992) 'Organisational Influences on the New Product Development Process in Financial Services', *Journal of Product Innovation Management*, 9(4): 303–313.
Tidd J. and Bodley K. (2002) 'The influence of Project Novelty on the New Product Development Process', *R&D Management*, 32: 127–138.
Tidd J., Bessant J. and Pavitt K. (1997) *Managing Innovation. Integrating Technological, Market and Organizational Change*. Chichester: Wiley.
Tolbert P.S. (1985) 'Resource Dependence and Institutional Environments: Sources of Administrative Structure in Institutions of Higher Education', *Administrative Science Quarterly*, 30: 1–13.
Tolbert P.S. and Zucker L.G. (1983) 'Institutional Sources of Change in the Formal Structure of Organizations: The diffusion of Civil Service Reform, 1880–1935', *Administrative Science Quarterly*, 30: 22–39.
Tolbert P.S. and Zucker L.G. (1996) 'The Institutionalization of Institutional Theory', in Clegg S.R., Hardy C. and Nord W.R. (eds.), *Handbook of Organization Studies*, London: Sage, pp. 175–190.

Trice H.M. (1993) *Occupational Subcultures in the Workplace*. Ithaca: ILR Press.

Tripsas M. and Gavetti G. (2000) 'Capabilities, Cognition, and Inertia: Evidence from Digital Imaging', *Strategic Management Journal*, 21(10): 1147–1161.

Tushman M.L. (1977) 'Special Boundary Roles in the Innovation Process', *Administrative Science Quarterly*, 22(4): 587–605.

Tushman M.L. and Anderson P. (1986) 'Technological Discontinuities and Organizational Environments', *Administrative Science Quarterly*, 31(3): 439.

Tushman M.L. and O'Reilly C.A (1997) *Winning through Innovation. A Practical Guide to Leading Organizational Change and Renewal*. Boston: Harvard Business School Press.

Twiss B.C. (1980) *Managing Technological Innovation*, 2nd edn. London: Longman.

Ulwick A.W. (2002) 'Turn Customer Input into Innovation', *Harvard Business Review*, 80: 91–97.

Utterback J.M. (1994) *Mastering the Dynamics of Innovation*. Boston: Harvard Business School Press.

Ven A. van de (1986) 'Central Problems in the Management of Innovation', *Management Science*, 32(5): 590–607.

Ven A. van de (1995) 'Managing the Process of Organizational Innovation', in Huber G.P. and Glick W.H. (eds) *Organizational Change and Redesign. Ideas and Insights for Improving Performance*. New York: Oxford University Press, pp. 269–294.

Ven A.H. van de and Hargrave T.J. (2004) 'Social, Technical, and Institutional Change: a Literature Review and Synthesis', in Poole M.S and van de Ven A.H. (eds), *Handbook of Organizational Change and Innovation*. New York: Oxford University Press, pp. 259–304.

Vermeulen P.A.M. (2005) 'Uncovering Barriers to Complex Incremental Product Innovation in Small and Medium-Sized Financial Firms', *Journal of Small Business Management*, 43(4): 432–452.

Vermeulen P.A.M. and Dankbaar B. (2002) 'The Organization of Product Innovation in the Financial Sector: an Exploration in the Netherlands', *The Service Industries Journal*, 22(3):77–98.

Vermeulen P.A.M., van den Bosch F.A.J. and Volberda H.W. (2007) Complex Incremental Product Innovation in Established Service Firms: a Micro Institutional Perspective, paper forthcoming in *Organization Studies*.

Verschuren P. and Doorewaard H. (1999) *Designing a Research Project*. Utrecht: Lemma.

Veryzer R.W. (1998) 'Discontinuous Innovation and the New Product Development Process', *Journal of Product Innovation Management*, 15: 304–321.

Volberda H.W., van den Bosch F.A.J., Flier B. and Gedajlovic E.R. (2001) 'Following the Herd or Not? Patterns of Renewal in the Netherlands and the UK', *Long Range Planning*, 34(2): 209–229.

Washington M. and Ventresca M.J. (2004) 'How Organizations Change: the Role of Institutional Support Mechanisms in the Incorporation of Higher Education Visibility Strategies, 1874–1995', *Organization Science*, 15(1): 82–97.

Weick K.E. (1993) 'The Collapse of Sensemaking in Organizations: The Mann Gulch Disaster', *Administrative Science Quarterly*, 38(4): 628–652.

Weick K.E. (1996) 'Drop Your Tools: an Allegory for Organizational Studies', *Administrative Science Quarterly*, 41(2): 301–313.

West M.A. and Farr J.L. (eds) (1990) *Innovation and Creativity at Work: Psychological and Organizational Strategies*. Chichester: Wiley.

West M.A. and Altink W.M.M. (1996) 'Innovation at Work: Individual, Group, Organizational, and Socio-historical Perspectives', *European Journal of Work and Organizational Psychology*, 5(1): 3–11.
Wester F. (1995) *Strategieën voor kwalitatief onderzoek*. Bussum: Coutinho.
Wheelwright S.C. and Clark K.B. (1992) *Revolutionizing Product Development.*, New York: Free Press.
Wicks D. (2001) 'Institutionalized Mindsets of Invulnerability: Differentiated Institutional Fields and the Antecedents of Organizational Crisis', *Organization Studies,* 22: 659–692.
White H. (1992) *Identity and Control: A Structural Theory of Social Interaction.* Princeton: Princeton University Press.
Wolfe R.A. (1994) 'Organizational Innovation: Review, Critique and Suggested Research Directions', *Journal of Management Studies*, 31: 405–431.
Yin R.K. (1994) *Case Study Research: Design and Methods*. London: Sage.
Zald M.N. (1996) 'Culture, Ideology, and Strategic Framing', in McAdam D., McCarthy J.D. and Zald M.N. (eds), *Comparative Perspectives on Social Movements. Political Opportunities, Mobilizing Structures, and Cultural Framings.* Cambridge: Cambridge University Press, pp, 261–274.
Zaltman G., Duncan R. and Holbek J. (1973) *Innovations and Organizations*. New York: Wiley.
Zeithaml V.A., Parasuraman A. and Berry L.L. (1985) 'Problems and Strategies in Services Marketing', *Journal of Marketing*, 49(2): 33–46.
Zucker L.G. (1977) 'The Role of Institutionalization in Cultural Persistence', *American Sociological Review*, 42: 726–743.
Zucker L.G. (1983) 'Organizations as Institutions', in Bacharach S.B. (ed.), *Advances in Organizational Theory and Research*. New York: Jai Press, pp 1–47.
Zucker, L.G. (1987) 'Institutional Theories of Organization', *Annual Review of Sociology,* 13: 443–464.
Zucker L.G. (1988) 'Where do Institutional Patters come from? Organizations as Actors in Social Systems', in Zucker L.G (ed.), *Institutional Patterns and Organizations. Culture and Environment.* Cambridge: Ballinger, pp, 230–52.
Zucker L.G. (1991) 'The Role of Institutionalization in Cultural Persistence' in Powell W.W. and DiMaggio P.J. (eds), *The New Institutionalism in Organizational Analysis*. Chicago: The University of Chicago Press, pp. 83–107.

Index

Figures are indicated in *italic*